Working with People with Learning Disabilities

Working with People with Learning Disabilities

Theory and Practice

David Thomas and Honor Woods

Jessica Kingsley Publishers
London and Philadelphia

First published in the United Kingdom in 2003
by Jessica Kingsley Publishers
116 Pentonville Road
London N1 9JB, UK
and
400 Market Street, Suite 400
Philadelphia, PA 19106, USA
www.jkp.com

Copyright © 2003 David Thomas and Honor Woods
Second impression 2003
Reprinted twice in 2004
Fifth impression 2005

Library of Congress Cataloging in Publication Data
Thomas, David, 1962 Apr. 24-
   Working with people with learning disabilities : theory and practice/David Thomas and Honor Woods
      p.cm
   Includes bibliographical references and index
   ISBN 1-85302-973-4 (pbk : alk paper)
   1. Learning disabilities. 2. Learning disabled children. I. Woods, Honor, 1950-II. Title.
RC394.L37T46 2003
362.3'8--dc21

2002043373

British Library Cataloguing in Publication Data
A CIP catalogue record for this book is available from the British Library

ISBN-13: 978 1 85302 973 8
ISBN-10: 1 85302 973 4

Printed and Bound in Great Britain by
Athenaeum Press, Gateshead, Tyne and Wear

Dedication

To Mary, Harold, Jill, Emma, Amie, Ben
and Laura, and to John and Ben

CONTENTS

ACKNOWLEDGEMENTS

We would like to thank all the people that have helped and supported us throughout the process of writing this book. In particular, and at the forefront, we would like to thank our immediate families and friends for their understanding and support. Each has played a crucial part through their encouragement, time spent listening to ideas, reading and debating. A very special thanks is extended to Mary, Greta and Jill for their time and inspiration given so readily. We would like to thank the many people with a learning disability who have provided us with information, understanding and insight and have taught us so much. The support provided by the publishers has been greatly appreciated and their guidance on how to transform ideas into a manuscript and then into a book has been invaluable.

DISCLAIMER

The case studies used within this book are based on realistic working situations; however, the people appearing in the studies are all fictitious. Any resemblance to people living or dead is purely coincidental. The authors have been meticulous in making certain that confidentiality has not been breached.

Introduction

'Learning difficulty' or 'learning disability', which term should be used? This is a difficult question to answer and one about which views vary. Ideally people should be referred to by name and not be labelled with a definition that encompasses many different ability levels. In the 1980s the term 'learning difficulties' started to replace the use of the term 'mental handicap'. The use of learning difficulties emerged essentially from the Warnock Report which introduced it as a term to embrace all children with special educational needs. In part, its introduction focused on being more positive and reducing stigmatization. The term was generally applied to children in education; however, there were and still are some who apply it to adults. Later, learning disabilities became the definition more regularly used in relation to adults. In reality the terms 'learning disability' and 'learning difficulty' are, to an extent, used interchangeably to describe someone who has 'intellectual functioning that is more limited and is developing or has developed more slowly than is the case for most of the population' (Thomas and Pierson 1996, p.201). The debate over definitions and labels will continue; however, we will use the term identified by the Government and used by many others. Therefore throughout the book we will predominately refer to people with learning disabilities. No offence is intended to people who prefer to use the term 'learning difficulties'.

Working with People with Learning Disabilities: Theory and Practice was conceived during the authors' working relationship as practice teacher and social work student studying for the Diploma in Social Work. Both authors have a particular long-term interest in the field of learning disabilities and have diverse practical experience in residential, day care and community based services.

Over a number of years both explored theories and their transferability to direct working practice and identified the difficulties in finding appropriate literature that placed theory into learning disabilities based practice. Some texts examined theoretical perspectives, whilst others focused on people with learning disabilities and various aspects of their lives. A combination seemed to be missing and thus the idea for the book was developed.

The book is written to be used in two ways. One as a book, the contents of which make a journey which starts from the initial understanding of a learning disability. It moves through the process of theory to practice, looking at oppression, discrimination and the use of different theories leading towards a way forward in using theoretically based practice.

The book can also be used as a text that can be dipped into as required, each chapter standing on its own. As different areas of study or work are undertaken, specific chapters can be used. Case studies are given in most chapters and are presented in a way that draws evidence and reasoning from the general theories being discussed. Each case study highlights how theory can be used to inform and underpin practice and thus positively support and empower people with learning disabilities.

The authors have considered not only the practice teacher and student roles but the diversity of people who may use theory to inform and underpin practice within the field of learning disabilities. It appeared logical to write a book that could be used as a learning tool for students and a learning guide for practitioners. The book is consequently aimed at any person who is actively involved with, or has an interest in, people with learning disabilities. For example, people within:

- social care
- social work
- nursing
- voluntary sector care
- private sector care
- university and college social care, social work and nursing courses.

It is hoped it will also be of interest to anyone who may have a family member or friend that has a learning disability and wants to understand in more depth some approaches that are used in care and support. Whilst they predominantly focus on the social model of care, case studies are used that are applicable to all sectors of the readership.

The book therefore is designed to be broadly accessible and a practical guide to a variety of theoretical perspectives and their application. It also gives references enabling a deeper insight into areas as required. It is hoped that each chapter will provoke thought, raise questions and enable development of the care and support roles.

The authors have aimed to show the importance of theory informing practice and how this can enhance personal and professional development.

1

What is a Learning Disability?

INTRODUCTION

In this initial chapter we will explore what is meant by a learning disability from a variety of perspectives. The exploration will start with a definition and to offer contrast will identify names and descriptions used over the previous 100 years or so. Through this we hope to develop an understanding of how some terms previously used to describe learning disabilities are still apparent and in use today. The implications of using outdated terminology in the present complex care structure will be explored.

Consideration will be given to the medical and social models of disability as each holds its own values and powers, both positive and negative. The influence of the different models will be examined and the effect they have on people with learning disabilities highlighted. The methods used to diagnose learning disabilities and some relevant terminology will be explored. The need to categorize and label a person in a given model and the attendant potential for discrimination will be considered. Two case studies based in practice settings will be used to illustrate some issues raised in this chapter.

WHAT IS A LEARNING DISABILITY?

To begin the exploration of what is meant by a learning disability we will give an initial definition: 'the Government-approved term for intellectual functioning that is more limited and is developing or has developed more slowly than is the case for most of the population' (Thomas and Pierson 1996, p.202). As the quotation indicates, a learning disability is the terminology used to label people that function at an intellectual level that is significantly lower than the average level of people in society. Many different forms of terminology have been used in the past. The labels and titles used have changed many times over the past century and the changes have been driven by several influences. These have included ideological considerations of the time and through developing theoretical conceptions challenging and exploring the way people with learning disabilities are thought about and cared for. Subsequent legislation has tended to reflect such changes.

We hope that understanding the evolution of the labels used will provide insight into the changing attitudes of today's society towards people with a learning disability. We have chosen to consider the evolution of terminology over the past 100 years and recognize that more could be learnt from looking back further into history. It is not intended to give a definitive historical guide, rather an overview of terminology and its development. We will highlight some of the terminology used and show how it has been reflected in various pieces of legislation.

In the early part of the 1900s the term 'feebleminded' was often used to describe people with learning disabilities. This was reinforced in 1908 with the *Report of the Royal Commission on Care and Control of the Feebleminde*d (Royal Commission 1908). The introduction of the Mental Deficiency Act in 1913 used some similar terminology such as 'feebleminded' but additionally described people as 'idiots, imbeciles and moral imbeciles'. The terminology of 'moral imbecile' was changed to 'moral defective' in the Mental Deficiency Act of 1927.

In the post war years the Beveridge Report (1942), *Social Insurance and Allied Services*, promoted a sense of collective responsibility. This had limited impact on people who were 'moral defectives'. The promotion of the medical model of control and care at the time reinforced the custodial nature of many institutional hospitals. This approach continued for some years. The findings highlighted by the 1954–57 *Royal Commission on Law Relating to Mental Illness and Mental Deficiency* were startling. In 1952, there were over 54,000 in institutions with 70 per cent of people having been retained in excess of five years (HMSO 1957). In this report many areas of care were criticized including educational opportunity, care facilities and release opportunities. Terminology used in the summing up makes interesting reading:

> The idiot, the imbecile and feeble-minded are an integral part of the human race; their existence constitutes an unspoken demand on us. The extent to which we guard their right to the fullest and most useful life, the extent we guarantee to them maximum freedom which they can enjoy and the extent to which we help their families to give them the love they need, is a measure of the extent to which we ourselves are civilised. (HMSO 1957)

Even though the idea was positive the terminology used remained, from today's perspective, negative and discriminatory.

In the USA in the 1950s the term 'subnormal' was introduced. This was followed by the vogue description of the time, 'backward'. In 1946 the Association of Parents of Backward Children was founded and as this association evolved it changed its name and is currently known as Mencap.

The Mental Health Act 1959 used the terms 'subnormal' and 'severely subnormal'. In the 1970s the terminology 'the mentally handicapped' came into use. Handicapped was used as a term to identify people unable to look after themselves, requiring support or charity from others. In 1972 the British Institute of Mental Subnormality was formed; this has now been changed and is known as the British Institute of Learning Disabilities, often referred to as BILD.

In the 1980s 'people with mental handicap' became the preferred term of those in power. For the first time acknowledgement was given that people with learning disabilities were firstly people. The introduction of advocacy and the People First movement in the mid-1980s brought people together and started the process of enabling people with learning disabilities to have a voice. At that time the consensus of people with learning disabilities was to be called 'people with learning difficulties'. This term is still used and is generally applicable to children in education. However, this term still does not escape criticism; the main concern is its vagueness. A learning difficulty may not necessarily be related to people who function at an intellectual level that is significantly lower than the average level of people in society. A conflict arose between the labels placed upon people and what the people themselves wanted to be called.

In 1990 the Department of Health officially adopted the term 'people with learning disabilities'. This has been predominantly used since that time even though many individuals and advocacy groups have challenged it. The original wish of the advocacy groups and self-advocates was recognized by the Central Council for Education and Training in Social Work (CCETSW 1992). This was effected by using the term 'learning difficulties' throughout the paper that looked at new services for people with learning disabilities.

PRESENT LEGISLATION

Terminology used to define a learning disability will now be explored in relation to legislation (legislation is covered in more depth in Chapter 10).

The key piece of legislation that underpins community care is the National Health Service and Community Care Act 1990. Specific terminology such as learning disabilities or learning difficulties is not used in the Act, as a different way of describing people is given. In this the generalized term of 'vulnerable' is used to identify people who should receive assessment. To find out how 'vulnerable' is defined requires use of a different piece of legislation, outlined below.

Section 29 is a part of the National Assistance Act 1948 and provides a definition of 'vulnerable people':

> Persons who are eighteen or over who are blind, the deaf or dumb, or who suffer from mental disorder of any description, and other persons aged eighteen or over who are substantially and permanently handicapped by illness, injury, or congenital deformity or such other disabilities as may be prescribed. (National Assistance Act 1948 in Brayne and Martin 1997, p.280)

This wording shows how many of the terms used in the past century are still apparent in practice now. Other legislative material used within the learning disabilities framework such as the Chronically Sick and Disabled Persons Act 1970 rely on the same definition of Section 29 clients to identify whether eligibility criteria are met. The Department of Health (1993) endeavours to provide some definition of what is meant by 'deaf, dumb and handicapped'. If you have a particular interest in this area, it would be worth obtaining a copy of the circular.

The above legislation illustrates the development of derogatory and stereotypical terms over time and how these terms are still being used. The power of using and imposing such labels as 'dumb' or 'handicapped' should not be underestimated. Awareness of the power issues involved will support the ongoing challenge to the oppression and discrimination faced by people with learning disabilities.

MODELS OF DISABILITY

The definition of disability has mainly come from two perspectives, medical and social. It is useful to understand the difference and the theories underpinning each. This will place them in context and enhance understanding of many issues raised throughout this book when we look at medical and social need. Each definition uses the term 'disability'; this can relate to physical disability or learning disability. We will look at the definitions and focus specifically on a learning disabilities perspective.

The medical model of disability

The model most often used to define disability during the 20th century was predominantly developed through the paradigm of Western medicine. Medical understanding has also been reinforced by religious beliefs and the broader scientific underpinning that medicine has evolved from. These have played a part in the development of what 'has become known as the medical or "personal tragedy" model' of disability (Drake 1999, p.10).

This model relies on 'the understanding of a person's problem, behaviour or condition in terms of illness, diagnosis and treatment' (Thomas and Pierson 1996, p.220). The definition essentially refers to the location of disability in the person, not necessarily in strictly medical terms, but as a characteristic of the person. The medical model 'has been criticised as leading to fragmented help being offered according to specialisations which treat clients as problems rather than as whole beings' (Payne 1997, pp.21–22). Through treatment by the medical profession or related professions that implicitly accept the medical model, aspects of the whole person may be neglected.

In the 1970s the World Health Organisation (WHO) developed a way of differentiating between 'impairment', 'disability' and 'handicap':

- impairment: the loss of physiological or anatomical function. The functions of the body or its structure

- disability: the impact of the impairment on everyday life

- handicap: the social disadvantage that the disability caused.

This mainly focuses on how the body works and neglects to consider the non-medical causes of disability. Additionally it appears to suggest that if a person does not fit into the same category as the majority then the person has an 'abnormality' (Oliver 1990). The diagnosed impairment is often perceived as the cause of the disability. Oliver reinforces the concern that this approach places the disability as the property of the individual and can only be resolved through medical or therapeutic intervention (Oliver 1990, 1996).

This begins to highlight the power held by the people who diagnose or categorize using criteria that have been developed against what is seen and accepted as normal within society. People who have had their presenting characteristics medically defined as a disability have to live and survive in a society that has been built on the social norms of the majority. If the environment and society were better able to adapt to different needs then people with disabilities would be less disabled by society.

The social model of disability can be used to explore this further.

The social model of disability

In the 1970s the Union of Physically Impaired Against Segregation, otherwise known as UPIAS, was formed. In particular, this group challenged the medical model of disability and its definitions of impairment, disability and handicap. UPIAS suggested the following:

- impairment: 'lacking part or all of a limb, or having a defective limb, organism or mechanism of the body'

- disability: 'the disadvantage or restriction of activity' caused by the contemporary social organizations that take very little account of how physical impairments may exclude someone from accessing the majority of society

- handicap: was ignored by the Union and not seen as worthy to be included.

(Union of Physically Impaired Against Segregation 1976 pp.3–4)

The Union's focus on disability looked at the impact that society had on restricting people that were not like the majority. It challenged the norms and values that society held, looking at aspects such as the accessibility of buildings and public transport. If society did not meet the needs of all the people in it irrespective of their physical ability and their mental intellect, then it was society that was causing the disablement, not the medical condition used to explain the function of the person's mind or body.

The contrast between the medical and social model of disability

To aid consideration of the contrast between medical and social models we will provide some initial thoughts about each. We are suggesting these as general ideas and not necessarily specific in every given situation.

The benefits of the medical model may include:

- making a medical diagnosis

- ongoing research into disability

- increasing the understanding of specific diagnosis

- promoting higher expectations of individuals with a disability after a diagnosis has been made

- providing a diagnosis that may be used to support funding of care.

The medical model may limit its consideration of the whole person with a disability, either directly or indirectly, for a number of reasons, based on such factors as:

- the focus remaining on diagnosis through academic medical insight

- treating people as medical cases that need to be cured

- focusing mainly on continuing to strive to eliminate impairment and disability

- the thought that physical or mental impairment is the cause of disability

- labelling, stereotyping and subsequent stigmatization

- lack of inclusion of the person, 'drawing on a "medical model": acting as an "expert" who decides what to do without reference to the people concerned' (Thompson 2000, p.134).

A social model of care and support has many positive attributes that empower people with learning disabilities; these include:

- focusing on the person and not the disability

- challenging social exclusion within the wider society

- focusing on the environmental and social barriers excluding people with a disability from mainstream society

- understanding the need for informed medical diagnosis and health care support

- acknowledgement that even with barriers removed, issues associated with impairment and chronic illness will continue to need addressing

- presenting a continual challenge to institutionalized oppression and discrimination.

The social model can also be challenged since reliance on this model alone might:

- not be fully realistic and may be seen as an idealistic approach

- restrict the opportunity for diagnosis and miss the opportunity to help inform and understand an individual's medical situation

- restrict funding due to lack of medical diagnosis.

The above suggestions about the two models are in no way intended as a definitive guide. Some omissions may be identified by the reader that promote discussion or criticism. The aim, however, has been to show the impact, whether positive or negative, that both models can have on people with learning disabilities. A medical model of disability should not be confused with health care provision or practice. Enhancing a person's ability through health care intervention should promote and enable well being and is an important part of enabling a person within society. Health care and social provision are complementary in making appropriate provision for people with learning disabilities. We will highlight this by considering the support a person may require in practice. A health care and social skills assessment may be required to identify the care and support needed. A health care assessment would look at health needs, take diagnosis into account and include appropriate medication and therapeutic treatment. A social model assessment might look at the broader aspects of care, the social environment, what the person's choices are, where the person might live, the level of care and support required and social opportunities. Joint working, health care and social care assessments may be required to ensure full assessment, funding and support is given to meet individual needs.

People who provide medical care may provide some level of social support or care and people who provide social care may work towards meeting health needs. The medical model and social model of care are two different approaches that go towards explaining the impact of disability within society. Through having an understanding of each and how, to an extent, they overlap, a more informed approach to practice can be taken.

THE CLASSIFICATION OF A LEARNING DISABILITY

The classification of a learning disability (mental retardation) includes a combination of factors, and these factors include both medical and social aspects:

> Mental retardation is a condition of arrested or incomplete development of the mind characterized by the impairment of skills and overall intelligence in areas such as cognition, language, and motor and social abilities. Also referred to as intellectual disability or handicap, mental retardation can occur with or without any other physical or mental disorders. Although reduced level of intellectual functioning is the main characteristic feature of the disorder, the diagnosis is made only if it is associated with a diminished ability to adapt to the daily demands of the normal social environment. (WHO 2000)

If someone is assessed as fitting the above description, that person would usually be diagnosed with a learning disability (mental retardation). The American Association on Mental Retardation (AAMR) offers the following definition which makes the criteria clearer:

> Mental retardation refers to substantial limitations in present functioning. It is characterized by significant subaverage intellectual functioning, existing concurrently with related limitations in two or more of the following applicable adaptive skill areas: communication, self care, home living, social skills, community use, self direction, health and safety, functional academics, leisure and work. Mental retardation manifests itself before age 18. (AAMR 1992)

Significantly sub-average intellectual functioning relates to an intelligence quotient (IQ) test score of 70–75 or below on a standardized individual intelligence test. The term 'related limitations' refers to a person's limitation of adaptive skills. The 1992 AAMR definition moved on from the concept of identifying a person's level of mental ability by only using an IQ test. It also considers patterns of limitations by looking at how a person functions in a variety of situations in everyday life. The AAMR definition does not limit itself purely to intellectual and adaptive skills assessment. A multidimensional approach is used to aid consideration of a person's ability to include four different dimensions: present growth, environmental changes, educational activities and therapeutic interventions.

The AAMR's concept of intervention and support refers to resources and strategies that can be provided to a person with mental retardation to enable them to enhance their independence, productivity, community presence and personal satisfaction. Support may be provided through technology, individuals, agencies or services. Eight types of support function are described:

1. befriending

2. financial planning

3. employee assistance

4. behavioural support

5. in home living assistance

6. community access and use

7. health assistance

8. teaching.

One of four different levels of support would be identified using the AAMR concept:

1.   intermittent or as needed support

2.   limited support, needed regularly but for a short period of time

3.   extensive support

4.   pervasive support.

The AAMR draws together the above concepts and provides a three step procedure for classifying and identifying the required support:

1.   to determine the eligibility for support (IQ 70–75 or below, onset prior to the age of 18 and significant disabilities in two or more of the adaptive skill areas)

2.   to identify the strengths and weaknesses and the need for support across the four dimensions (present growth, environmental changes, educational activities and therapeutic interventions)

3.   to identify the kind of support and the intensity required for each of the four dimensions.

(Adapted from Hawkins-Shepard 1994, p.2)

This concept highlights the diversity of information that is required and used to help identify a learning disability (mental retardation).

Human functioning, disability and health are drawn together by the WHO to provide a structured explanation and framework. Their *International Classification of Functioning and Disability* deals with:

> functional states (i.e. mobility, social integration, etc.) associated with health conditions. It recognises the fact that a diagnosis of diseases and disorders, while important for public health needs, is not sufficient to describe the functional status of the individual and also to predict, guide and plan the various needs of such an individual. (WHO 2000)

The overall aim of the international classification ICIDH-2 is to provide a structured and coherent frame and language to describe 'human functioning and disability as an important part of health' (WHO 2000). Functional states that are associated with health conditions are considered at different levels:

- at body level: functions of the body systems and the body structure

- at an individual level: simple to complex activities performed by a person

- at a society level: simple to complex areas of the person's life, the society the person is involved with or has access to and societal opportunities.

A person's immediate and general environment is also considered.

ICIDH-2 is a multi-purpose classification designed to serve various disciplines and different sectors. It aims:

- to provide a scientific basis for understanding and studying the functional states associated with health conditions

- to establish a common language for describing functional states associated with health conditions in order to improve communications between health care workers, other sectors, and disabled people/people with disabilities

- to permit comparison of data across countries, health care disciplines, services and time

- to provide a systematic coding scheme for health information systems.

(WHO 2000, p.2)

There are many people with learning disabilities who were diagnosed prior to the changing of definitions and methods of assessment discussed above. Many people may have been assessed predominantly through IQ testing. Some case files and records may show an intelligence quotient (IQ), mental age (MA) and chronological age (CA). It is important to recognize that mental age does not describe the level of ability and the nature of the person's life experience or capability to function within society or community living. Mental age is derived from chronological age and intelligence quotient, and thus a fixed mental age cannot be given, as this will vary with chronological age. To enable a better understanding of the levels we will briefly describe the five categories that were often used: borderline, mild, moderate, severe, and profound. We will highlight the difference between each classification identified through IQ testing as these are often referred to:

- *Borderline* is measured within the IQ range of 70–80. This would be characterized by the person having had some learning difficulties at school. In adult life the person should be able to have good social relationships, be a part of, and contribute to, society as a whole.

- *Mild* is measured within the IQ range of 50–69. This would predominantly be characterized as above.

- *Moderate* is measured within the IQ range of 35–49. This would be seen as someone who had very identifiable developmental delays in their childhood. The person should have been able to learn and develop some skills of independence in areas such as self-care, communication and learning skills. An adult would need varying levels of appropriate support to be able to function in the community.

- *Severe* is measured within the IQ range of 20–34. The need for continuous support is very likely.

- *Profound* is measured by an IQ of under 20. This level of IQ would show that there are severe limitations in self-care, communication and mobility. The need for long-term continuous care would most likely be essential.

(Adapted from Grossman 1983; Holt, Kon and Bouras 1995)

The AAMR and the WHO definitions and approaches used to identify a learning disability draw together the medical model IQ testing and social model adaptive functioning. The complex nature and the changing face of classification remains a prevalent issue and one that will continue to impact on people with learning disabilities.

HOW MANY PEOPLE HAVE A LEARNING DISABILITY?

As classification is often both difficult and complex it is hard to gain an accurate figure of how many people there are with learning disabilities. In the 1980s The Arc (1982) identified that approximately 2.5 to 3 per cent of the general population have a level of learning disability. This was reinforced in The Arc's report and the World Health Report in 2001, where as many as three out of every 100 people are thought to have some level of learning disability (The Arc 2001; The World Health Report 2001). It would be possible to go to each county and check how many people are known to social services and to health services. This, however, would not give an accurate picture as many people may not receive services.

We will briefly provide some published figures for the UK. The DoH researched and estimated that in 1992 there were between 120,000 and 160,000 adults in England that had a severe or profound learning disability (DoH 1992). Many people who have a mild or moderate learning disability may function without the services providing support. In 2001 approximately 210,000 people in England have a severe learning disability and 1.2 million have a mild or moderate learning disability (DoH 2001a).

In Scotland there is limited detailed information about the number of people with learning disabilities. However, it is estimated that three to four people for every thousand have a profound or multiple disability and twenty people out of every thousand have a mild or moderate learning disability. This equates to approximately fifteen to twenty thousand people in Scotland with a learning disability (Scottish Executive 1999).

In Wales the Learning Disabilities Advisory Group suggests that there are approximately four to five people per thousand with a severe learning disability. This equates to approximately 10,800 people with a severe learning disability living in Wales. People with mild learning disabilities have been estimated at twenty five to thirty people per thousand population (Learning Disability Advisory Group 2000).

In Northern Ireland we were unable to locate a comparative document to those above. In discussion with the consultation team for *Improving Civil Rights for Disabled People* (Northern Ireland Executive 2001) we were told that no similar document was yet produced; however, it was suggested that the figures would in all likelihood be comparable to those of the UK mainland.

Mencap state that there are 'nearly...one point five million people with a learning disability living in the UK' (Mencap 2002, p.1). The Foundation for People with Learning Disabilities (2001) suggests that between 580,000 and 1,750,000 (1–3% of the population in the UK) have a mild learning disability and between 230,000 and 350,000 (0.4–0.6%) have a severe learning disability. These figures lend insight into the overall numbers of people that have some level of learning disabilities living within the UK. With the improvement in medical knowledge and people living longer the number of people with learning disabilities will continue to increase.

WHAT ARE THE MAIN CAUSES OF A LEARNING DISABILITY?

The causes of learning disabilities can be divided into two areas, 'genetic' and 'environmental', although these may at times overlap (AAMR 1992; Russell 1985). A learning disability can be caused by any condition that impairs the development of the brain either before birth, during birth or within the childhood years. It has been suggested that several hundred different causes have been discovered. However, even with so many causes identified the reason remains unknown for approximately one-third of the people that have a learning disability (The Arc 2001).

The causes of a learning disability may relate to:

- genetic disorders, e.g. phenylketonuria
- chromosomal deviations, e.g. Down's syndrome, Fragile-X syndrome
- cranial malfunctions, e.g. hydrocephalus
- congenital factors, e.g. maternal disease, substance exposure, prematurity, perinatal concerns
- psychosocial and environmental factors.

These causes can be explored in greater depth in medical journals, research documents and through the work of The Arc, BILD, Mencap and various support groups and societies.

LEARNING DISABILITIES AND MENTAL ILLNESS

It is important to reinforce the difference between a learning disability and mental illness as these are often confused even in today's society. We have explored the terminology of a learning disability in depth. In contrast a mental illness can be explained as abnormal feelings, thoughts and behaviour which can lead to an inability to function in everyday life. These are conditions that with medical intervention and medication may be improved and alleviated. Recognizing the difference between mental illness and a learning disability avoids misconceptions.

At the beginning of the 1900s people with either of these diagnoses were frequently confined in the same institutions. As time has moved on, different services have developed including institutional care and today's separate service provision. Many social service departments have separate mental health and learning disabilities teams enabling a better understanding of the different needs. Even though a learning disability and mental illness are different it should not be overlooked that a person could have both.

As discussed there are many different syndromes and diagnoses that are found within the learning disabilities field. It can be useful to have an understanding of specific conditions in order to improve the support and care role. Additional information relating to specific diagnoses and medical and social implications can be found in many medical and social work journals, texts and reference books.

LABELLING

In this chapter we have explored how diagnosis and classification when identifying a learning disability takes place. Such classification often creates a label as a means of identification. The label may be 'learning disability' or of a particular syndrome; whatever the label is, it can impact upon a person throughout his or her life. We will now consider this in more depth.

Being labelled

Labels can be placed on individuals as well as groups and the impact and implications of being labelled may be far reaching and should not be underestimated. Labels can be seen as both positive and negative. They have the potential to create negative influence, to stigmatize and affect the person who is labelled. Some of the causes of oppression and discrimination associated with the labelling process will be highlighted.

Consideration will be given to the need for labelling in order for a person to receive a service. An assessment needs to take place and a diagnosis made of, for example, learning disabilities or mental health for the purposes of service allocation. A person not only has to be labelled to receive many support services but also has to face the impact of being so labelled. These issues will be explored by investigating labelling theory.

Labelling and its background

Initially we will explore what is meant by a label and consider the power of labelling. One definition of a label is: '[Something] attached to an object giving information on it…to classify…to describe' (Hawker and Hawkins 1996). The label placed on someone may be there to provide information to others about that person, to categorize them, to identify who they are or what they do. Each person can carry a multitude of labels. These may include labels that identify ethnic or cultural background, family position such as husband, wife, partner, parent, brother, sister and child. They may also relate to class, work, employment or student status. Specific job titles such as 'nurse', 'social worker', 'care worker' may have the same effect. Each label informs others of who and what we are and a level of expectation will usually be attached to the various labels.

Many of the labels just mentioned will largely be seen as positive. In reality labels are not always positive; this may be due to personal interpretation or society's perception affected by stigma and stereotyping. Labels such as 'unemployed' or 'single parent' may have some level of stigma attached by some people and not others. The impact of labels such as 'sex offender' may have lifelong implications. This is not intended as a guide to the hierarchy of labels or those that are positive and negative; it is intended to provoke thought about the diversity and power of labels. Each of us may perceive labels in different ways. This will be affected by our understanding of the label and, to an extent, if we know the person or not. Labelling is not an exact science but open to interpretation and misinterpretation.

Within the health and care fields labels are often placed on a person to categorize a condition and to help identify whether services should be provided. The label of learning disabled is not placed on a person to be deliberately negative. However, being identified as having a learning disability, and being called something that reinforces and informs others of this, does not appear to be particularly supportive or empowering.

Thomas and Pierson offer a different perspective with their explanation of labelling and labelling theory. 'The process whereby people holding positions of power or influence sometimes attribute generalized negative characteristics to particular categories of individuals, tending to produce or amplify those behavioural characteristics attributed' (Thomas and Pierson 1996, p.200). This definition places a strong emphasis on the power that a person holds when placing a label on someone else. By considering the origins of labelling from its sociological perspective a clearer understanding of its part in today's care work can be gained.

Becker (1963) and Lemert (1972) were key people in the development of labelling theory. Becker (1963) explored the links between the sociological perspective of 'symbolic interactionalism' and labelling. Symbolic interactionalism (Blumer 1969; Mead 1934) considered the way in which understanding and explanations materialize through the study of interactions of people. They explored the meanings given to bodies, feelings, situations and the wider social worlds in which we exist. Much of the work focused on a person's deviance from society's 'normal' expectations. If a person deviated from the normal, then society often treated the person in a negative or oppressive way. The idea that deviance was caused by society's oppressive responses to people's labels gained acceptance in the 1960s and 1970s (Rosenham 1973).

Goffman (1961) looked at labelling in terms of how and why people were defined by others, and explored the effect of the labelling process on people's subsequent behaviour. Goffman suggested that labelling essentially creates deviance or abnormality because the individual adjusts their behaviour to that of the label. Becker (1964) and Lemert (1967) considered deviancy theory in the broader context of any person or group that deviated from the 'normal'. Society's responses to people with a learning disability may not be against specific deviant behaviour but in response to deviance from the accepted societal norm.

The link between sociological understanding and the impact of labelling can be used to explain some aspects of human and social behaviour. Becker (1963, 1964) raised the following points:

- Human behaviour is influenced to a high degree by the social expectations that others have on individuals and groups.

- Though labels can operate as a negative process they do not always successfully explain deviant behaviour.

- Labels used in a widespread way increase the likelihood of stereotypical conceptions of particular categories or groups of people which can lead to exclusion through ignorance, mistrust or misinformed understanding.

- Institutional labellers such as state agencies and those in control of health and social welfare possess power to place labels on people that can have a radical influence on their lives.

Becker suggested that people in a position to label others must always consider the impact of that labelling. This included the power held by the person placing the label, the impact of the label on the person and how this might affect his or her acceptance within society.

The stereotyping and stigma faced by people with certain labels that are still prevalent today are reinforced by media coverage, bad press and, at times, ignorance. The term 'mentally handicapped' is still heard on the television and read within news reports. The difference between learning disability and mental illness is often confused, increasing the level of stigma and stereotyping both groups may face. The labels 'learning disabilities' or 'learning difficulties', although perhaps today's politically correct descriptions, may be derogatory. Rowitz described this terminology as 'a nice catch-all phrase to explain anything relative to mental retardation' (Rowitz 1974, p.265). The terminology of handicapped, mentally impaired or retarded can conjure up pictures that restrict or show ignorance of the true abilities of the person labelled. This reinforces the idea that it is often ignorance or misunderstanding of given labels, or the wider restriction of society in response to them, that may oppress or cause discrimination.

The placing of labels

We have touched upon why labels are placed upon people and will go on to explore some of the issues further. Many of the labels that describe people who have a learning disability have derived from medical definitions. Historically the label of 'mental impairment' was used and this can be found in policies and legislation that are in use today. For example, it can be found in legislation such as the National Assistance Act 1948 and the Chronically Sick and Disabled Persons Act 1970 (Brayne and Martin 1997) (see Chapter 10 for more information about legislation). Oliver (1990) suggests that the mere fact that a medical definition is used to describe disability only achieves marginalization and dehumanization of the person.

The impact of being classed as disabled is another label that can affect people with a learning disability. Disablism considers the impact of functional disability by focusing on the combination of 'Social forces, cultural values and personal prejudices that marginalizes disabled people, portrays them in a negative light and thus oppresses them' (Thompson 1997, p.107). People with a learning disability can face both disablism and discrimination due to the label they are given. They can be further disabled and discriminated against by the confusion of mental impairment and mental illness. Perceptions around and acceptance of these labels can increase pressure upon the person. Multiple oppression may occur through additional labelling associated with gender, age, culture or race. An understanding of labelling theory can help unpick the implications of the names, descriptions and titles given to people.

We mentioned earlier that the initial work of social interactionalism and labelling focused on deviance from the normal. Wolfensberger (1972) undertook work that focused on 'normalization' (see Chapter 4). Labels such as 'learning disabled' are given to people because their functioning ability and IQ are lower than 'normal'. A person is diagnosed as physically disabled if unable to achieve what 'normal' able bodied people can achieve. Any criteria that relies on a label being placed, which is measured from a 'normal' standpoint, is fraught with danger. This concept looks at adjusting the person in relation to the majority. It may continue to promote the exclusion of people who are not measured as 'normal'.

Who has the right to decide the definition of 'normal' and how it is measured? Care and support providers are often involved in the process that decides what label to give someone. This may be defined by medical or social criteria. Whether or not a service is provided may hinge upon the label given to that person which best describes their medical condition or need and how that person fits into specific eligibility criteria. However, labels can also be helpful in accessing services, claiming benefits, diagnosing illness and accessing correct treatment. It is also worthy of consideration that many of the tests and criteria used to diagnose and label are measured from specifications that are white, middle-class and western European (Baxter *et al.* 1990). This may further oppress and discriminate through racial and cultural bias and should be taken into consideration when providing support. Whatever label is placed, the person should remain central.

The label placed on a person can have a major impact on how the individual copes or is accepted within society. However, without various labels it would be difficult to access many of the services restricted by rigid eligibility criteria. By considering and understanding the impact and power of labelling the risk of stigmatizing or marginalizing can be reduced.

We have explored some of the complex aspects of the medical and social models of disability. The relevance of each model and their intertwining when providing care is an intrinsic part of working in the learning disabilities field. The impact of classification and labelling has also been explored. The following case studies will highlight aspects of these perspectives in a practice context.

CASE STUDY ONE

Ivan referred himself and his son Serge to social services as he was finding it increasingly difficult to cope with Serge. Serge required a variety of support to enable him to function and participate both at home and in the community. Ivan also knew he himself would soon have to go into hospital for an operation and wished to pre-empt a crisis when this occurred as he clearly could not leave Serge on his own at home.

An initial assessment was undertaken by a social worker. The family were unknown to social services and the social worker was unsure whether Serge had a learning disability or not. The social worker contacted the GP who had no definite diagnosis for Serge. In consultation with Ivan and the social worker the GP referred Serge for a fuller medical assessment and diagnosis.

Application in practice

Ivan was struggling to cope with his adult son. Ivan's two other sons had recently left home and without their support and presence Ivan felt increasingly isolated and overwhelmed. The family were not known to social services; until this time they had always supported Serge within the family group. The family had come to live in Britain when Serge was already an adult so there were no childhood records of him. The problem for the social worker lay in the fact that without a diagnosis she could not allocate Serge's case to a specific team and thus it would be difficult to access resources for Serge and Ivan.

In this instance even the resources of social services relied upon the Western medical approach, the medical model, of needing a diagnosis to ensure eligibility before structured support could be put in place. It would have been theoretically possible for the social worker to make an assessment of need without the formal diagnosis by talking to Serge and Ivan and others involved. This however may not fit within the protocol and procedures and subsequently not be acceptable in the face of restricted resources and budget allocation. The diagnosis gave credence and enabled allocation to a specific team and the subsequent arrangement of a care package.

CASE STUDY TWO

Evalyn had lived in the family home with her parents and later with her niece Lillian. Evalyn was 58 years of age and had become increasingly forgetful. In the recent months she seemed confused at times, forgetting the names of some of those familiar to her and the names of some common objects. Evalyn had also become aggressive on a few occasions, which was most unlike her usual even temperament. She also started to wander in the night, on two occasions had left the house in her nightdress, and had been found by passers-by.

Lillian began to find it increasingly difficult to cope with Evalyn and her friend suggested she contact social services for help. Lillian explained the situation to the duty social worker, who arranged for an initial assessment visit to be made by someone from the learning disabilities team. It was also arranged that Lillian have a carer's assessment in order to look at her needs.

At the assessment they all agreed a suitable care package to support Evalyn at home. At this point the social worker suggested that Evalyn should see her GP again in order to get a formal medical assessment and firm diagnosis in relation to her medical support needs. Evalyn was referred to a specialist for further investigation and diagnosis. When this was complete it was confirmed that Evalyn had Alzheimer's disease.

Application in practice

To receive a social needs assessment Evalyn first had to have some form of label, in this instance learning disabilities. She could then be assessed by the community learning disability team. As main support provider Lillian had the label of carer placed upon her, thus enabling a carer's assessment to be undertaken.

Due to the increased risks Evalyn was presenting through medical causes, it was necessary for her to have a specialist medical assessment and to be diagnosed and labelled as having Alzheimer's disease. This enabled her to access additional funding and thus additional support. It also meant that the community psychiatric nurse became involved and could further support both Evalyn and Lillian.

In this case Evalyn was 58 years old before she became known to social services and formally labelled as having learning disabilities. This was done with the positive intention of assessment to provide a support package. Ultimately, Evalyn having the additional label of Alzheimer's disease helped Lillian to understand some of her behaviour and support needs. It also enabled Lillian to gain the support of the community psychiatric nurse and to be put in touch with a carers' support group, all of which proved positive for Lillian and her care of Evalyn.

CONCLUSION

We have identified what a learning disability is and shown that its classification is by no means a straightforward process. Consideration of aspects of diagnosis and classification enables a more structured understanding of the developing approaches for working with people with learning disabilities. Whilst classification and labelling may enhance understanding and enable care provision, the impact of such classification and labelling can be powerful, discriminatory and oppressive. By listening to people with a learning disability we can work towards a greater holistic understanding of the impact of being labelled learning disabled.

It is important to remember that whatever title, label, diagnosis or syndrome has been given to a person that they are firstly that – a person. It is not about concentrating solely on meeting the needs identified through specific diagnosis or classification, it is about spending time to get to know and understand the person holistically.

Key points

- Learning disability and learning difficulty are two descriptions used to mean the same thing. There is an ongoing long-term debate about which, if either, should be used.

- There are many other terms and descriptions used to describe people with a learning disability; these are especially found in legislation. Many of these terms are outdated and unacceptable in today's society.

- There are various degrees of learning disability; these are identified through IQ testing and functioning assessments.

- A medical model perspective locates the disability in the person – not necessarily in strict medical terms, but as a characteristic of the person.

- A social model perspective focuses on the person's social needs and focuses on how individuals can be supported within society.

- The process of care between the two models is different and an awareness of the impact of each is important.

- Labelling theory has its origins in sociological perspectives.

- Labels can be both positive and negative.

- Everyone has some type of label placed on them; for example, mother, son, colleague, friend, nurse or care worker. Many of these labels may be perceived as positive.

- Labels can lead to the stigmatization and stereotyping of people; for example, labels such as 'learning disabled' and 'mentally ill'.

- Legislation plays a part in reinforcing definitions and labelling people. Some pieces of legislation used today in the learning disabilities field are over 50 years old and contain archaic terminology.

- At times labels are required to enable a person to be categorized to gain financial support.

- The impact and power of labels should not be underestimated.

2

Application of Theory

INTRODUCTION

In this chapter we will explore the importance of developing an understanding of what theories are, the diversity of where theories may originate and how they can be used. We will introduce three of the main theoretical perspectives, social science, psychology and political science, that provide a structural framework for many of the theories that are used to inform day to day social and health care practice. Throughout this book we seek to demonstrate how theories can link directly to practice and the benefits of using them in a variety of applications. The importance of knowledge and theory being integral to practice is reinforced when considering the Central Council for Education and Training in Social Work criteria. 'It is essential…that students…demonstrate that they not only know about a range of social work methods and theoretical approaches, but that they can select and make skilled use of them in their practice' (CCETSW 1996, p.17).

We will explore how support and practice can become informed support and practice through the use of a theoretically based approach. Following chapters will go on to explore specific theories and their use in day to day practice. Two case studies will be provided, one to illustrate how theories can be used to inform practice, the other to illustrate the importance of developing informed practice using reflective learning underpinned by theory.

WHAT IS MEANT BY THEORY?

One definition of theory is: 'a set of ideas formulated to explain something; opinion, supposition; statement of the principles of a subject' (Hawker and Hawkins 1996, p.333). In the dictionary of social work, theory is described as 'a set of propositions or hypotheses that seek to explain phenomena' (Thomas and Pierson 1996, p.380). Both definitions place an emphasis on theory being developed from ideas, drawn together to formulate an explanation. If a theory is to have credibility and be accepted then two things appear common to its success: the credentials of the person or people suggesting the ideas and some form of proof either through testing or research that validates the concept. The likelihood of having the knowledge, skills and financial ability to fund the research required to develop a theory may belong to only a few – those with knowledge, resources and time. This raises an issue that theory may in reality only be suggested and created by a limited amount of people. If this is the case then those able to develop a theory may hold a position of power over those to whom the theory will be applied.

An understanding of the origin of a theory can provide insight into the perspective from which it comes. For example, theories based on medical or social need, developed for political reasons or for advancement of a specific area of study. Whether theories take into account diversity, ethnicity, race or culture may also impact upon their validity. These factors all have relevance to the development and reasons for theories being created.

Many of the theories that have a relation to social, medical and health care come from a social science perspective. We will briefly consider some of the different areas of social science that have provided theoretical perspectives which can be used in the learning disabilities field.

SOCIAL SCIENCE

There are various disciplines associated with the term 'social science'. We will highlight three that have particular relevance: sociology, psychology and what is sometimes referred to as political science. Sociology and an area of political science, social policy, are explored in more depth in Chapter 10.

Sociology

It is not an easy task to find one explanation that clearly and fully describes the diversity of sociology and sociological studies. An explanation formed through reading and interpreting many authors' perspectives is that sociology is a study of the social structures that surround us, what they are, what they do and how they have evolved. The study of sociology focuses on people's different life experiences within these social structures. Explanations of structural influence through social class, gender and race can all be made with an understanding gained from sociological studies.

Sociology enables and informs an understanding of the social institutions and relationships that affect individuals and groups. Sociology has highlighted patterns of inequality that have affected and impacted on those within society. It presents different perspectives of social forces and provides insight into issues of social stability and social change. Sociology can also provide explanations on the nature of deviance.

Sociological studies can inform us on a variety of issues:

- culture and society
- culture and behaviour
- socialization
- norms and values
- status and role
- theories of society
- views of human behaviour.

(Haralambos and Holburn 1991, pp.2–18)

This reinforces an argument that the area of study of sociology is immense and deserves further consideration. Other texts provide information in the context of social work (Dominelli 1997b), and care provision for people with learning disabilities (Iphofen and Poland 1998).

Psychology

Psychology can be described as the scientific study of behaviour and of the mind. This includes the mental processes that are undertaken by each of us, including memory, thinking, perception, understanding, social relationships and social interaction. Specific psychology for social care and social work will not be explored in depth here; other texts undertake that task (for example, Messer and Jones 1999; Robinson 1995).

Psychology is able to offer conceptual and theoretical insight that can have an impact on social care and support work. Many different theories or therapeutic strategies are used in the care and support of people with learning disabilities. Often there is not an awareness of the links these approaches and methods have to psychology and psychological research. Some of these theoretical approaches and methods of working are:

- systems theory
- crisis intervention
- loss and bereavement
- group work

- counselling

- psychotherapy

- behaviour modification

- social interaction work.

(Adapted from Herbert 1981)

In many working situations more than one theory can be used to inform and enhance practice. For example, following a crisis situation; insight may be gained from the use of systems theory and, subsequently, counselling may be helpful once the crisis has been worked through. Using theories from different disciplines can also inform and enhance practice.

Political science

Political science focuses on studying power and the distribution of power within different types of political systems. Aspects of political power might include:

- the sources of power

- how power is exercised and used

- how constraint is achieved

- how control is operated

- those that win and those that lose power struggles.

The diversity of those involved in policy making includes various political institutions, political parties, the state and interest groups. Political systems may also be influenced by such institutions as the European Union and worldwide political agendas. All have relevance to how policy creation may influence and affect people with learning disabilities, either directly or indirectly.

Political science and policy making can be explored specifically in relation to disability policies. As discussed in Chapter 1, the medical and social perspectives of disability affect the way policies are created. Medical perspectives often hold power in setting criteria and accessibility to services defined by specific policies created by the state. 'Human values and aspirations are realised by an exercise of power channelled through some process, system or conduit and that which converts understanding and definitions of disability into tangible policy is the state' (Drake 1999, p.18).

In the case of disability policy, a commissioned piece of research or specific area of inquiry is usually carried out. This may result in a Green Paper, which is a format for discussion about a policy that the Government would like to become a piece of legislation. When all the comments received have been studied, the paper is returned and becomes a White Paper; this is put forward before Government as a Command Paper. It will contain specific measures that are intended to become law. The Bill then has to be discussed in both the House of Commons and the House of Lords. This is undertaken three times, each having a committee stage and a report stage in each House. The Bill is read through line by line and any negotiated amendments will be made. If the Bill passes through both Houses it goes for Royal Assent and then is passed into law as an Act of Parliament. There are other methods by which a Bill may be put forward, either by backbenchers of the governing party or from an opposition MP, if they have been successful through ballot in introducing the proposal. Bills may relate to health care, social care, benefits entitlement or education, all issues that can have a direct effect upon people with learning disabilities.

We wish to highlight the potential and real power that is held by Government and suggest that it may be better understood with a knowledge of political science. This then underlines the influence that the Government and those holding power have over the rest of society. The people affected, in this case people with learning disabilities, have little chance to challenge policies and their effects, although they may have an opportunity to be part of a consultation process. Further study on policy relating to disability can be found, for example, in Drake (1999) and Priestley (1999).

SOCIAL WELFARE AND PRACTICE

Sociology, psychology, political science and many of the theories developed from these main perspectives can be used to explain and provide insight into situations that occur in day to day practice. For example, understanding political science can inform the practitioner as to why certain policies and structures are used in various aspects of care. Legislation has influence over how services are provided, resources that are available and financial expenditure. Policy and legislation play a vital part in informing everyday practice and underpinning social welfare provision.

Midwinter (1994) suggested that social welfare consists of 'four common threads by way of solution':

...some balance of public and private provision is normally to be found; there are compromises as to whether the services are organised centrally or at more local levels; there are constant debates as to whether treatments should be delivered personally, at home, for instance, or whether recipients should be treated in institutions; there are likewise decisions to be made about making provision in cash or kind. (Midwinter 1994, p.1)

The above threads can be seen as pertinent to the learning disabilities field. The number of places that are provided by the statutory sector and those provided by the private and voluntary sector are all dependent upon funding. The management of fund holding is likely to affect the amount of money available to meet the medical, health care or social needs of a person. Fund holding may be managed jointly between health and social services or independently by one or the other. The rights of someone to receive care at home may be restricted by resources affecting the availability of home care support, housing rights and benefits that can be claimed. A reliance on voluntary or family support to enable a person to continue living in the community may mean the funding is decreased. This may lead to an inaccurate guide to the real cost of community support. The complexity of social welfare provision, the limitations of resources and the benefits structure can impinge upon the rights of individuals and their care.

The nature of welfare provision in society and how society itself has developed holds a key to how services are provided, the number of services available and subsequent limitations. The influence on society of political ideals and other external factors at any given time impact upon the provision of social, medical and health care. These are reliant on realistic funding to meet the needs of the people being supported. Services are often resource led, the resources available are identified and the person needing a service will be fitted in accordingly. We suggest it is preferable to work in partnership and jointly assess need, identify the support systems required and then provide a needs-led care package. As the last one hundred years of care for people with learning disabilities has shown, a service-led process has been the norm.

Understanding the origins of theories and why they have been developed plays an important part in enabling practice to become informed practice.

INFORMED PRACTICE

Thompson (1996) explains the principles of theory and practice in health and social welfare settings. A core issue suggested by Thompson is that of informed practice. The benefits of using an informed approach are summed up as necessary to:

- do justice to the complexity of the situations social and health care workers so frequently encounter

- avoid assumptions, prejudices and stereotypes that can lead to discrimination and oppression

- lay the foundations for a developmental approach, one which permits and facilitates continuous personal and professional development

- ensure a high level of motivation, challenge and commitment.

(Thompson 1996, pp.1–2)

Informed practice is suggested as being achieved through what Thompson refers to as 'thinking and doing'. The idea comprises the notion of learning from experience. When people undertake practice they should think about how they have been working and reflect on their practice. This can be achieved by thinking about:

- What went well?

- What did not go well?

- What are the reasons it did not go well?

- What could have been done differently?

- Why should anything be done differently?

When considering what could have been done differently or better, the use of one or more theories may highlight how aspects of work could be improved next time. This provides the opportunity to learn from experience. A reflective approach enables practice to be explored and adapted to meet the needs of the person being supported and to provide insight into areas of oppression and discrimination that need challenging. This should lead to 'improved levels of practice; increased opportunities for job satisfaction; a basis from which to justify decisions made and actions taken; continuous professional development' (Thompson 1996, p.111).

THEORY IN PRACTICE

Theory can provide guidance and insight to inform and aid reflection and analysis of practice. Specific theories can provide a structured approach to working that can promote confidence and understanding for care and support workers. In some working environments the workers may be left to work predominantly on their own where practice may not frequently be observed or examined. This could lead to an environment mainly reliant on a 'we have always done it this way' approach rather than a theoretically informed approach. Goffman (1961) wrote of the ongoing institutionalized behaviour of support and care workers through a learnt behaviour strategy, rarely challenging or questioning working practice or ethical issues that surround care:

> Social workers [and care workers of any description], to be truly effective, need to be constantly asking why. It is in this quest for understanding about, for example, why situations arise, why people react in certain ways and why particular interventions might be utilised, that theory informs practice. (Coulshed and Orme 1998, p.9)

Each person and situation should be seen as individual; however, knowledge, skills and the understanding of theories can be used to inform and enhance all aspects of practice.

The first case study that follows will illustrate the application of theory and provide an example of how individual theories discussed later in this book can be used to help practice become informed practice. The second case study will reinforce the benefit of reflecting upon and analysing how a person is supported and of using theory to inform the development of practice.

CASE STUDY ONE

Four young people had recently moved from residential school into a staffed house in the community. They were all students on full-time courses at the local college. A few weeks into term the staff noticed that the four residents were finding it difficult to get up and get ready for college in the mornings. The staff attributed this to too many late nights and decided to instigate a 10pm bedtime for the residents during the week. This would then enable them to get up earlier and get to college on time.

Application in practice

This case study can be considered from a variety of perspectives. The wider picture of care and support in residential homes within the community can, in part, be explored through sociological theory. There are many sociological studies that have been undertaken that look at the structure of society and the expectations of people within it. For example, there are studies on care provision and how people should be supported, educated and, at times, controlled.

Psychological theories can inform and lend insight into why people behave in certain ways. Every person has some level of learned behaviour or family scripts informing him or her of the 'best' way of doing things. Looking at the practice in this case study, to the staff it appeared that the 'best' way of doing things was for the residents to go to bed earlier. Through the staff's family scripts, they had learnt 'early to bed, early to rise' and imposed this upon the residents. The staff's approach, however, did not allow the residents to learn from their own experience. If the residents had been able to continue their late nights and experience the consequences of lateness or absence from college they may have been able to adapt their habits accordingly. However, it should also be considered that the social care remit to provide a safe and supportive environment might, on occasion, require protection and control to minimize the risk of harm. Balancing rights and risks requires working in partnership with the individuals involved.

In this instance the staff had oppressed the residents and discriminated against them as adults by their imposition of a 10pm bedtime (see Chapter 3). The staff were aware of college expectations concerning attendance but their practice did not allow the residents to learn this for themselves. If the 'learned' approaches had been evaluated and used in conjunction with theories such as role theory (Chapter 9) or social learning theory (Chapter 8), then more informed practice may have taken place.

CASE STUDY TWO

Mtembe had been key worker to Jacob for six months. Jacob had limited verbal communication and used Makaton to communicate. Jacob had become increasingly frustrated in his general communication in recent weeks leading, on occasion, to him hitting himself.

Mtembe brought Jacob's case for discussion at the staff meeting to look at how the work was approached and reflect upon the methods used and how they could be improved. On reflection it was clear to Mtembe that he did not have enough knowledge about communication methods to provide the required support. Mtembe needed to inform his practice and adapt his ways of working. Thus he requested to attend a communication course to improve his ability to work with Jacob. On the course Mtembe learned to look more widely at aspects of communication including the use of symbols and computer software. He also learned about environmental and other barriers to communication.

Application in practice

Through Mtembe's reflection about Jacob and his communication needs he had identified factors that could be improved. Mtembe was fairly fluent in Makaton but recognized certain staff were not; it was not a signing environment. When the staff team discussed their approaches, inconsistencies were identified in the systems (Chapter 9) around Jacob and a more uniform approach was decided upon when working with him.

Through reflection upon his work Mtembe thought that a better understanding of communication methods (Chapter 5) and of possible barriers that restricted communication would improve his knowledge and skills. This informed practice would enable him to be a more effective key worker to Jacob. Mtembe was thinking about his own and others' practice, what worked well and what did not work so well and what could be done differently.

Mtembe thought about what he had learned and used these ideas in partnership with Jacob and staff to enhance Jacob's quality of life. Mtembe was thinking and doing, using theory to enhance practice. From the doing they could decide what was most helpful to Jacob and what was not so helpful and further modify practice. Thus, support and practice became informed support and practice.

CONCLUSION

The use of theory is summed up by Payne (1997):

> ...theory is practically useful, and...its variety and confusion can be organised and understood. The relationships and oppositions between theories provide a context in which their value can be assessed against one another, and against the modern social context in which they must be used. (Payne 1997, p.71)

An understanding of what a theory is and the diversity of theories that can be used in day to day practice has been suggested. The benefit of the use of theories is twofold: meeting the needs of the person who is being supported and as a way of learning. Theories are important in developing personal understanding and insight into providing effective care that can be assessed and validated in its delivery. We have looked at theory informing practice and the use of an underpinning theoretical framework. We will progress chapter by chapter to provide a more in-depth theoretical framework that can be used when working with people with learning disabilities.

Key points

- Theories originate from many different perspectives and are tried and tested methods of explaining and informing given situations.

- Theory can be used to provide insight and guidance and to aid reflection upon and analysis of practice.

- Theories can be used to inform practice by providing an understanding about different ways of working and supporting people with learning disabilities.

- More than one theory can be used at a time.

- Theories discussed in this book can be used to help inform practice with other groups such as older people, those with mental health issues and children and families.

- Social work and health care training bodies reinforce the importance of theory being used to inform and underpin practice.

3

Anti-Discriminatory Practice
and Anti-Oppressive Practice

INTRODUCTION

Anti-discriminatory practice and anti-oppressive practice are terms often heard within care and support work. In this book we are focusing on people with a learning disability, but we must stress that the principles discussed can be applied and used to inform practice in other fields of care work.

In this chapter we will start by briefly exploring some of the underpinning ideas that help to highlight issues of discrimination and oppression. We will go on to explore what is meant by discrimination and oppression. This will be achieved by considering some of the forms each can take. Exploring these different forms will develop a focus upon the impact each can have. The information gained will subsequently provide and reinforce an understanding of how a theoretical framework can be used to promote an anti-discriminatory and anti-oppressive approach.

The idea of anti-discriminatory and anti-oppressive practice is fundamental; it should underpin day to day practice and will consequently be used throughout the book. The importance of this as an intrinsic part of practice will be emphasized as this chapter unfolds. An anti-discriminatory and anti-oppressive approach will be placed in a practice context of working with people with learning disabilities through two case studies.

UNDERPINNING IDEAS

An understanding of issues relating to discrimination and oppression has predominantly developed from sociologically based studies. Some psychological work has further informed specific situations. Sociological explanations of the structure of society provide insight and an understanding of the impact created by difference. For example, insight is gained through studies undertaken on race, deviance, sexuality, gender and class. Within any structure where there is difference, power bases may be affected. Majority and minority groups develop and attitudes between different groups may conflict. Such conflict could then lead to discrimination and oppression. Payne (1997) discusses the impact of sociological studies on our understanding of discrimination and oppression and subsequent anti-discriminatory and anti-oppressive practice. We intend to explore the concepts of discrimination and oppression and show their impact upon care and support work with people with a learning disability.

DISCRIMINATION AND OPPRESSION

To introduce this section on discrimination and oppression we will explore what is meant by the terms. Discrimination is the unfair or prejudicial differentiation or treatment of individuals or groups of people. Discrimination is found in all areas of society and faced by many people in a variety of different ways. Through discrimination, judgements may be made about individuals or groups of people. These judgements may be made from non-relevant criteria, criteria which may, however, be predominant within society.

Oppression describes the unjust treatment of individuals or groups of people through the exertion of power, both individual and structural. Power is used to implement unfair judgements, often widely, over specific people or groups within society.

In this chapter we will explore perspectives of anti-discriminatory and anti-oppressive practice in a practice context. A definition of each will be given; this will provide a basis from which to understand how discrimination and oppression can be identified and subsequently challenged. Anti-discriminatory practice: 'A term used widely...to describe how workers take account of structural disadvantage and seek to reduce individual and institutional discrimination particularly on grounds of race, gender, disability, social class and sexual orientation' (Thomas and Pierson 1996, p.16). Anti-oppressive practice 'attempts to confront or resist injustice or the abuse of power. Anti-oppression can refer to either individual or personal experience and to structural arrangements' (Thomas and Pierson 1995, p.19).

As the chapter unfolds we hope these definitions will become more accessible. They will be placed in the context of social and care support within the learning disabilities field and practical applications will be used to support understanding. The definition of anti-discriminatory practice given above raises the issue of the multiplicity of people and groups that may be affected through race, age, gender, disability, class and sexual orientation. This type of discrimination is sometimes referred to in the context of an 'ism'.

'Isms'

An 'ism' can be used to group descriptions of people who are affected by discrimination and relates to an ideology of superiority. The supposed superiority is of one group over another and is imposed on those 'inferior' groups. Such imposition is often used as a method of trying to justify oppression and unfair judgements on others. We will explore some of the isms and examine how they can be used to provide an understanding of areas of discrimination.

Racism relates to discrimination against people from different races, ethnic groups and countries, and against some collective groups within society. The discrimination can be manifest in people's ideas, attitudes and behaviours. The discrimination is supposedly justified because the oppressing group of people believe in a presumed inherent biological superiority over those that are oppressed. Ageism focuses on discrimination and prejudice against people due to their age. Bytheway describes ageism, highlighting its diversity: 'Ageism is about age and prejudice...it appears in all sorts of situations and affects people of all ages' (Bytheway 1995, p.3). Sexism relates to discrimination on the grounds of a person's sex or gender. It particularly focuses on the discrimination and oppression of women by men and the male dominant attitudes found within parts of society.

Over time other isms have developed. Classism relates to the effect of discrimination and oppression through class hierarchy. The conflict arises where one class believe themselves superior and oppress people of another class. Disablism, sometimes spelt as disableism, relates to the impact of discrimination and oppression on people who are seen as disabled in comparison to the majority of society. Thompson describes disablism as 'the combination of social forces, cultural values and personal prejudices which marginalises disabled people, portrays them in a negative light and thus oppresses them' (Thompson 1997, p.105).

Other areas of oppression occur that do not necessarily have a specific ism to their name. We will highlight some of these to underline how wide the issues of discrimination and oppression are within society. An individual's sexual identity may have an impact on how they are, or are not, accepted. If a person is a male homosexual, lesbian, bisexual or transsexual this may have an impact on how they are viewed and accepted by society. Different values or beliefs may affect how a person is treated. Equal opportunities policies are used by some employees as a way of reinforcing that people should not be treated differently due to their sexuality. Although acceptance may be increasing in society, the discrimination and oppression faced by a person due to his or her sexuality needs to be considered and challenged. A person's religious beliefs may affect others. Expectations through religious understanding may be deliberately, or inadvertently, placed on others. Religion and religious beliefs can be fundamental to a person's life-guiding actions and moral principles. This in turn can create a level of cultural normality where different cultures, religious beliefs or non-religious beliefs may not be accepted or understood.

The language used by a person may not be understood or accepted in the wider society. An example of this could be a first language that is different from the majority. Languages often link closely with ethnicity:

> [Ethnicity]…relating to or characteristic of a human group having racial, religious, linguistic and certain other traits in common…relating to the classification of mankind into groups especially on the basis of racial characteristics. (*Collins Dictionary* 1986, p.524)

Within different ethnic groups communication used may differ through dialects and localized language which can vary from region to region. Through these differences marginalization of individuals and groups may take place.

The culture of a person or a group also has an influence. Culture combines a shared understanding, a way of seeing things, of thinking and a way of carrying out tasks. 'The character and validity of a culture is to a large extent language dependent. Language helps to preserve traditions, shape modes of perception, and profoundly influences patterns of social intercourse' (Carter and Atchinson in Hume and Pryce 1986, p.18).

Any factors that relate to a person being perceived as different from the majority increase the possibility of discrimination and oppression. This extends to groups as well as individuals and this type of discrimination and oppression is prevalent and can be seen on a daily basis on the news and within media coverage. The media has a great amount of power in reinforcing stigmatization of people and groups. The methods and style used for reporting on issues relating to mental health is a good example of the media's power to stigmatize. Often mental illness is portrayed as schizophrenia, paranoia and associated disorders related to murders or major criminal acts. This reinforces the notion that all people with schizophrenia or paranoia are likely to commit heinous crimes, which is clearly far from the truth. The negative response to mental illness is both discriminatory and oppressive to the person who has issues of mental ill health. Labels such as mentally ill, schizophrenic and paranoid hold a tremendous power over the people so labelled and how they are perceived. Labelling is explored in more depth in Chapter 1.

Discrimination and oppression are often found when considering people with learning disabilities. In part this may relate to the confusion between mental illness and learning disabilities and also the way people with learning disabilities have been perceived over time. Thompson suggests four distinct models that can be used to inform society's views and provide understanding of how people with a learning disability are perceived: 'The threat to society model; the medical model; the subnormality model; the special needs model' (Thompson 1997, pp.151–152).

The first model illustrates the predominant view of society at the beginning of the 20th century. The view that people with mental impairment were 'morally deficient' was reinforced by the eugenics movement, and the perception of them as a threat to society and its social norms increased discrimination and oppression against people with learning disabilities. This increased to the point of institutionalization and segregation. The second model links to the National Health Service in the 1940s. Britain's response to mental impairment was such that it was seen as a medical 'problem' that could be controlled through medical intervention. The medical model of care and control became dominant. The third model relates to the measurement of mental impairment and the ability to achieve educationally. An IQ test could be used to diagnose a learning disability and to identify whether the IQ level was below 'normal' (see Chapter 1). If it was below normal then subnormality was diagnosed. The fourth model considers integration into society but relies on the identification of the special needs of an individual. The special needs model highlights people's difference and thus barriers against integration may be erected. People are fitted into society and society does not adapt or change to accommodate them.

Thompson suggests that elements of each of these models may affect current societal attitudes. Each could play its part in explaining the reason for discrimination and oppression towards people with a learning disability. 'What all these models have in common is a tendency to marginalize and disempower, to a greater or lesser extent, people with a mental impairment' (Thompson 1997, p.152). Another type of discrimination and oppression is found within the structure of society. Issues of poverty, mental illness and homelessness may be seen as the person's fault; there is a 'blaming the victim' attitude towards these inequalities. Banks (1995) highlights a further issue using an example considering the 'colour blind' approach. If all people, no matter what their colour were treated with equal rights and choice, then in theory all people would be treated the same. However, this does not take into consideration ethnic or cultural difference or needs. A colour blind approach can dismiss the importance of respecting an individual's identity and of learning and understanding the implications of difference. Banks challenges equal opportunities policies that have such statements as 'everyone will be treated equally irrespective of race, gender or religion'. This type of statement does not 'recognise institutional or structural discrimination and therefore do[es] not recognise the need for positive action to promote change' (Banks 1995, p.39). Multiple discrimination and oppression can occur which then have further impact upon the person or group. If someone is disabled and elderly, black and lesbian, white and male homosexual and disabled then the discrimination and oppression they face increases. This could have a major impact on the person concerned and how he or she manages living in society.

The multiplicity of discrimination and oppression and its effects upon people or groups is extensive. We have identified only some of the ways it can occur, but by doing so hope to have emphasized the need for, and importance of, an anti-discriminatory and anti-oppressive approach. It is important, however, to be aware that discrimination and oppression can occur in many different forms.

TYPES OF DISCRIMINATION AND OPPRESSION

We will now explore and highlight some of the forms that discrimination and oppression may take and give brief explanations of them.

Prejudice relates to an opinion formed beforehand; it is often unfavourable and one which is based on inadequate facts. Prejudice is the holding of such opinions and using them to reinforce intolerance or dislike for people of a certain culture, race, religion, sexuality or ability. An example could be of a group of motorcyclists being asked to leave a pub in the belief that they would cause trouble.

Stereotyping is characterized by a standardized image or understanding by the majority of a social group. Stereotyping fails to take into account the complex nature of individuals and attributes homogeneous images, often derogatory.

Marginalization can be seen as the process that relegates a person or group to the margins of the majority or mainstream. Being out of the central focus can make the person or group marginalized appear unimportant and to hold little, if any, significance. A person who uses a wheelchair and is not able to access the local night club due to the physical barriers created by stairs and doors, is marginalized.

Covert discrimination is usually not obvious to the person being discriminated against. For example, when someone with a learning disability applies for a job and the employer rejects that person based on his or her learning disability but says it is because the position is already filled. Another example of covert discrimination is that of accommodation being advertised and the caller being told the accommodation has been let when it has not, because the advertiser has a prejudice against the caller's accent, dress or looks.

Overt discrimination is openly done. An example of this may be found in pubs with signs saying, 'Travellers will not be served'. Another example of overt discrimination is that of accommodation-to-let postcards in windows that state people on benefits need not apply.

Positive discrimination is permitted when it is used in the context of education, teaching or welfare to meet the special needs of a person or a particular group. An example would be advertising for female-only staff to work in a teenage mother unit.

Discrete discrimination may occur, for example, when a woman goes for a job interview and is asked about her intentions regarding marriage and children but a male candidate is not asked the same question. The treatment of one person less favourably than another due to colour, race or ethnic origin are other examples.

An example of *indirect discrimination* is when there is a requirement for someone to speak English where a person using a different first language could carry out the job equally well.

Individual, group, institutional, structural and *societal discrimination* can occur. Studying the feminist perspective of social work in authors such as Taylor and Daly (1995) can provide a valuable insight into the developmental process of oppression. Taylor and Daly considered the historical development of women's roles as being subservient to that of men, this being prevalent in many aspects of life such as social convention, law, and medical and religious practice. This is another example of the power that can be held by one group in society over another.

Some areas of discrimination and oppression have been challenged by sections of society, and legislation has been introduced to try to address them.

LEGISLATION

Various pieces of legislation have been introduced over time as part of the ongoing battle against discrimination and oppression.

The Sex Discrimination Act 1975 was set up to eliminate discrimination in relation to gender. This focused on employment, education, housing, goods, facilities, services and advertising. A main part of the Act supported women who faced discrimination through marital status when applying for employment and when jobs were being advertised. The Act was updated by the Sex Discrimination Act 1986. The Act made it illegal to discriminate on the grounds of a person's gender and applies to both men and women.

The Race Relations Act 1976 was set up to promote good and positive relationships between ethnic groups. The ideal was to combat and alleviate racial discrimination. The Commission for Racial Equality was formed through this legislation. The Commission was set up to investigate alleged discrimination with the aim of ordering organizations to amend their policies and practice.

The Disabled Persons (Services Consultation and Representation) Act 1996 was intended to make improvements for people who had physical disabilities, learning disabilities and issues of mental health. The Act was to support assessment, representation, consultation and service development. Unfortunately not all sections of this Act were implemented, probably due to cost implications.

The Criminal Justice Act 1991 required the Home Secretary to provide and publish annual information to support the justice administrative system in not discriminating on the grounds of race, sex or any other 'improper' grounds.

The Disability Discrimination Act 1995 was introduced to alleviate discrimination on the grounds of disability, it being defined as 'a physical or mental impairment which has a substantial and long term adverse effect on ability to carry out normal day to day activities' (Disability Discrimination Act in Brayne and Martin 1997, p.416). It is unlawful to discriminate on grounds of disability in employment, except for education, the police, the armed forces, the prison service and any firm that employs less than 20 people. Discrimination should not occur in services such as shops and restaurants and in property selling and letting. This piece of legislation appears weak in challenging discrimination. It may well highlight some of the issues and start to challenge and alter culture but does not appear powerful enough to abolish it. In Hansard the Act is described as 'riddled with vague, slippery and elusive exceptions making it so full of holes that it is more like a colander than a binding code' (Gooding 1995).

The Children Act 1989 provides specific instruction to authorities stating they must give regard to racial groups. When making day care arrangements for children or selecting foster parents, racial needs must be taken into consideration. The decision has to be made with the best interest of the child at the forefront of concern. This means that a child may or may not be placed with a person of their own racial background or nationality.

The Children (Scotland) Act 1995 focuses on the rights of children and the responsibilities of adults and public bodies to provide care and protection for them. The Act encompasses the broad principles of commitment to children made under the United Nations Convention on the Rights of Children and the European Convention on Human Rights.

The National Health and Community Care Act 1990 requires planning at community level. Services are to be devised that meet the needs of the population. The statutory authority has a duty to plan and provide an assessment of need; however, it is at the discretion of the authority whether or not to provide services. Therefore the needs of minority groups may not be met.

The Human Rights Act 1998 was intended to create a cultural shift focused on individual rights. The intention appears to be far reaching, including playing a part in the decision making of Government and legal systems. The understanding that people with disabilities have the same human rights as any other person is not something that society has historically been supportive of:

> The withdrawal or restriction of medical services, the abuse and degrading treatment of disabled people in institutional care, and prejudiced judgments...are just some of the areas where the Human Rights Act may help disabled people live fully and freely, on equal terms with non-disabled people. (Daw 2000, p.i)

The Disability Rights Commission will work with other organizations towards achieving equality. At the moment the effectiveness of this legislation is being observed. Until challenges are made to human rights violations through the court system and legal decisions are given clarifying such violations the full impact of the Act cannot be accurately judged.

The Adults with Incapacity (Scotland) Act 2000 introduces a new structure of supporting people who do not have the capacity to make decisions for themselves due to mental disorder or an inability to communicate. Doctors will be involved in assessing capacity, completing certificates of incapacity and treatment. The Act recognizes that incapacity is not an 'all or nothing' situation and that some adults may be able to make simple or straightforward choices. However, some may not be able to decide on more complex issues involving money, property or their own personal welfare. The Act introduces new provisions that will enable adults with incapacity to maximize their ability, encourage the development of new skills and ensure that whatever intervention is provided it is the least intrusive possible. This may help to challenge many issues of oppression and discrimination faced by 'Adults with Incapacity'.

The majority of agencies, statutory, voluntary or private should have their own policies and procedures to challenge discrimination and oppression within their specific practice. These should be readily available to enable them to be studied and implemented.

We hope to have shown that discrimination and oppression occur in many different forms and legislation has been implemented to try to challenge these. However, the limitations of the legislation, the weakness of wording and restricted implementation all indicate that this has not been altogether successful. The majority of the issues discussed so far in this chapter are pertinent to working with people with learning disabilities. Working in an anti-discriminatory and anti-oppressive way is far from easy in a society and legislative framework that frequently does not support equality. In the next sections we will start to explore methods that inform working in an anti-discriminatory and anti-oppressive way and practice examples will be given in case studies.

INFORMING, DEVELOPING AND USING AN ANTI-DISCRIMINATORY AND ANTI-OPPRESSIVE APPROACH

There are various theories that can be used to inform an anti-discriminatory and anti-oppressive approach. The first theory that will be explored and used in the context of people with a learning disability will be Thompson's PCS Analysis (Thompson 1997).

The PCS Analysis provides a clear and understandable method of considering discrimination and oppression in the context of personal, cultural and societal levels. Thompson describes the interlinking and overlapping of each and how one can inform, impinge upon or relate to another. To emphasize this approach Thompson's explanations will be quoted and the link between the three highlighted:

> P refers to the *personal* or *psychological*; it is the individual level of thought, feelings, attitudes and actions. It also refers to *practice*, individual workers interacting with individual clients, and *prejudice*, the inflexibility of mind which stands in the way of fair and non-judgemental practice. (Thompson 1997, p.20)

We are each individual and have our own beliefs and values. These may have developed through learning over our lifetime and may at times be seen as no more than common sense. However, each belief, value and attitude will have been learnt, and to a varying extent reinforced, until it becomes intrinsic in a person's individual value structure. Values may have been learnt from a variety of sources including parent or parents, schooling, neighbourhood or through culture and religion. The structure of society, political influence, the media and worldwide actions may all influence personal beliefs and values. A person may have learnt not to talk to people who are homosexual or to stay away from people who appear or act differently through mental illness, learning or physical disability. This type of personal learning may vary tremendously between different cultures and through ethnicity, religion and individual upbringing.

Personal development is influenced by the culture that we live within. The cultural norms and expectations can influence an individual to conform. Culture can place a heavy influence on the forming of opinions, beliefs and values. This can subsequently guide actions and how behaviour and perceptions are understood. This leads into the C of Thompson's PCS Analysis. The C encompasses personal beliefs and values:

> C refers to the *cultural* level of shared ways of seeing, thinking and doing. It relates to the *commonalities* – values and patterns of thought and behaviour, an assumed *consensus* about what is right and what is normal; it produces *conformity* to social norms... (Thompson 1997, p.20)

In each culture certain social and cultural values will be exercised. These values influence our individual perceptions of what is acceptable and how we treat certain people. Cultural views can underpin how we act towards people with disabilities, people of other races, ages or of a different sex. Learnt personal views and wider cultural influences may lead to discriminative and oppressive attitudes. Thompson emphasizes that P views are not always influenced by cultural views but that personal values and beliefs need to be explored within the cultural structure.

The P and C level in turn are encompassed by the S level:

> S refers to the *structural* level, the network of *social divisions*: it also relates to the ways in which oppression and discrimination are institutional-ized and thus *'sewn in'* to the favric of society. It denotes the wider level of *social forces*, the *sociopolitical* dimensions of interlocking patterns of power and influence. (Thompson 1997, p.20)

The structure of society includes the complexity of social division and the powerful influence of social acceptance. Class, gender, age and disability can all be affected through social division and the power of society in deciding what is acceptable, which groups of society require support and which do not. Society influences cultural views, which may in turn impact upon personal values and beliefs. Thompson suggests that the three levels at which discrimination and oppression operate need to be understood and the way they affect each other acknowledged.

Having awareness of the different types and ways that discrimination and oppression can occur is a starting point in the process of anti-discriminatory and anti-oppressive practice. It is important to examine per-sonal views and beliefs to see if they are negative or condone discrimination and oppression. At a personal level there is a greater ability to challenge and re-evaluate practice. A worker can challenge discrimination and oppression at a cultural level but the ability to succeed in changing attitudes becomes more limited. The wider the context in which discrimination and oppression are challenged, the more difficult for the individual it can become. Neverthe-less, as individual workers a part can be played in the important task of pro-moting anti-discriminatory and anti-oppressive practice:

> This involves individuals playing their part in challenging collectively the dominant discriminatory culture and ideology and, in so doing, playing at least a part in the undermining of the structures which sup-port, and are supported by, that culture. (Thompson 1997, p.23)

There are other theories and methods that can inform understanding and ways to challenge discrimination and oppression. Dominelli's (1997a) work enables consideration and strategy development in challenging discrimi-nation in the context of racism. Dominelli suggests eight 'avoidance strategies' that occur as ways of not having to deal with racism. We would like to suggest that these strategies can be transferred and, to an extent, used to look at some of the avoidance tactics used when considering attitudes towards people with learning disabilities:

1. Denial – a refusal to accept that people are discriminated against for having a learning disability.

2. Omission – the non-acceptance of disability, saying everyone is equal and thus ignoring the implication of the learning disability.

3. Decontextualization – accepting discrimination happens, but not in their lives or locality, it is a problem elsewhere, not here.

4. The colour-blind approach – treating everyone the same and not seeing and accepting each person for the individual she or he is.

5. The 'dumping' approach – blaming the person with a learning disability for the discrimination faced.

6. The patronizing approach – accepting people with learning disabilities for their ways as they cannot help being the way they are.

7. Avoidance – not wanting to get involved in the debate of discrimination and equality.

8. Exaggeration – if we have an equal opportunities policy in place everything will be fine.

(Adapted from Dominelli 1997a, pp.72–73)

Consideration of these eight avoidance strategies raises awareness of how they may be used every day to discriminate. This type of reflection upon discrimination and oppression can be a powerful tool in identifying and challenging it.

Banks (1995) reinforces the argument that anti-oppressive practice is, to an extent, achievable through challenging structural oppression:

> ...that is, challenging the systems of beliefs, policies, institutions and culture that systematically discriminate against and demean women, Black people, differently abled people, lesbians and gays, working class people and other oppressed groups. (Banks 1995, p.114)

Dalrymple and Burke's (1995) work on drawing together various thoughts and ideas includes the work of Norton (1978) who suggests development of a practice model that involves the worker and client in partnership, both committed to working toward change with the purpose of achieving a greater level of equality within society. Working in partnership could include: developing individual ideas, achieving change, influencing society and challenging political action so that discrimination and oppression can be addressed within the wider society.

The importance of and need for an intrinsic value base that promotes equality through an understanding of the structure of discrimination and oppression is clearly highlighted within the requirements for nursing evidence based practice (UKCC 1992) and social work training (CCETSW 1989, 1995, 1996).

Why is a value base needed?

We will initially highlight the importance of values and having an informed value base to underpin practice. Values and beliefs can be both implicit and explicit and they underpin the ways that things are carried out. Values determine what people think ought to be done, and are intricately linked with moral and ethical codes, whereas beliefs are what people think is or is not true. Values and beliefs contribute to shared meanings, understandings and expectations which are distinctive to a particular group and are passed on to new members (Louis 1980). It is with these links in mind that the importance of a structured, tried and tested value base is reinforced. Various professional training courses state the requirement for a clear value base to be used to enable the development of evidence based practice.

Within nursing training the need to develop evidence based practice is highlighted. The UK Central Council for Nursing, Midwifery and Health Visiting (UKCC) states:

> As a registered nurse, midwife or health visitor, you are personally accountable for your practice and, in exercise of your professional accountability, must maintain and improve your professional knowledge and competence. (UKCC 1992, Clause 3)

The value requirements identified in 1996 by CCETSW for social work training help to reinforce the importance of a sound and structured value base in practice. The rules and requirements state that a social worker's practice 'must be founded on, informed and capable of being judged against a clear value base' (CCETSW 1996, p.18). The values identified are as follows:

- to identify and question their own values and prejudices, and their implications for practice

- to respect and value uniqueness and diversity, and recognize and build on strengths

- to promote people's rights to choice, privacy, confidentiality and protection, while recognizing and addressing the complexities of competing rights and demands

- to assist people to increase control of and improve the quality of their lives, while recognizing that control of behaviour will be required at times in order to protect children and adults from harm

- to identify, analyse and take action to counter discrimination, racism, disadvantage, inequality and injustice, using strategies appropriate to role and context

- to practise in a manner that does not stigmatize or disadvantage either individuals, groups or communities.

(CCETSW 1996, p.18)

These must all be 'consistent' and require 'thoughtful integration' into practice (CCETSW 1996, p.18).

Thompson's PCS Analysis, Dominelli's avoidance strategies, CCETSW's value base and the importance of using evidence based practice can all provide insight and understanding. We will illustrate the use of anti-discriminatory and anti-oppressive practice through the following two case studies.

CASE STUDY ONE

Iyawo was 70 years of age and lived with her niece, Adaku; both were African-Caribbean. Adaku was unexpectedly rushed into hospital with a serious medical condition. This meant that Iyawo, who had a learning disability and could not manage to live alone, was placed in emergency respite care in an older persons' home.

Iyawo seemed to settle in without too much distress. She joined in social activities with other residents and said she liked her room. Iyawo was given support in personal care including bathing and washing her hair. After washing her hair, the combing of the hair afterwards caused problems as some broke off during the process and the member of staff did not know how to plait or twist the hair in Iyawo's usual manner. Over the week Iyawo's skin also became dry and noticeably patchy at the elbows and knees. In addition, Iyawo told staff that she missed her niece's home cooking and asked if she could have some food prepared in the same way as at home.

Application in practice

Iyawo was admitted in an emergency and at that time thought was not given to her cultural needs as finding her a bed took precedence. Iyawo was visited by a social worker once she was safely placed but her personal care needs were not raised as a specific issue by her or by the residential staff.

The staff in the home were all white and did not have experience of the cultural needs of an African-Caribbean person. They were without experience in how to offer appropriate personal care for Iyawo. None of this was questioned by them or by management staff. They had wrongly assumed that the regular shampoo found in the bathroom would be suitable. They had also assumed they would be able to comb Iyawo's hair in the way they tended to the other residents who were white. They were then unable to style Iyawo's hair which left her looking unkempt and took away her dignity.

Due to staff not thinking about Iyawo's cultural needs, she was discriminated against both in her personal care and in her diet. Iyawo may have used the regular shampoo, but in fact at home used a specialist shampoo and conditioner which should have been checked out. At home Iyawo also always used body oil to condition her skin after bathing and this also was neglected.

Iyawo was expected, along with the other residents, to choose from the two main meals on offer, although this did not take into account the type of food she particularly enjoyed and was used to at home. Whilst this was not intentionally done, the lack of thought about her cultural needs meant that Iyawo did not receive the appropriate care that she was entitled to. Lack of thought about practice resulted in discrimination.

CASE STUDY TWO

Heinrique had recently moved from a residential home in another part of the county into a specially adapted house for people who used wheelchairs. He liked his new home and had formed a good friendship with another person in the house. Heinrique was able to continue to attend his college course and joined a local youth club. Before the move Heinrique had regularly attended church and this was important to him.

In his new locality the local church of his denomination was reached by a flight of steps and there was no wheelchair access. Due to lack of suitable transport, Heinrique also needed to be accompanied by a member of staff to enable him to get to and from church and the staffing levels did not allow for this.

Application in practice

Heinrique was oppressed and discriminated against in several ways. As a person with learning disabilities he was not accepted by some people within his local community or by some people in wider society. As a wheelchair user he was also denied access to many places due to inaccessible kerbstones and doorways. Additionally, there were no local taxis that were wheelchair accessible to enable him to go out independently without staff.

Heinrique required support but resources were limited and did not allow for a regular one to one ratio to enable him to attend church. Nor was he able to attend his preferred church due to the inaccessibility of the building.

The local vicar was able to offer Heinrique the opportunity to attend a service she held in a local residential home once a month. This was accepted but did not prevent the discrimination faced by being unable to access the church building and church services. Additionally, it meant Heinrique having to rely upon others for support when he would have preferred independence.

CONCLUSION

Various types of discrimination and oppression have been explored and isms have been considered. Theoretical approaches that go towards explaining and challenging the structure of discrimination and oppression have been highlighted. These provide a framework that suggests how anti-discriminatory and anti-oppressive practice can be continually developed.

In reality, care and support workers can challenge discrimination and oppression but are, to an extent, restricted by the legislative and structural framework of care provision. The promoting of rights, choice, positive education and awareness in society must play a key part in achieving equality. The following points may help in reflecting upon practice in a positive, person-led way, taking into consideration the power that comes with a care or support role:

- The ability to recognize and challenge discrimination in a positive way.

- Having a universal commitment to equality within the learning disabilities field.

- Understanding the misuse of power.

- Having access to anti-discriminatory practice training.

- Being aware of the need to use non-jargonistic language.

- Remaining open and critical to personal working practice.

- The use of theories such as Thompson's PCS model to understand how inequalities and discrimination feature in social circumstances.

- The use of advocacy and consultation groups through independent advocacy services.

- An awareness of the conflicts of duties and powers working within the NHS and the Community Care Act 1990 and other relevant legislation.

(Adapted from Thompson 1997)

These perspectives can help to provide part of the structure that is required for realistic anti-discriminatory and anti-oppressive practice. They are just some of the ways that anti-discriminatory practice can be worked towards and should be an intrinsic part of everyday practice. The consequence of not practising in such a way and of the person being diminished or treated in a tokenistic way is powerfully summed up by Thompson:

> ...practice which does not take account of oppression and discrimination cannot be seen as good practice, no matter how high its standards may be in other respects. For example,...intervention with a disabled person which fails to recognise the marginalised position of disabled people in society runs the risk of providing more of a disservice than a service. (Thompson 1996, p.10)

Key points

- Discrimination and oppression can take many different forms. Sometimes it is clearly visible and at other times subtle and more difficult to identify.

- Discrimination and oppression can be faced by people for many reasons, e.g. due to race, colour, culture, gender, age, class, ability, religious views and sexuality.

- Personal, cultural or societal views and understanding can impact on the level of discrimination and oppression a person or group of people may face.

- There is legislation that challenges aspects of discrimination; however, legislation does not support all people and all situations.

- Theories can aid understanding and subsequently inform the challenging of aspects of discrimination and oppression. Theories can be used to underpin the majority of care and support work undertaken within the learning disabilities field.

- The value base suggested as an underpinning to social work training highlights the need for anti-discriminatory and anti-oppressive practice to be an intrinsic part of care and support work.

- Informed, evidence based practice is crucial.

- Anti-discriminatory and anti-oppressive practice needs to be an integral part of everyday practice.

4

What is Normalization?

INTRODUCTION

In the 1970s and 1980s, normalization was a theory of great influence informing the field of learning disabilities. Today it still holds an important place in explaining how learning disability services and care provision have developed. In this chapter, brief consideration will be given to what is meant by normalization and where the idea originated. We will then go on to explore in more depth what impact normalization and related theories have on today's care structure. This chapter is not intended to be a definitive guide, rather an introduction to the concept of normalization. Two case studies will be used to help place normalization into a practice context.

NORMALIZATION AND THEORETICAL LINKS

Wolfensberger provided a statement of the normalization principle as: 'The utilization of culturally valued means in order to establish and/or maintain personal behaviours, experiences and characteristics that are culturally normative or valued' (Wolfensberger 1977 in O'Brien 1981, p.2).

Thomas and Pierson provide their definition of normalization as 'a concept (originating in Scandinavia and further developed in North America) that emphasizes the desirability for people with learning disability to live a lifestyle as close as possible to the norms of the surrounding society' (Thomas and Pierson 1996, p.249). Normalization is a concept that focuses on people with learning disabilities being able to live and function within the same structural norms as the rest of society. This may be a sound ideal and one desired by many people including those who provide support and care services. However, identifying the ultimate goal desired does not make it any easier to achieve in practice.

The ethos and principle of normalization originated in Scandinavia and focused on the need for services to be available for people with learning disabilities so that they could have similar lifestyles to others (Bank-Mikkelsen 1980; Nirje 1969). Wolfensberger (1972) developed the theoretical basis of normalization from a different perspective. In North America, Wolfensberger used deviance theory as a way of explaining the stigma faced by people that were seen as different and often perceived in negative ways within society. Wolfensberger (1983) went on to develop his initial thinking and reformulated normalization as 'social role valorization', which stressed that people should be able to occupy socially valued roles within their communities. This was described as: 'The creation, support and defence of valued social roles for people who are at risk of devaluation' (Wolfensberger and Thomas 1983). The notion of being able to undertake social roles and then fulfilling those roles is of key importance. Wolfensberger stated:

> It is a well established fact that a person's behaviour tends to be profoundly affected by the role expectations that are placed upon him. Generally people will play the roles they have been assigned. This permits those who define social roles to make self-fulfilling prophesies. (Wolfensberger 1972, pp.15–16)

Eight general roles that may be applied to people who are part of disadvantaged groups were suggested by Wolfensberger and Thomas:

- subhuman organism
- menace
- unspeakable object of dread
- object of pity
- holy innocent
- diseased organism
- object of ridicule
- eternal child.

(Adapted from Wolfensberger and Thomas 1983)

Wolfensberger and Thomas suggested the possibility that such terms could devalue and label people and consequently could be used as powerful social influences and methods of control. If people are treated in a particular way by society according to the label placed upon them, they may face oppression and discrimination (see Chapter 1 for labelling theory). If people are seen as 'objects of pity' or as 'eternal children' they may be treated in a way that does not enable them to develop a new role; they may not have the opportunity to move on from the restrictions created. Although Wolfensberger developed his ideas about social role valorization, in some quarters this was criticized as complex (for example, Brown and Smith 1994). However complex the ideas, they have been influential in developing understanding and changing perceptions about people with learning disabilities and the sort of opportunities that should be available to them.

As in some other countries, the principle of normalization was used in the UK by people endeavouring to act in the interests of people with learning disabilities. Additionally, there were other factors that influenced change to the way care was being provided – factors such as the quality of care provision and the political pressure faced over the high cost of hospital based care. Thus, a combination of these aspects played a part in influencing change to the structure of care provision in the UK. These ideas can be studied further, for example, through the works of Emerson in Brown and Smith (1998), and Race in Malin (1987).

NORMALIZATION IN THE UK

During the 1960s and 1970s in England and Wales there were scandals reported of neglect and abuse that had occurred within 'hospital' settings, Howe Report (Department of Health and Social Security 1969). The normalization principle played its part as a factor in identifying and persuading policy makers and relevant professionals to reject long stay hospital based services in the UK for people with learning disabilities (Kings Fund Centre 1980). Additionally, other factors, including the belief that community care would be a cheaper option, reinforced the need for change. The emphasis was placed on services needing to deliver a high quality of life for people with learning disabilities. This would supposedly be achieved by reproducing the lifestyle that was experienced by people who were non-disabled. This would be realized if:

- day to day living was achievable
- progression through the course of life took place
- there was the ability to choose and have self-determination
- there was the opportunity for equality in economic standards.

Emerson summed up normalization thus: 'Normalization becomes a statement about how services can reflect the basic rights of people with learning difficulties in an Egalitarian society' (Emerson in Brown and Smith 1998, p.3).

In the UK, much of the work undertaken by academics and policy makers in the field of learning disabilities focused on the concept of 'An Ordinary Life'. The idea of An Ordinary Life was proposed by the Ordinary Life Movement (Kings Fund Centre 1980). The initiatives and principles were based on the idea of ordinary homes in ordinary houses in ordinary streets rather than hospitals and hostels. It also included the understanding and acceptance that people with learning disabilities have the right to live as others do within their local community; to share in using ordinary facilities and to widen educational, work and leisure opportunities.

Community living

The ideas of An Ordinary Life helped to pave the way for the development of services, which enabled many people with learning disabilities to move into and live in their 'ordinary' houses. We now see many different models of living within the community. These range from people with their own tenancies to individuals living in houses with 24 hour staff support, and all the designs for living in between. Unlike hospital or large group living, this range of housing options better promotes choice and inclusion and better enables people with learning disabilities to live 'in the mainstream of life', thus achieving part of the Kings Fund goal (1980).

Allen (1994) highlighted that although the initiatives of An Ordinary Life had a considerable impact on the way residential services were provided they did not have equal impact on day care service provision. We will now briefly highlight the development of day services to enable an understanding, and the impact of ideas influenced by the normalization principle.

Day care provision

In the 1960s, the need for day care provision within local communities for people with learning disabilities was highlighted through legislation. The Mental Health Act 1959 (in Scotland 1960) gave local authorities the power to provide day care services within the community. P.Williams (1995) identified that by the 1970s many Adult Training Centres, often referred to as ATCs, were set up in most local authorities. These day centres offered often in excess of one hundred places for people and the main focus was industrial training. Over time, the value of ATCs was questioned by some; it was thought that they provided limited opportunity and the work carried out was often mundane and repetitive. There were also concerns of exploitation due to the minimal monies offered for the tasks completed (Allen 1994). The National Development Group (1977) was a body set up by the Government to advise on policies in relation to people with learning disabilities. Recommendations were put forward for ATCs to become 'social education centres' and to focus on people's education, social and daily living skills. In line with the development of day services, legislation was also developing and guiding the way forward.

The White Paper *Better Services for the Mentally Handicapped* (DHSS and Welsh Office 1971) and the Scottish counterpart (Scottish Home and Health Department 1972) were published, setting targets for change and the development of community based services. The English and Welsh Office recommended an expansion of day care places. In 1970, there were approximately 26,400 places available. The recommendations suggested that this should increase to over 75,000 during the following 20 years. In part, the increase was supposed to enable people leaving the long stay hospitals to receive day care; however, the targets were never achieved. There were two factors that played a part in this: first, the difficulty in releasing monies from hospitals and, second, the changing views, rights and roles of people with learning disabilities within society. O'Brien was key in highlighting and suggesting how their rights could be better enabled and achieved.

The work of O'Brien has had considerable impact upon the ideas and development of community based services in the UK and internationally. O'Brien suggested the notion of 'five accomplishments' that should be aimed for and ideally met by community based services. These five accomplishments are described below and each is followed by an explanation of how it can be related to practice within the learning disabilities field.

O'Brien's Five Accomplishments (Adapted from O'Brien 1987a)

Community presence

People with learning disabilities who have supportive networks and who are able to be active in the life of the community through work, leisure or just as a part of it are more likely to have positive roles within the community. This can safeguard against being treated in negative ways by society. This accomplishment refers to the many positively valued roles they may undertake within society such as consumer, employee, friend and neighbour.

Choice

A basic and fundamental right is to have autonomy and control over decisions about all aspects of life, day to day issues and about major life events. Promoting the rights of people with learning disabilities and treating them with respect and dignity is a core activity for the caring services. It means making sure that opportunities are provided for them to learn about and exercise their rights, to learn how to choose effectively and accountably.

Competence

People with learning disabilities should have the opportunities to develop skills and reach their full potential. This relates to how the caring services assist them to use the same facilities, be in the same places, and do the same sorts of things as other people, at the same times of the day, week and year. It requires effort to ensure that they are visible in valued ways at home, work and in leisure.

Respect

This refers to the rights of people with learning disabilities to be able to have a valued role within society, to have opportunities to develop their roles, to learn and grow in the sense of their full humanity, from skills and social competence to feelings and self-awareness. To be competent in a range of ways helps in other areas of life and increases the chances that they can contribute to their own and others' lives.

Community participation

A key feature of community life is that a person develops a wide variety of relationships with a range of people, from casual acquaintances and neighbours, to deep, warm friendships and lifelong partnerships. It is necessary for the caring services to find ways that people with learning disabilities can be supported in developing an extensive network of others to interact with, in positive and meaningful ways. It is about being an active participant in everyday life.

O'Brien's five accomplishments can help guide the process of integration and inclusion with people with learning disabilities. They highlight the importance of people with learning disabilities being supported in having their own social networks, living accommodation, relationships, and work opportunities similar to others in society. *Ties and Connections: An Ordinary Community Life for People with Learning Difficulties.* (Kings Fund Centre 1988) highlighted the need for paid employment in preference to tokenistic 'pocket money' payments and it also highlighted the need for access to education. Another key issue was the importance of people with learning disabilities being treated in a manner that was appropriate to their chronological age, not their mental age as identified through, for example, IQ testing. With this in mind, the philosophy developed that they should be supported to speak for themselves and to take a level of risk in achieving their aims and objectives. This could be achieved in part through them making informed choices either with or without assistance or additional support.

O'Brien (1987a) highlighted the complexity of normalization and choice and provided some suggestions as to how they could be achieved:

> Choice is the experience of autonomy both in small and everyday matters (e.g. what to eat or what to wear) and in large, life-defining matters (e.g. with whom to live or what work to do). Personal choice defines and expresses individual identity. Without focused effort to increase available options and provide support for decision making, people with severe handicaps will be passive and without voice or the ability to escape undesirable situations... People with severe handicaps can challenge others' ability to detect personal preferences; some may depend upon a guardian to choose their interests. Valued activities will increase the variety and significance of the choices that a person makes. (O'Brien 1987a, pp.177–178)

The development of advocacy services (see Chapter 6) such as People First motivated and highlighted the rights of people with learning disabilities to have a say in the way their lives developed. This was a clear progression from the role of a paternalistic social care movement (Croft and Beresford 1990). It was also a move away from the medical model of care and control (Smith 1990). The principle of normalization and the subsequent work of O'Brien have been widely adopted by many of the care and support services for people with learning disabilities. Using these models as guidance, the work undertaken upholds the importance of choice and inclusion as central components in the accomplishment of effective services. Social care provision for people with learning disabilities during the 1980s and 1990s showed that the principle of normalization has not been free from problems when put into practice. We will go on to identify some of the difficulties and limitations of the perspective.

SOME DIFFICULTIES WITH NORMALIZATION

We will provide some brief examples that highlight some of the difficulties in achieving a structure that ensures that people with learning disabilities will be able to undertake a full and active part within their own community. The right of people marginalized by society to be supported and enabled to have equal opportunities within society is critical. However, this in itself is one of the difficulties of the concept. It raises the question whether it is the services that negotiate the parameters of normalization rather than the people themselves. This leads on to issues of power, where the power lies and if this needs to be challenged.

> Normalization offers a theory of how to improve services. As services are controlled by professionals, normalization has enabled professionals to retain a key role in the debate…it has enabled professionals to adapt to deinstitutionalization by developing new models of practice. It therefore continues to legitimize their authority. (Chappell 1992, p.40)

The Disability Discrimination Act 1995, established to promote and protect the rights of people who are seen as disabled, is an example of legitimized authority. The act is flawed by unmeasurable terminology, such as 'normal' and 'reasonable'. The Act relies on the use of the term 'normal' to decide if needs are identified: 'A physical or mental impairment which has a substantial and long-term adverse effect on ability to carry out normal day-to-day activities.' (Disability Discrimination Act 1995 in Brayne and Martin 1999, p.416). A person with learning disabilities has a right to be able to participate in normal activities. However, the way normal activities are identified and defined may be contentious. If such a person needs specific care and support that is normal for them, then this should be available. Should people be excluded from receiving services due to the wording of the Act? The term appears to rely on majority normal in preference to individual normal needs. The same argument could be put forward about social norms and the need to fit within them. Social norms will vary, and consideration of different groups and cultures may increase the complexity of thinking about this. In the UK, current social norms may focus predominantly on white Western philosophies and this could further devalue a person with learning disabilities who is black or from a different minority group or culture (Blaxter, Hughes and Tight 1998). This highlights the importance of considering minority groups and the impact of structural norms upon them.

Structural oppression that restricts people from minority groups is apparent in many different areas of society. Support or care workers are faced with dilemmas in day to day work where they are expected to help people 'fit into' available services:

> ...the role of [support or care workers] in challenging it [structural oppression] is emphasised, in practice much of the work they do is about helping people with disabilities 'conform' to what is accepted as 'normal' behaviour. (Banks 1995, p.116)

The power that care and support workers hold in adapting someone to fit into society's norms should not be underestimated. If the person does not conform and adapt they may not be seen as successful in the normalization process. The appropriateness of people being excluded from receiving care if they do not conform to what is considered normal is clearly questionable. This can also be considered in the wider context of society's barriers; for example, a lack of awareness and understanding by those in society of the needs of people with restricted mobility may have adverse effects upon less mobile individuals. Additionally, the physical barriers found within society may impede day to day living. Examples of physical barriers include buildings and transport that do not have wheelchair access. These barriers accentuate the difficulties of fitting into the norms of society. The ideological base of beliefs and attitudes needs fundamental change to promote an inclusive society, to enable and support people with learning disabilities to have fulfilling roles and equal rights.

ROLES AND RIGHTS

In Chapter 9 we will highlight the impact of roles, perceived or real. The role that someone is perceived to undertake can impact upon them. A person's role may affect the success of inclusion and can seriously impinge upon a person's rights. The labelling or stigmatizing of people as different or deviant can be detrimental:

> ...instead they are to be seen as full members of society, to be treated as anyone would wish to be treated, albeit with extra support and assistance. It follows that treatment methods must be ones which people offering the treatment would find acceptable for themselves. (Brigden and Todd in Todd and Gilbert 1995, p.142)

People with learning disabilities should have the same rights as others; for example, in making informed choices about the sort of care to have, where to live and what to do during the day. When people are empowered and develop self-determination they should have the right to decide what they want or need. Real empowerment includes the full involvement of people with learning disabilities throughout the process of deciding what is wanted and needed. Real inclusion needs to address the poverty and inequality faced within society's structures and not just focus on services to support inclusion. The marginalization of tasks such as providing shelter and accommodation at night and recreation during the day time (Fulcher in Barton 1996) needs to be challenged. There is a need to move forward from tokenistic normalization of day and night time care to that which is fully inclusive: day to day living that allows and enables people with learning disabilities to integrate fully into society. As part of the process of full integration, there may be occasions when decisions made by people with learning disabilities are considered inappropriate or potentially harmful.

Support and care workers need to give careful thought to decisions where the personal choice of individuals may be overruled. Negotiations should take place with the individuals concerned. In some instances, there will be multi-disciplinary negotiation and decision making. Each may play a part in overruling decisions of people with learning disabilities and place constraints or restrictions. For example, if a person's choice entails abuse, is potentially harmful to the individual or to others, contains a high risk or is life threatening, the decision to overrule the individual clearly may be appropriate. At times, a legal duty will be apparent and intervention guided by legislation will be required. However, the informed choice of individuals is of paramount importance and needs to be supported within the legislative framework. The legislative structure is constantly changing and in Chapter 10 we provide some examples of how legislation is playing its part in promoting inclusion and participation. Advocacy is an important process in enabling informed choice and supporting people in achieving their rights to gain independence within society. The principles of advocacy and empowerment will be explored further in Chapter 6. This process is often very effective as a method of diminishing power imbalances. This can start to be achieved by looking at how voluntary advocacy services, independent of health and statutory provision, support empowerment, participation and inclusion. Enabling people to make informed choices, so that they be included in decision making and be involved in service development, is central. Those providing care and support must have equal commitment to the process of inclusion as this is of key importance to its success. Advocacy services have been playing an important part in enabling some service users to move forward the service that they receive.

In 1998, the Social Services Inspectorate found that many more opportunities were becoming available within day care services. These included:

- attendance at further education colleges
- using leisure facilities in the community: swimming pools, gym and leisure centres
- running cafés
- supported employment
- other work related opportunities
- involvement with community based volunteer workshops
- small, rural, community based day services.

These types of day time activities help promote independence, respect, choice and community presence and clearly reflect the importance of the work of normalization in general, and in particular, the work of O'Brien. O'Brien's five accomplishments are an important reminder of the need to check constantly that the rights of individuals are being met and that opportunities to develop the maximum independence possible are available.

We felt it important to try to sum up what normalization is about and also what it is not about. Whilst researching we found an explanation provided by the Faculty of Health and Community Care.

Normalization is about:

- the way that you treat people
- the way that you talk to people
- the things that you call people
- the activities that people have access to
- the buildings that people live in.

(Faculty of Health and Community Care 2002, p.1)

Most importantly, however, normalization is about treating people with disabilities in ways that show they have equal value and worth to you.

Normalization is not about:

- making people *normal*
- giving people treatment
- changing the individual.

(Faculty of Health and Community Care 2002, p.1)

Tyne and O'Brien (1981) have identified many of the difficulties faced by people with learning disabilities. The Faculty of Health and Community

Care suggests that the principle of normalization can help 'to break the vicious circle' faced in day to day living by:

- changing others' expectations
- giving greater exercising of rights and responsibilities
- encouraging more decision making by service users
- encouraging more self-advocacy.

(Faculty of Health and Community Care 2002, p.1)

We will now place the principle of normalization into a working context using two case studies. The first will provide an example of where it would have been more empowering to have used O'Brien's accomplishments to inform practice. The second case study will focus on normalization, and the positive attributes in promoting and developing self-esteem and self-confidence.

CASE STUDY ONE

Melina lived in a residential home that provided care for six adults with complex needs. Melina used a symbol board to communicate. Melina's aunt was her closest relative, visited frequently and attended reviews and meetings to support her. The home Melina lived in was the only one in the area that provided a service for people with multiple disabilities. The home had recently undergone major change through being taken over by a different service provider with its own management structure.

Melina seemed less happy, unsettled and appeared quite withdrawn to her aunt. In discussion with staff, Melina's aunt discovered that with the management changes there had also been changes in the workers' shift patterns and working practices. The key worker in Melina's bungalow had changed.

After careful communication with Melina, her aunt was able to establish that Melina was generally upset by so many changes. She was specifically upset due to the change of her key worker and at no longer being able to attend her social club.

Application in practice

Whilst some people had been consulted, Melina and the other residents in her home had not been consulted about the changes that took place. The changes had been imposed upon them as part of a strategic plan in that locality. They had been informed of the changes before they occurred but the reality of how this would affect them was unknown at the time.

As the service users had not been part of the consultation process, their choice and interests had not been promoted. One of the most important people in Melina's life, her key worker, had been changed without consultation and without Melina having a say in the process, which upset her greatly. That Melina had not attended her club was due to staffing levels over the summer, which therefore affected her ability to get out into the community.

Melina was in a position of depending upon others to meet her needs. Through her aunt's intervention, Melina's wishes were listened to more carefully. A plan was made to enable a handover time to say goodbye to her previous key worker and for Melina and her new key worker to get to know each other.

On this occasion Melina was treated in an institutional way and was restricted in the service she received through having little available choice. After the event and following her aunt's intervention, recognition was made of the amount of changes Melina and other residents had had to cope with as part of the strategic plan. If the principles of O'Brien's five accomplishments had been considered and had underpinned practice, then Melina may have been better empowered and included. She could have played an active role in the process of change instead of being made a passive recipient.

CASE STUDY TWO

Sid and Reggie were good friends and had lived for 12 years in a residential home housing 16 people. Over time they had seen other residents move on to group homes and houses in the local community and decided they also wished to do this. Sid and Reggie contacted their local advocacy service for support. They were at first seen separately by members of the advocacy unit. Later, at their request, Sid and Reggie were then jointly supported by an advocate to discuss this issue with residential staff and later with a social worker from the local team.

Through meetings with their advocate, they were enabled to talk through their hopes and fears concerning a move and were advised of their rights. Sid and Reggie considered the type of housing they wanted that included having a garden, as both were keen gardeners. If possible, they wanted to be near the bus route so they could be as independent as possible. Their advocate helped them consider what options were available and the time this process might take.

The community support team were involved, and through talking to Sid and Reggie and assessing their skills and abilities they worked in partnership to identify aspects of support needed. Through this process, they were able jointly to identify the level of support Sid and Reggie would require when living in the community. The process also stimulated independent actions such as Sid joining a Budgeting for Beginners class run at a local college.

Over a year later Sid and Reggie moved into supported housing run by a housing association in their local area. They have been settled there for five years and their only regret was not starting the process sooner.

Application in practice

If the process that Sid and Reggie went through is looked at in terms of O'Brien's five accomplishments then it was, in the main, successful. In terms of status and respect, Sid and Reggie had their own network of friends and acquaintances that they had built up over time. They were active in their local community and participated in it as valued members socially, through work and through their daily presence.

Sid and Reggie were able to make informed choices and had autonomy and control over the decisions made. They were strengthened in this through the process of advocacy and had support from residential staff and the community support team. Their interests were respected and they were supported to think through the process of moving and to look at different aspects of exercising their rights.

Sid and Reggie were valued in different areas of their lives. Sid was valued at work and Reggie at the day centre, and socially both participated in the same places and same ways as others in the local community, according to their personal choice. The wish to move on came from Sid and Reggie; they had opportunities in their lives for growth and development, which had strengthened their skills, social competence and self-awareness. These opportunities had enabled them to network further and indeed had led them to their local advocacy unit for support.

Sid and Reggie had an active life in the community and friendships through some of the clubs to which they belonged, including the local football supporters' club. They had relationships in different forms: their long-term friendship, friendships with others within and outside the residential home, friends and acquaintances at their clubs and as valued customers at local shops. Sid and Reggie were part of their community and participated in that community.

CONCLUSION

Many texts can be found that explore the principle of normalization in greater depth and some of these have been highlighted during this chapter. This introduction to normalization has been written as a way of exploring the idea, to acknowledge both its positive attributes and its shortcomings. That society needs challenging, educating and developing to enable equality for people with learning disabilities is the underpinning message. We believe that this needs to be considered from birth, through childhood, schooling and into adult life. The processes and structures that promote exclusion need to be identified, recognized and challenged.

Key points

- Normalization was a dominant theory in the learning disabilities field in the 1970s and 1980s. Although times have moved on, it can still provide insight into a variety of service development ideas.

- Normalization played a part in the development, recognition and importance of integration and inclusion and reinforced the belief that people with learning disabilities should have the same rights and roles as others to live within society and be part of it.

- Society needs to adapt and change to support and enable people with learning disabilities to live within the mainstream.

- Five accomplishments were suggested by O'Brien: community presence, choice, competence, respect and community participation (1987a). These have provided an underpinning and guidance for service development and support.

- Advocacy, empowerment, participation and involvement are key issues when considering making informed choices about life. Having the opportunity to make informed choices and to be a valued member within a community is a fundamental right of all people with learning disabilities.

The continual development of advocacy, empowerment and inclusion plays a key part in promoting and supporting equality within society. The idea of moving on from looking after people with learning disabilities to working with them is crucial.

5

Communication Methods

INTRODUCTION

In this chapter we aim to explore different aspects of communication. We do not, however, intend to explore in any depth how communication develops or give an overview of communication theory as this is a vast area and one that could not be satisfactorily achieved within the remit of this book. Many other authors have undertaken the task of exploring developmental communication and developmental theory and we will signpost some of the relevant texts. We intend to focus predominantly on the practicalities and methods of communication in practice. Communication can take many forms including written and spoken word, signing such as British Sign Language (BSL) and Makaton and use of word boards. Non-verbal communication such as body language can extend from the full use of the body and a whole range of facial expressions, to communication through a single movement or flutter of the eye. Each method can be enhanced through knowing the person being supported, befriended or cared for and understanding individual needs and styles of communication.

Effective communication can be restricted by various barriers, including: power imbalance, lack of confidence, fear, anxiety, place and expectations of those involved. We will explore some of these barriers and suggest ways that they can be challenged and overcome.

Throughout the chapter we will promote the need to be flexible and adaptable in approach. The ability to listen to the person with a learning disability and to use relevant services that have a clear knowledge about communication is important. We will highlight alternative and additional methods that can enhance communication. Two case studies will be used that will place the importance of effective communication in a working context.

GENERAL COMMUNICATION

The reason for approaching communication in a general context is to reinforce the diversity and range of methods that may be used by people with learning disabilities. Some individuals may require specific support that enables their communication needs to be recognized and met. Each person is unique and differently abled, and fully supported communication should enable participation in all areas of life. We will start by considering what is meant by communication.

'Communication – the exchange of information, or the use of a common system of symbols, signs, behaviour, etc for this' (*The New Penguin English Dictionary* 2001, p.278). In today's society communication is associated with the exchange of information through a variety of methods. Exchanges occur through speaking, writing, use of pictures, diagrams and computer generated images, each one dependent on the information to be exchanged. The diversity of methods used for information exchange are often commonly associated with the use of machines or electronic aids:

- mobile phones

- text messages

- faxes

- electronic mail (e-mail)

- data transfer

- computer disks

- CD ROMs.

These different forms of communication and their individual usage may vary across the world. Within some areas of society and within some developing countries the use of electronic aids may be limited; reliance may be upon word of mouth, the written word, radio communication, visual sign or sound. All methods are dependent upon those who use them and societal expectations, and can be affected by financial and resource constraints.

Each method of information exchange has value in individual situations such as personal, family, social, educational or business. Communication takes place all the time in a variety of contexts – it is the methods used that differ. There are many barriers that can restrict successful communication, some of which are given below:

- limited verbal communication or ability to sign
- being unable to read or write
- not speaking the same language
- inability to access and/or use services or equipment such as telephone or computer systems
- a lack of awareness or understanding of the many different forms communication can take
- physical disability restricting the communication processes such as writing, using a word processor or getting out and about
- a visual or hearing impairment
- the lack of ability to concentrate and focus on communication.

Many methods of communication are taken for granted in our day to day living such as an ability to hold a conversation or telephone each other. Understanding some of the restrictions that may impede the process provides a basis for promoting and increasing good communication. If restraints to effective communication are identified then ways of reducing or removing these barriers can be sought.

HOW DOES COMMUNICATION TAKE PLACE?

As discussed in the previous section, communication can be carried out in a multitude of ways. None of the methods highlighted are, in principle, excluded from use by people with learning disabilities, although the person's ability may restrict use of some methods. Many people with learning disabilities use speech, write, use computers and mobile phones; however, not all are able to make use of what is often taken for granted by many people in society. Another aspect to be considered is the process of developmental learning. By exploring aspects of developmental learning we can begin to understand how we learn to communicate and the implications if development and learning are restricted.

The developmental process can be considered from a variety of perspectives, including those of Birch (1997); Daniel, Wassell and Gilligan (1999); Davenport (1996); Rosengreen (2000). Communication difficulties within the learning disabilities field can be explored from a childhood perspective (for example, Gaag and Dormandy 1993) and from an adult perspective (for example, Law and Parkinson 1999).

We will provide two examples of how an understanding of developmental learning can lend insight into communication. A study carried out by Trevarthen and Richards (in Davenport 1996, p.30) related to a sample of five babies being studied for an hour a week during the first six months of life. The study identified the communication differences between babies lying in the cot looking at overhead mobiles to those in contact with their mother. The toys were explored and played with, but they observed a 'sort of conversation with their mother':

- From two months of age the babies would open their mouths when their mothers spoke to them. No sound was emitted.

- At approximately four months the babies and mothers took turns in communicating – one speaking, the other quiet. When the mothers stopped speaking the babies made sounds.

- This continued and developed not only as a method of gaining care but as a mutually enjoyable experience. The body and face were used in communicating, moving in time with what was occurring. This is referred to as 'interactional synchrony'.

(Adapted from Trevarthen and Richards in Davenport 1996, p.30)

Stern (1977) looked at the use of face to face behaviour, holding eye contact, looking away, smiling and moving head and hands in time with what was being said. Stern suggested that this behaviour all related to fun and mutual enjoyment of the communicating experience.

These explanations of developing attachment and communication all relate to a child who can see, hear and has the mental ability to develop in line with the majority of children in society. What these studies neglect is disability and the impact of disability upon development and communication. As mentioned, other studies provide further insight into these issues; for example, from a child perspective (Gaag and Dormandy 1993) and from an adult perspective (Law and Parkinson *et al.* 1999). We suggest that the developmental process of a person and the individual's opportunity to develop can help inform how that individual has learnt to communicate. Eye contact, head or hand movements, hearing and concentration may be affected for people with learning disabilities. The person's individual communication style and ability needs to be identified and understood. Thus having an understanding of development and the effect this may have upon communication can play a part in removing barriers to effective communication.

METHODS OF COMMUNICATION ASSOCIATED WITH CARE, SUPPORT AND EDUCATIONAL WORK

We wish to identify some of the methods of communication found in our practice experience. This is not an exhaustive list but we hope that it will reinforce the idea of the many different ways that communication takes place.

Verbal

Many people labelled as having a learning disability are able to hold a verbal conversation. The learning disability may have only a minimal influence on the ability to communicate. People with a profound or severe learning disability may be able to use specific words or short phrases or sounds to mean words. Support and care workers need to consider methods and options for promoting effective communication for people being supported.

British Sign Language (BSL)

In our experience of working in the learning disabilities field we have found BSL to be used in limited ways. Those who were taught and had used it from birth through having deaf parents were notable exceptions and as signing was their first language they were both confident and fluent in it. What they often lacked later was a signing environment where they could express themselves and be understood. The use of either single or two hand spelling and signing is reliant on dexterity, fine motor control and co-ordination. It also requires the ability to remember and to be able to spell out words or string many signs together. BSL also uses the movements of the hands, eyes, face, head and body that are watched and deciphered by the people communicating. Clearly this is not a method accessible to all.

Makaton

Makaton is a licensed type of sign language that appears to be used predominantly by people with a learning disability. Licensed type refers to one that is registered and often has a copyright; software, books, educational packs and the licence have to be purchased. Makaton is particularly used with people who have limited verbal expression and it makes use of a limited amount of signs underpinned by BSL. The specially selected vocabulary is considered as the most essential and useful in providing basic communication. Makaton is structured in stages of increasing complexity. It follows a pattern of language development; the first stage provides signs to express essential needs. Subsequent stages expand vocabulary and more complex language is introduced.

Makaton is an important and useful method that can be used to facilitate learning and to indicate wants and needs. An example of this could be learning the sign for drink and subsequently using it to get a drink. It is useful to consider who decides which words and signs someone has the opportunity to learn. In our experience Makaton is generally used to reinforce verbal communication.

Paget–Gorman sign system

This is a more sophisticated manual sign language used with people who have hearing difficulties or specific language disorders.

There are some formats of communication more associated with people who have some level of visual restriction.

Braille

This is a system that uses embossed or raised dots on a paper; each set of dots represents a letter of the alphabet. Braille consists of two levels: grade one is where each word is fully spelt out and grade two uses contractions to explain groups of words that are frequently used. This alleviates the need to spell out each word. Braille relies on the ability to be able to feel, and move the fingers over many dots and understand their meanings.

Moon

Moon is a form of tactile reading used by people with visual impairment and uses a simplified version of the Latin alphabet. This method is sometimes used as a way of communicating with people with a learning disability and visual impairment.

Bliss

Bliss is a symbolic communication system designed for people who have limited speech and hand functions. The system can range from very basic to quite sophisticated and is often used before moving on to more complicated methods of communication. The symbols are often set out on a board and their meanings relate to the individual using Bliss. The indication of the symbols may be made by hand, fingers, eye contact, pointers or electronic aids. Sometimes the symbol might be quite different to the actual word's meaning; for example, the symbol might be of a cat but the word that is meant is animal. It is therefore very important to be aware of the meaning of the symbols to that individual.

Word boards

Electronic word boards or keyboards are a further development of the Bliss concept. The signs pressed can spell out the required words onto a screen, or may be attached to some form of voice synthesizing unit. A speaking unit enables the person's chosen signs to be voiced. There are many different ways that these can be operated: with a hand, finger, pointer and attachment. With the fast moving development of technology new ideas are emerging that may further enhance the effectiveness of electronic communication.

Body language and non-verbal communication

We all use non-verbal communication, perhaps far more often and in many more ways than we realize. Body language is apparent through gesture, expression and posture. Other non-verbal communication may extend wider than this; for example, to the clothes we wear. People may dress differently for different occasions. What is worn for an evening out, to attend court, or to go for a walk may be different. People dress for specific purposes and also for a specific look; it may be to achieve respect, look important, or to make the person feel more confident. Our mode of dress may provide unspoken information about us, our profession, standards or attitude.

Non-verbal communication is usually specific to the setting and those who it is between. A quick glance at a close friend could mean something quite different from the same glance to a stranger. The meanings of non-verbal communication are dependent upon the shared social understanding and relationship of the people involved and of the situation.

Argyle suggested that non-verbal communication can serve many different purposes:

> Assisting speech – Such as emphasising important words by stressing them heavily, and saying them more slowly than other words.

> Replacing speech – For example, shrugging the shoulders to say 'I don't know'.

> Signalling attitudes – Such as adopting a bored facial expression when forced to listen to someone whose opinion you are not interested in.

> Signalling emotions – Such as hugging a close friend that you haven't seen for some time to express your pleasure at seeing them. (Argyle 1975 in Hayes 1996a, p.514)

There are various ways that non-verbal communication can be achieved, including:

- facial expression
- eye contact
- posture and gesture
- proximity
- dress style.

(Adapted from Hayes 1996a)

If this particular area of communication is of specific interest, more can be learnt by reading appropriate texts that study the psychology of communication.

Widget

Widget is a licensed computer software program that provides a method of working with symbols. It enables words that are typed into the computer to be reinforced with a picture above them. The program also has a speech facility so that when words are typed they are heard through the computer speakers. A written document can be read by the computer either as a sentence, paragraph or in its entirety. The range of pictures available is fairly extensive which enhances its use. The program appears to be used more often in educational settings than in social or medical ones.

There are other methods of communicating that have not been mentioned here that may suit different individuals and their circumstances. Exploration of different formats can promote communication tailored to individual needs.

Exploring the environment where communication takes place can provide insight into how it may impact upon an individual. For example, a person may be able to sign but others within the environment may be unable to. Thus the non-signing environment inhibits the individual's communication style. The use of assisted and augmented communication is dependent upon the environment and a working example to reinforce this is given in case study one.

We will now go on to explore support facilities that can enhance communication.

SUPPORT FACILITIES

There are various support facilities that can be found either within the expertise of a person or in a developmental programme aimed at increasing communication opportunities.

Interpreting

The use of interpreters can be beneficial in promoting and opening communication channels. In a multicultural society we may work with people whose first language is not English and it is important to effectively communicate. This may be achieved through the use of an interpreter. Interpretation services extend to people who use different forms of communication. This can include specialist signers in BSL, Makaton, deaf-blind signing, or in reality most of the communication methods already highlighted.

There are particular issues that can cause dilemmas whilst using interpreters, so their use should be carefully considered (Freed 1988). An interpreter is useful as a channel for communication between two parties. Confidentiality, neutrality and providing accurate interpretation of the tone of the interaction and of the information being discussed are all critical aspects of good interpretation. The person being supported may be put in the situation of having to share personal information with the interpreter as well as the worker or supporter involved and this could affect the conversations.

An interpreter may have a personal view of the information being given; however, a trained interpreter would be aware of this and remain neutral in accurately relaying information. The use of an independent interpreter can obviously have an advantage over using family members or people from the person's community. The independence provides objectivity, autonomy and confidentiality. Consideration of cultural expectations is important as these can have an impact and influence upon the work being undertaken (Ahmed 1990).

Speech therapy

A speech therapist is an expert in assessment and diagnosis, treatment and support of communication and aspects of feeding. A formal assessment and observation are combined to identify the nature of the support that is required. These might include aspects such as:

- pre-language skills – skills required that underpin the first words spoken

- language – focusing on the use and understanding of words

- sound systems – focusing on the sounds and composition of words that are used when communicating

- articulation – looking at how the lips, tongue and facial muscles are used when speaking

- fluency – looking at how speech is structured and how it flows when being used

- voice – whether a voice is present or not, the quality of the voice and subsequent success in its use.

Speech therapists work with individuals and groups with the purpose of enhancing certain skills. This work is often achieved through games and by using the particular interests of those being supported. If the use of verbal communication is problematic then the speech therapist may look at alternative systems. We have discussed some of these earlier in the chapter – systems such as Bliss, Makaton, Paget–Gorman and BSL.

Physiotherapy

A physiotherapist works towards optimizing the physical function of an individual. This is achieved by facilitating and developing fine motor and sensory performance and co-ordination. The physiotherapist can assess and analyse movement and work with physical aspects such as neuromuscular, muscoskeletal, cardiovascular and respiratory symptoms. If someone is supported in developing or improving his or her fine motor control, breathing, or eye to hand co-ordination this can then assist communication. Physiotherapy intervention can include the treatment of acute clinical conditions such as respiratory problems and orthopaedic injuries. Through motor and sensory stimulation a person's mobility, positioning, balance and co-ordination may all be improved. Physiotherapists also undertake group work to stimulate social awareness and interaction. Many of the above activities could be seen as having little to do with communication; however, all could be relevant to its enhancement.

Occupational therapy

The role of the occupational therapist, as that of the physiotherapist, may not be immediately apparent when considering communication. The occupational therapist is a specialist in identifying the ability of a person to undertake everyday tasks. These may include:

- interpersonal and social skills
- activities involved in having a job
- occupational activities
- activities for daily living
- management of personal needs.

Occupational therapists use their training and skills to enable people to develop an awareness of themselves and their environment. This in turn can promote and increase confidence and independence. A learning environment that is informal and encourages concentration is ideal for a development or interaction programme to be carried out. Such programmes can include:

- daily living activities such as housework, self-care, hygiene, dressing
- assisted activities such as shopping, budgeting, use of transport
- use of equipment and environment adaptations
- work skills training
- use of cognitive skill; personal development.

In each of these programmes communication between the person and the occupational therapist has to take place, some of which may be used purely to achieve the designated task. Other programmes may relate to finding the most appropriate way to communicate and then supporting the individual's skills development. This may include looking at various types of augmented and assistive communication technology and assessing, introducing and monitoring the use of the equipment.

A combination of specialist supports can help in promoting and developing communication. Each situation needs to be assessed and the most appropriate and least restrictive method of providing support used. The benefits of developing confidence, self-esteem and self-worth play their part in promoting a person's ability to communicate.

In addition there are a variety of therapies using different media and methods that also promote communication skills. Art, drama and music therapy can be used in enabling learning and development. The use of these therapies encourages communication, role play, imagination, relaxation and group interaction. The methods and way the sessions are used can be adapted to the needs of individuals and can be used with people of different abilities. The aim of these therapies is to develop physical and mental responses, promoting confidence and communication. By their very nature these therapies are not dependent upon the ability of individuals to verbalize their feelings. Self-expression through different methods is an important way of promoting inclusion. As with many services the cost and availability may vary depending upon the locality. A wider exploration of the support and resources available may be necessary.

Listening

Listening is another aspect of interpersonal skills, a key part of communication. Finding different ways to enable effective communication is obviously important, but holds little value if the information being exchanged is not heard. Listening skills require both a cognitive and social dimension. The cognitive part is about the listener understanding what is being said. This understanding must include the overall context of the conversation and the specific relevant details. The listener being able to understand these details is not the only or final issue. The listening ability needs to include clarifying the information received with the person concerned, and making certain that it has been fully understood. The social skills aspect focuses on enabling the person being supported to communicate and, if required, discuss relevant issues. This needs to be done in such a way that all the relevant information is shared and that important parts are not ignored. McLeod (1993) suggests that cognitive and social skills can be combined to inform our understanding. This is about making connections between what you see, what you hear and what you do when communicating. This may include such aspects as:

- empathy
- body language
- facial expression
- body posture
- appropriate encouragement and reassurance to the person providing the information
- accurate and clear listening
- hearing what is actually being said
- summarizing and checking the information

- monitoring what is being said

- evaluating your own intervention, checking it is supporting and not leading or influencing the information being given

- giving time and having patience to work at the person's own speed and not to rush them.

(Adapted from McLeod 1993)

In the use of a task centred approach (see Chapter 9), Reid and Epstein (1972) suggest that communication and listening are founded on two principal approaches: being systematic and being responsive. The systematic approach focuses on the ability to keep the person being supported working at the task in hand, thus enabling the targeted problem to be resolved. The responsive nature of the approach relates to being empathetic and enabling the person to be truly involved in the process.

The two approaches mentioned above highlight the importance of active listening and hearing what is being said. When working with people with learning disabilities flexible and adaptable methods are required. Getting to know the person and his or her communication style is a key issue in identifying how to maximize listening and interpersonal skills.

BARRIERS TO COMMUNICATION AND THEIR REMOVAL

Throughout the chapter we have highlighted potential barriers to successful communication. So much relies on the flexibility and adaptable nature of the support and care workers. Within the present care context where many services have to be bought from care providers, money may restrict the availability of resources and some resources may be scarce in a particular area. Having an awareness of the different ways of enhancing communication is a major step forward in removing some of the barriers.

When we communicate it is usually related to something we have seen, heard, thought, felt, need or want to find out. Communication involves reciprocal giving, assimilating and responding to information. When we receive information we need to evaluate it and then respond to it; this process enables feedback to be given. The person who has received information can then undertake the same process. This exchange will, to an extent, be affected by beliefs, values and perceptions (Nelsen 1980). If the information we have been given is misunderstood, or our values and beliefs distort the meaning of it, then feedback could increase the confusion between the parties communicating. This type of situation can lead to an information processing block. The majority of actions that a person takes can be seen as methods of communicating. Verbal and non-verbal methods of communi-cating are not the only way a person can 'say' something; consideration should be given to silence and absence. If we are totally silent or even absent from, for example, a meeting that we should have attended, our actions can be interpreted by others. Our silence or absence conveys a message which is open to interpretation. Consider a person who becomes mute following trauma or abuse – the lack of spoken communication may in itself speak volumes.

Lishman (1994) suggests ways that communication can be enhanced by developing working relationships:

- being genuine
- showing warmth
- having acceptance
- providing encouragement
- giving approval when required and appropriate
- having empathy
- being able to be responsive
- sensitivity.

(Adapted from Lishman 1994)

There are many different ways that communication can be undertaken and understood. However, it is not only the methods that are important for its success, it is also the skills of listening and working in a way that ensures equality. The way information is processed, the evaluation of beliefs and values and how a person listens and talks are key issues in using communi-cation methods in practice. Information given should be listened to carefully and checked that it has been heard correctly. Likewise information given should be accessible and understandable to those involved. Combining a thoughtful approach with relevant support should ensure equality and inclusion. The awareness and use of other theories can also help in this process.

Communication has strong links to many other theoretical approaches. Systems theory and the interaction of the systems a person functions within will be affected by communication. If a person is unable to effectively com-municate with or understand other people within a system then he or she is likely to become marginalized or excluded (see Chapter 9). Some aspects of behavioural work rely upon the interpretation of what a person communicates. The decision to undertake behavioural change may be considered in light of the information gained through discussion or observation of an individual. If the communication has been one-sided or the person's views misunderstood then the use of behavioural approaches may be questioned (see Chapter 8). In considering people's roles and role theory, if individuals are perceived as unable to communicate in the same way as the majority then their role in society may be affected. Subsequently, a person may be excluded from particular social or working roles and thus be denied access to some areas of society (see Chapter 9).

We will now explore aspects of communication through the following two case studies.

CASE STUDY ONE

Kim had attended residential school from the age of 11 years. The school used BSL in conjunction with speech to create a signing environment. Having finished school Kim attended college for a further year. She then chose to attend a day centre for three days per week and additional training sessions with the disability employment adviser. Kim hoped to gain paid employment.

Kim found the transition to the day centre somewhat difficult. Only one other person from her college was joining her in the move. Kim found it hard to integrate with the established groups. She also found communication frustrating as some people did not readily understand her speech and few people within the day centre used BSL. Day service staff had also noticed her isolation and had looked at ways of including her more. These issues were discussed at Kim's six week review.

Application in practice

Identifying the communication difficulties experienced by Kim was important. The environment that Kim had moved into was not one that readily used BSL; the impact on her was profound. The six week review enabled joint discussion of how the situation could be improved. Kim's base group within the day centre was changed to one where the staff member had level one BSL and was keen to undertake level two. Joint signing better enabled Kim's inclusion and encouraged issues of importance to her to be discussed. Kim also joined a group facilitated by a staff member and speech therapist as part of a multi-disciplinary approach. The group focused on the personal interests of members and enhanced communication. The speech therapist was also able to identify some individual speech work with Kim.

With Kim's consent, her base group worker contacted both her previous college and school to gain ideas of improving communication. It was evident that in the wider systems of education and social services that similar methods were not being used. It was disabling to Kim to have come from a signing environment to one which was not predominantly signing and this caused frustration. The lack of conformity between services needed to be addressed, to look at continuity for those moving from one service to another and at removing barriers to communication.

CASE STUDY TWO

Yasmin was behaving in a way that challenged people in the day centre she attended and this was unusual for her. Yasmin had very little speech but could communicate in several ways. She could make sounds indicating pleasure and displeasure and was able to indicate preferences by using her own pictorial book, photographs and by pointing to people or objects. A day centre staff member tried to talk to Yasmin to establish what was upsetting her but was unable to find out. She then discussed the situation with Yasmin's parents. They too had been experiencing difficulties with Yasmin and she had hit her mother on two recent occasions. Yasmin's parents said they would like some help as they did not know what else to try. Yasmin was referred to her community learning disabilities team for support.

The worker took time to assess the situation and consider the systems surrounding Yasmin. He spent time with Yasmin, her parents and day centre staff. He visited Yasmin both at home and at the day centre to see if there were any obvious clues to the situation. He spent time looking at Yasmin's photographs with her and realized she was indicating one particular photograph showing her sitting in a garden. He then investigated this further and discovered that this photograph showed Yasmin at the children's respite unit that she no longer attended. Further discussion with her parents and staff indicated that Yasmin's changed behaviour had started fairly soon after this respite care had ended and her new respite care had begun.

Application in practice

Yasmin could not speak her unhappiness at no longer attending a favourite respite unit or the loss of her friends there. She communicated her unhappiness through her actions both at home and in the day centre. This was recognized through careful work with her. The worker particularly spent time in getting to know Yasmin, building a relationship and communicating with her. He also took the time to talk to everyone else involved.

Through this process of building a relationship and better understanding, working in a holistic way and not focusing solely on the aspect of behaviour, the worker was able to identify the cause of Yasmin's distress. He was then able to work out a plan with Yasmin and her parents to try some different options for respite until she found an alternative that suited her. Yasmin's non-verbal communication had been powerful in effecting change.

CONCLUSION

There are two concepts that we would like to look at as a conclusion to communication: these are the dissemination of information and the way to move communication forward.

Disseminating information

Some of the intricacies of communication and ways of enhancing it have been highlighted. These can then be taken a step further. Organizations, whether social, medical or educational, need to provide information about their services. This needs to be quality information. There is no point writing pages of service specification if it cannot be read and understood by the people for whom it has been written. The information needs to be in accessible formats. These may include video with signing, audio, large print, picture and word and picture format. It needs to explain the function of the agency or service and what can be provided. The information should not use jargon or be written in a way that prevents it being understood. What we are suggesting is that real meanings are not obscured by the latest vogue terminology. Information should be presented in a clear format that avoids the chance of misunderstanding.

Health and social care agencies need to develop effective channels to enhance communication. Collaboration and working towards a joint goal of easily accessible information is important. The involvement of people with learning disabilities in developing this process is of paramount importance. They are the experts in understanding their communication needs. Communication and its importance in social care practice can be studied in more depth through the work of, for example, Banks (1995), Coulshed and Orme (1998), Nelsen (1980,1986), Payne (1997) and Trevithick (2000).

The way forward?

The prioritizing of information as being accessible and understandable for as many people as possible, independent of someone else supporting them, promotes equality and the opportunity of making informed choices. The use of people independent of social and medical care services can be important in providing objectivity. Advocacy has increased dramatically over the past few years and its value and importance are acknowledged within the learning disabilities field. At times, someone independent of the services being provided can get to know the person in more depth and in a different way than service providers. With the advocate's involvement within the assessment process the person can often be supported in a way that enables better representation to be made. In Chapter 6 we explore advocacy in a wider context.

Understanding the many different forms of communication will ultimately be empowering for people with learning disabilities. This in turn will help to challenge the oppression and discrimination that can be faced in day to day living and lead to non-tokenistic inclusion and equality.

Key points

- Communication takes many different forms and is not solely about verbal communication used by the majority of people within society.

- Learning to communicate is part of developmental learning. If the developmental process is restricted then communication may be affected; however, this does not mean that a person is unable to communicate.

- An awareness of the barriers that might restrict successful communication is critical.

- Within the learning disabilities field there are many recognized methods developed to enable communication; these include: signing, picture format and computer programs.

- There are a variety of people trained to help others to increase communication skills, and their specialist knowledge and training can be invaluable.

- Listening is a critically important part of communicating; if what is said by a person is not actively listened to, then the communication taking place holds little value.

- There are a variety of specific theories that can provide insight and help inform this area of study.

- Working closely with a person, by getting to know the individual and how he or she communicates, is a key factor to success.

6

Advocacy, Empowerment, Participation and Choice

INTRODUCTION

In this chapter we will initially introduce and then explore the concept of advocacy, highlighting the various ways that it can be used. The link between advocacy and empowerment will be made and consideration will be given to how both can be used as practical methods of helping and supporting someone with learning disabilities. These methods may include empowering the person, supporting participation and providing the opportunity to make informed choices – thus enabling more control of his or her life. The ultimate aim of the approach is to make sure that the voices of people with learning disabilities are really heard and not just acknowledged as a tokenistic gesture.

The development and practical application of advocacy and empowerment will be considered and the barriers that are often faced explored. The links as to how advocacy and empowerment can play an important part in many theoretical approaches will be made. Two case studies showing advocacy and empowerment enabling participation and choice will reinforce the use in practice.

WHAT IS ADVOCACY?

One definition of advocacy is: 'the representation of service users' interests in order to improve their situation' (Thomas and Pierson 1996, p.11). It is important to note that the representation can come from many different perspectives. Before exploring the different forms that representation can take, we wish to consider the development of advocacy. There is a difference between 'independent advocacy' and of people advocating within the remit and guidelines of their jobs and working to their codes of practice. Payne

(1997) suggests that 'advocacy' has particular links in its origin to the legal profession. Solicitors and lawyers take on the role of being an advocate for the clients that they are representing. Payne also identifies the advocacy role as intrinsic to some professional codes. 'For example, UK professional codes enjoin nurses to undertake advocacy in the sense of raising problems in the resourcing or management of services which might lead to detriment to their patients' (Payne 1997, p.267). In these examples the power can be seen as very one-sided and mainly held by the person with the skills and abilities to deal with the relevant information. A lawyer has the professional training and has the knowledge to guide the client through the legal process. An understanding of the law, court procedures and legal expectations all play a part in that particular advocacy role. A nurse may personally see aspects of care that are not meeting the patient's needs. The concerns raised could then be taken by the nurse to identify the need to management. In each example the decision to represent the person predominantly lies with the professional, although patients and carers may make their own representations. This type of representation is being undertaken as part of the person's job and role and is not advocacy in the true context of 'independent advocacy' support.

In the 1980s much of the focus for advocacy was directed upon promoting the ability and increasing the quality of care and life for people in the fields of mental health and learning disabilities. There was an increase in awareness of advocacy and its uses as it became more widespread. This was linked to the changing views concerning long-term institutionalized care. With the increase in understanding of human rights and society's greater awareness of hospital based institutional care, the style and remit of care provision was challenged. The proposed introduction of community care and the move away from institutions reinforced the importance of people having their views and wishes heard. The advocacy development work undertaken in the field of mental health played a part in informing and supporting advocacy in the field of learning disabilities. The difference between mental health and learning disabilities must not be confused as they are, of course, each very different.

In the UK the United Kingdom Advocacy Network (UKAN) was formed by mental health service users as a way of supporting others with mental health needs. One of the ways of achieving this was by providing advocacy support. The Mental Health Task Force worked with and listened to people who were using mental health services. The aim was to understand what worked well for service users and what was less successful for them. This was seen as a major step in being able to develop services that met the individual's needs. To achieve this in more depth a user group representative organization was set up to carry out in-depth research: the Task Force User Group. This group commissioned UKAN to draw up a code of practice for advocacy.

The code of practice was drawn up following ten regional conferences in which service users took the opportunity to speak out with their views and thoughts. This identified four key areas to be considered:

- to inform and involve user groups

- to enable managers to understand the qualities that meaningful, independent, user-run empowerment and advocacy projects might be expected to establish and maintain

- to clarify the roles and functions of groups, advocacy and advocacy workers, in order to extend and strengthen advocacy

- to be used as a nationally recognized and approved basis for user training of both staff and users.

(King in Conlan *et al.* 1994, p.1)

The advocacy code was subsequently adopted by UKAN in 1994 and used in their advocacy handbook (Conlan *et al.* 1994). The work undertaken by UKAN and others played a key role in informing other areas of service provision of the development of advocacy services. In summarizing the variety of ideas and views of advocacy, it appears that the main focus is representing the interests, needs and wishes of people who may be perceived as powerless in society. Their interests, needs and wishes are represented to those who hold power and who control how care, support and social inclusion are structured in society. The development of advocacy in the learning disabilities field can be studied in greater depth through the work of Gray and Jackson (2001).

The definition given earlier by Thomas and Pierson (1996) suggests that advocacy relates to the representation of people. This definition needs to be expanded upon as representation can come from a variety of perspectives: family, friends, partner, key worker, social worker, nurse, doctor – the list could go on. Very importantly, the list should also include self-representation; it is critical to acknowledge that self-advocacy is a realistic concept for many people with learning disabilities. People can be empowered to be able to speak up for themselves. With the many different people that can take on the role of representation there is, of course, the risk of conflicts of interest and of personal agendas. This will be discussed later in the chapter.

Representation and advocacy work hand in hand with empowerment, which we will now briefly explore. This will be followed by a look at some of the different forms that advocacy and empowerment can take.

EMPOWERMENT

Empowerment is defined as: '...concerned with how people may gain collective control over their lives, so as to achieve their interests as a group, and a method by which social workers [and other care providers] seek to enhance the power of people who lack it' (Thomas and Pierson 1996, p.134). Payne's explanation also includes the issue of power and its part within empowerment: 'Empowerment seeks to help clients gain power of decision and action over their own lives by reducing the effect of social or personal blocks to exercising power and by transferring power from the environment to clients' (1997, p.266).

Empowerment has direct links with methods of working that aim to achieve equality for minority or other oppressed groups. In the 1970s a radical social work approach was proposed as a method of challenging the oppression faced by some groups in society. With a greater awareness of the needs and interests of minority groups then equality could be worked towards. Empowerment as a theory provides a framework that supports an understanding of the discrimination, oppression and devaluation faced by some minority groups. These groups could include people with learning disabilities and people with issues of mental health.

Feminist and anti-racist perspectives can be used to explain the principles of empowerment in practice. An understanding of the issues of power – who holds power and how it is used – is key to the success of empowerment. Without first identifying where the power lies, the ability to enable others to take power is bound to be unsuccessful. Without power people may not be able to make their needs and wishes heard. The decisions about what to do, when to do it and how to do it remain with others.

Without empowerment a person may remain helpless. Learned helplessness was a process suggested by Seligman (1975), who carried out research on how animals and humans learn. Further ideas about learned helplessness have been developed by Barber (1986), who considered it in the context of social care. Payne provides an explanation of how learned helplessness may occur:

> If people have important experiences which show that what they do does not affect what happens to them, they form the expectation that their actions will generally not produce any useful results. Their capacity to learn useful behaviour in other situations becomes impaired. People may lose motivation, become anxious and depressed and poor at thinking and learning. (Payne 1997, pp.283–284)

If people are rendered powerless at making decisions and over what happens in their lives, then they may go through a process of learned helplessness. This will have a major impact on their lives. Barber (1986) suggests that people who have gone through this process need to be able to experience being in control and achieving successful positive outcomes for their lives. Barber referred to this process as 'environmental enrichment'. We suggest that enrichment can, in part, be achieved through the process of empowerment.

One example of gaining enrichment can be explored through the work of Ahmed. Ahmed (1990) suggests that service users should be supported on a one to one basis, or through groups facing similar oppression within society. The aim is to empower the person or group, to enable them to take greater control of their lives. The need to sometimes use advocacy that will support and empower oppressed groups within society was suggested by Ntebe (1994) as an important part of a radical model of support and care practice. The link between advocacy and empowerment is reinforced as a key factor in achieving participation and choice.

We will now explore some ways that advocacy support can be provided and how the idea of empowerment should be intrinsic to these approaches.

DIFFERENT TYPES OF ADVOCACY

There are various ways that advocacy support can be provided and people enabled. Many of the styles that are mentioned in this text are not predominantly thought to be related to the learning disabilities field. By introducing and briefly explaining some of the advocacy styles, the aim is to raise an awareness of the diversity of advocacy and empowerment in practice. The different types of advocacy are not in any specific order as each holds its own importance and relevance in different situations.

Citizen advocacy was first developed in the 1960s in North America (Wolfensberger 1977). Citizen advocacy focuses on people who have a keen interest in helping and supporting people who perhaps do not have family or friends. The aim of citizen advocacy is to enable people to be represented so that they are not socially excluded and so that their needs and wishes are heard. The support is provided predominantly in a voluntary capacity to give independent, objective support. There are many voluntary advocacy agencies that advertise for volunteers, carry out checks on potential advocates, train them and supervise their supporting role.

> A valued citizen who is unpaid and independent of human services social workers creates a relationship with a person who is at risk of social exclusion and chooses one of several of many ways to understand, respond to and represent that person's interests as if they were the advocate's own. (O'Brien 1987b, p.3)

In the 1970s the approach was introduced in the UK and started to be used more within the changing role of social care and support for people with learning disabilities. The need for 'professional' advocacy services continued to become more apparent (Croft and Beresford 1990). The term 'professional' was used in the context of an independent service that had training, standards, a code of conduct and an operational framework. It did not mean an employed professional such as a nurse or social worker, as these would not be independent due to the nature of their work. The need for advocacy to be underpinned by principles that genuinely value the person and do not compromise the role are, of course, critical. There are many different types of advocacy support that have developed from the initial idea of citizen advocacy. Recognizing that clear principles guide quality advocacy and empowerment is important. We will go on to examine some of the various forms that advocacy support can take.

One to one advocacy (as citizen advocacy is now frequently referred to) is often used with people who have limited verbal ability and are more reliant on others to voice their views, needs and wishes. A longer term advocacy partnership may be set up so that someone independent can get to know the person requiring support. The time spent by the independent advocate with the person being supported and with others who have influence in that person's life may highlight specific issues that need addressing. As the advocate, it is hoped, gains a good working relationship and understanding of the person's needs, he or she is better able to put forward views developed from the working knowledge. This enables the person's voice to be heard, albeit through a third party. The individual need for an advocate can be varied and one to one support can occur in many situations. It may take place when someone is moving from hospital care to another style of living, trying for employment or lacks family support.

Group advocacy is sometimes known as collective advocacy or 'class advocacy' (Wolfensberger 1977). The principles of group advocacy lie in a group of people working together for a similar cause. These groups may be international, national, regional, local or within small community settings. Trade unions are one example of a group of people that campaign and, if required, legally represent their members. An example of a group voice within the learning disabilities field is Mencap. Many other organizations support specific groups. They campaign, represent and fight for the rights of people associated with particular forms of learning disabilities. These groups also highlight issues for people with learning disabilities in general and bring them to the attention of the public. There are many different forms of advocacy groups, both large and small, and the principles of people's rights are intrinsic throughout.

With the development of many housing association supported living projects, supported living advocacy groups have emerged. More people with learning disabilities are able to take on their own tenancy in housing projects designed and developed to meet specific need. There is a need for people to be able to voice their opinions. Advocacy groups provide the opportunity for people to compare the success of supported living and to jointly challenge any areas that are causing concern. This is a valuable way of developing and monitoring the projects by the people who actually use them.

Community advocacy groups are also being set up; predominantly they are for people with learning disabilities who live within the community. They are for people who may live with their parents, families or carers, have their own housing tenancies or live in their own homes. Community advocacy groups provide a forum for people to meet and discuss issues that may affect day to day living and draw together a voice to challenge discrimination and oppression faced. Sometimes these groups are facilitated by an independent person, at other times they may be run by the members of the group. Whatever format is used, community advocacy groups provide an important facility to support community living.

Of course, not all people with learning disabilities live within supported living or hold their own tenancies. Many people live in residential units run either by social services, health, private or voluntary agencies. Advocacy support is available to many people in their residential units. Home visiting advocacy focuses on an independent facilitator visiting perhaps once or twice a month and supporting the residents in discussing issues and seeking change. The day to day running and service development of the residential unit can be informed, guided and to an extent directed by those who are using the services. A similar process occurs in many of the day centres that operate for people with learning disabilities. These are sometimes referred to as user forums. Whatever the name used the process is clearly about empowerment, participation, inclusion and choice.

Self-advocacy groups can be found in any of the above examples of advocacy work. A self-advocacy group may be facilitated by an independent support worker working in a voluntary or paid capacity. The important factor is the independence of the support worker from the other services involved. Some self-advocacy groups focus on the people belonging to the group running it themselves without independent support. The organization People First has played an important part in the development of self-advocacy. Self-advocacy is also something a person can undertake without being part of a group. Self-advocacy involves more than just communication; it is about trying to achieve change. Self-advocacy involves more than just having choice; it is about having *real* choice. Real choice can only be made if it is based on having all the relevant facts to enable *informed* choice. Choice also involves individual responsibility and the recognition that choices have an impact on the individual and others. Self-advocacy is about balancing individual rights and responsibilities in achieving choice and change.

Other forms of individual advocacy may at times be required. If a person wants to deal with personal issues, family issues or make a complaint then a group setting may be an inappropriate place to do so. If the person is unable to self-advocate then an advocacy support system may be required. Should such issues cause distress for the individual then some form of crisis support may be required.

Crisis advocacy is often provided after a request is made for independent support following some form of crisis. This may result from many different situations and predominantly focuses on people's need for support, information and care during a time when they may feel they have little control over their lives. Crisis advocacy may be required following bereavement, eviction, arrest or change in health. These very different factors each present a particular time of difficulty for the individuals concerned. If specific issues relate to legal factors then legal advocacy may be required. Macmillan (1937) suggested that it is the legal advocate's job to present information to the relevant people in a way that the person him or herself would have done if he or she possessed the skills and knowledge to do so. This would still seem to hold true today. Of course, people do not only need support during times of crisis; support may be an important part of managing day to day living.

There are other types of advocacy services and support systems available in a variety of settings and we cannot cover them all. What we have tried to do is to show how advocacy is present and used in the care and support of people with learning disabilities. Advocacy plays a key part in empowerment and subsequent participation and choice. We will now explore its use as a practical method of working.

ADVOCACY AND EMPOWERMENT AS A PRACTICAL METHOD

Bateman (2000, pp.47–61) highlights the importance of principled advocacy; these principles are:

1. Always act in the client's best interests.

2. Always act in accordance with the client's wishes and instructions.

3. Keep the client properly informed.

4. Carry out instructions with diligence and competence.

5. Act impartially and offer frank, independent advice.

6. The advocate should maintain rules of confidentiality.

These principles can be seen as fundamental when using advocacy in practice. Without a clear framework from which to inform practice, negative, oppressive or discriminatory support could occur. It would be unrealistic to expect advocates to be so well informed that they could undertake any element of support on their own. Advocacy is also about joint working, taking into consideration confidentiality and being able to find the expert knowledge required to inform any given situation. 'Advocates…need to recognize when outside help is required and to know the limits of their expertise' (Bateman 2000, p.56). An inclusive approach working with the person requiring the advocate and with other people that can provide the knowledge in meeting need is crucial. An inclusive approach is a way of enhancing participation. Croft and Beresford (1994) reinforce the view that people have the right to be involved in the decision making process that affects their lives. An involvement in this process is fundamental to the ethics of good social and health care practice. The principles of Croft and Beresford's (1994) participatory practice are reinforced through four elements:

- empowerment
- control
- equipping people with personal resources
- organizing the agency to be open.

Empowerment focuses on being able to take charge of the decision making process that affects an individual's life and to challenge oppression. Control is gained through identifying and deciding upon individual need which, it is hoped, leads to the planning of needs-led care packages and resources. The ability to take power and develop confidence, self-esteem, self-worth, knowledge and skills, is a key principle of advocacy, empowerment, participation and choice. Advocacy and empowerment are not just about the individual and should be considered within the wider society. Social and political rights that are not being met, and are identified by people that are oppressed and discriminated against within society, should be acknowledged and play a key part in the development of care and support services (Oliver 1996).

Having explored the principles of advocacy and empowerment and their use and benefit as a practical method of working, we would now like to place these in practice. This will be done by looking at how advocacy can be used as part of practice within the learning disabilities field.

ADVOCACY IN PRACTICE

An advocate is someone who is independent of services and free from any conflict of interest, someone not in the paid employment of statutory social or health services. Often these are voluntary advocacy organizations or those that are independent but receive joint funding from social and health care services. The funding should not create conflict of interests as the organization's voluntary state supports its independence.

An independent advocate allocated to work with a partner should be able to offer impartial support. The first loyalty of the advocate should be to his or her partner, not to a group, relatives, carers or the people who provide services. However, a joint working strategy is not ignored and plays an important part in the secondary role of the advocate. The advocate should check that the person really wants to receive advocacy support. If communication issues make consent difficult then the advocate would need to work with the wider systems around the person as a way of reinforcing the appropriateness of the advocate's role.

If the advocacy partnership begins and communication issues make advocacy difficult, the advocate may ask questions on behalf of the person and make sure that the person's rights are safeguarded. As the partnership develops the understanding of the advocate about what his or her partner wants should become clearer. This then, it is hoped, leads to the partner being able to gain more independence and their voice in stating their needs and wishes. We suggest advocates should strive to enable their partners to:

- communicate what they want to say
- make decisions for themselves
- play an active role in their own lives
- have choices
- obtain their rights
- be able to express feelings and thoughts.

The purpose is to value the individual for the person he or she is, widen the individual's experience and promote participation and choice. Advocates should support their partners to speak up and to do things for themselves wherever possible. If this is not possible the advocate should ensure that his or her partner agrees to the advocate speaking or acting on his or her behalf. The key tasks of advocacy support are:

- to make sure a person is supported in speaking up
- to make certain the person's voice is heard
- to make sure that the person knows his or her rights in order to work towards gaining entitlements
- to remove barriers that restrict a person being able to move forward in life
- to make sure that the person receives the services that he or she needs.

Any of the above actions could be provided through the different styles that advocacy support takes: self, group and one to one/citizen advocacy. Each style can provide invaluable support in meeting people's needs, helping them gain control over their lives, in participating and making informed choices on aspects of day to day living.

We will now look at some of the difficulties, potential barriers and restrictions that can occur when using advocacy and empowerment in practice. By doing so we hope to provide an understanding of how people being supported can receive the maximum opportunity to participate, be involved and take control of their lives.

BARRIERS AGAINST ADVOCACY, EMPOWERMENT, PARTICIPATION AND SUPPORT

Advocacy is not an infallible system; the lack of advocacy facilities and the weakness of legislation are not particularly supportive in the overall picture of advocacy and empowerment. In this section we will consider some of the possible conflicts and difficulties involved in advocacy support.

If a person is in the role of social worker, nurse or support provider, he or she is not independent and therefore not in a position to provide independent advocacy support. However, the occasion may arise that an independent advocacy service or individual support is not available and a position of conflict could then occur. If a service user asks a residential worker or nurse to provide support in making a complaint about the residential home lived in, then he or she would be obliged to do so as part of the duty of care. Realistically, without the independence that an advocate brings, a role conflict may occur for the worker which could make it difficult to fully support the individual concerned. There may be other situations where role conflict could occur for the worker providing support and this could affect issues such as relationships, independent living and cultural and religious choice. Policies and procedures may also restrict the flexibility of approach. This could be specifically relevant when considering risk assessments. The rights of an individual to undertake an informed risk might conflict with the organization being concerned about being held responsible if something goes wrong. In any of these situations the benefit of an advocate who is independent of the service provider can be seen.

The issue of independence is taken a step further when considering self-advocacy groups. Members of self-advocacy groups may be people with a mild to moderate learning disability who can articulate well for themselves. If some of the group have more restricted abilities and are less able to articulate their wishes, then a power imbalance may come into force. The same argument could, of course, be made about independent people supporting groups. The structure and membership of each group needs to be considered when thinking about the success of advocacy work.

Legislation acknowledges advocacy and empowerment. However, it is not particularly supportive of it in practice. Kemshall and Littlechild (2000) discuss the principles of involvement being an integral part of the core mandate for social services. Alas, legislation is not forthcoming in putting the acknowledged requirements into practice as a legal duty. Government guidelines regarding care management and assessment clearly state that service users should have independent advocacy support available to them.

However, the reality is that advocacy remains a limited resource (Simons 1993). Sections 1 and 2 of the Disabled Persons (Services Consultation and Representation) Act 1986 set out the rights of authorized representatives of disabled people. This sounds very positive and supportive of the principles of advocacy. Unfortunately, these sections have never been implemented.

Other examples that illustrate the weakness of current legislation can be found (Kemshall and Littlechild 2000). The legislative weakness does not provide a satisfactory reason to stop challenging discrimination and oppression through advocacy and empowerment. There is a need to provide advocacy support for people from many different groups; these may include racial and cultural groups, those of different ages and abilities. People have the right to have their voice heard and an independent person to provide relevant support. Although lack of resources and funding may limit the setting up and development of independent advocacy services, the need for advocacy should continue to be highlighted. Through the need being demonstrated, additional funding can be argued for and secured.

GUIDING PRINCIPLES

Throughout this chapter we have talked about how advocacy can be used, the importance of empowerment and the fundamental right of people with learning disabilities to participation and choice. Advocacy and empowerment can have a direct involvement with many theories and approaches discussed in this book. We will briefly explore how advocacy and empowerment can be considered in the context of three theories covered in other chapters.

If communication took place and a person was unable, for whatever reason, to be involved in the discussion or in negotiating choice then disempowerment would occur. Finding the most appropriate and least restrictive way of communicating with a person is a form of empowerment (Chapter 5). Sometimes people are unable to communicate in the same way as the majority and extra time and support may be required. Individuals may need someone to advocate for them and help their voices be heard or arrange appropriate support networks to be set up. This type of involvement can promote the right of participation and choice.

When using a task centred approach (Chapter 9), the need to empower people so they are able to take a measure of control over the tasks they want to undertake is critical. Task centred work focuses on participation and the need for individuals to make choices about how they intend to approach a situation. If individuals face difficulties in considering the tasks ahead then an advocate or advocacy support may play a key part in helping them move forward.

If a person is facing concerns or anxieties over his or her role (Chapter 9), then advocacy based support can sometimes be useful. For example, if a person is facing conflict within the family setting concerning attending college, an independent person could work with the individual to help explore how the situation could be moved forward. The advocacy role could help empower a person to make choices.

We are not suggesting that advocacy is an infallible way of ensuring that empowerment, participation and choice happen. We are, however, suggesting that advocacy and empowerment can play an important part when considering ways of supporting people with learning disabilities in their day to day lives.

We will now put advocacy, empowerment, participation and choice into practice using two case studies. The case studies will demonstrate the use of advocacy concerning a tenancy and one involving day to day care. Our aim is to demonstrate the diversity of situations that advocacy can support.

CASE STUDY ONE

Rita had lived all her life with her sister and mother. Their family home was owned by the local council. Rita had an independent life, being employed and having friends and a social life. She belonged to a local community advocacy group for people with learning disabilities.

When Rita's mother died her sister, Angela, then held the tenancy for their house. Rita wished to have her name put on as joint tenant but her sister said the council would not do this. Rita took this problem to her community advocacy group where it was discussed. Some group members held joint tenancies with the local council and explained to Rita this was an option. The group thought about why Angela had said it was not possible. Some thought Angela might want the house for herself. They felt the best thing for Rita to do was discuss the subject of a joint tenancy again with Angela now she knew it was possible. One group member offered to support Rita in doing this and she accepted the support.

Angela was surprised when the subject of a joint tenancy was raised for a second time by Rita and her friend. Angela explained she had said it was not possible as she did not want Rita to worry about being liable for payment of rent. Once Angela realized that Rita understood about a joint tenancy, she suggested they go to see a housing officer together.

Application in practice

By having a forum in the community advocacy group, Rita was able to voice her concerns about her rights to tenancy and gained relevant information which she then used in discussion with her sister. Participation in the group enabled Rita to test out her ideas and gain support, knowledge and insight from others. Rita was then herself able to raise the issue with Angela for further discussion. Rita was able to make an informed choice about wishing to take on a joint tenancy and with it the responsibilities it involved. Whilst Angela had believed she was acting in Rita's best interest she had actually been denying her the opportunity to choose and participate. What Rita demonstrated, using the support and empowerment of her group, was that she had a voice, understood the responsibility of her choice and that she was the best person to know what was right for herself.

CASE STUDY TWO

Gerry was a citizen/one to one advocate for Albert, a man with learning disabilities living in a home for older people. They had built up a partnership since just prior to Albert's move from the hospital he had lived in for many years. Albert enjoyed Gerry's support and visits, particularly as he had no remaining family.

During one of Gerry's regular visits he checked with Albert to see if it was all right to talk with staff to see how things were going and Albert agreed to this. The staff described Albert as having been difficult and of having had two moments of anger in the afternoons. Gerry discussed the recent events with Albert. Albert said he was fed up because he was trying to follow the sport on the television in the lounge and every afternoon this was interrupted by an activity. Gerry asked Albert why he did not watch the sport on the television in his room. Albert explained that if he was not in the lounge then he did not get a cup of tea.

Gerry then went back to the staff to discuss the issue. He thought Albert's 'outbursts' were understandable given the situation. He negotiated that Albert could have afternoon tea served in his room so that he could watch the sport in peace and quiet.

Application in practice

Gerry represented Albert's wishes and supported him to gain his rights. Gerry questioned the institutionalized rules of the home and promoted flexibility to meet Albert's wishes. Gerry also advocated on Albert's behalf, pointing out that Albert's behaviour had been the product of an inflexible system and he thought this unfair.

Through building up a relationship over time and by networking with people in Albert's social systems, Gerry had built up knowledge and understanding. Gerry's representation enabled insight into a problem that was caused by the system and enabled the problem to be resolved in a satisfactory manner for Albert.

CONCLUSION

The right to be able to take control and make informed decisions about day to day living and other aspects that affect the life of a person should be fundamental. Decisions can be small or large and cover mundane issues such as what to eat or wear, through to life changing decisions about relationships or style of living. These decisions are taken for granted by the majority of the population but such choices are not always available to people with learning disabilities. The barriers that restrict integration should always be challenged, as anti-oppressive and anti-discriminatory attitudes are critical in the ongoing battle for inclusion and equality.

Thompson (1997) provides a powerful explanation of the use of empowerment to promote and achieve greater equality within society:

> Perhaps the central concept in the development of anti-disablist practice is that of *empowerment*. Traditional approaches to disabilities [in the context of this book, learning disabilities] continue to disempower people...to deprive them of aspects of control over their own lives. They are disenfranchised by marginalization, isolation and dehumanization at a personal level through prejudice and misdirected pity; at a cultural level through negative stereotypes and values; and at a structural level through a society dominated by capitalist notions of 'survival of the fittest' and charity for those who are 'handicapped' from competing. Empowerment amounts to working alongside disabled people to help overcome and challenge the oppression they experience. (Thompson 1997, p.130)

Thompson goes on to suggest that this is achievable through the use of person centred work, by developing the confidence of the individual and through the use of advocacy to help promote and reinforce the right to inclusion and equality within society.

In this chapter we have discussed how advocacy and empowerment can help to support and promote participation, choice and inclusion. The role of advocacy and the different ways it can provide support has been highlighted. One important aspect to consider is that whilst a person is being supported the supporter still holds the majority of power, due to the nature of the relationship. We believe that self-advocacy and self-empowerment are the ultimate goals as, when achieved, people have greater control over their lives:

> ...advocacy and empowerment represent an ideology of treatment which is radically different, or at least is experienced differently by client and, perhaps, worker. However, power *given* by a worker leaves the power with the worker. Clients must *take* power, and it is the role of social work to organise the institutional response which makes this possible and accepts it when it occurs. (Payne 1997, p.284)

Key points

- Advocacy can be used as a way of enabling people to speak up for themselves. This can be achieved through spending time getting to know people's views, by supporting them to speak up and by representing them.

- Advocacy support can take many different forms, e.g. citizen, group, community, individual and crisis.

- Empowerment focuses on people taking control and being able to make decisions about things that they want to do and factors that affect their lives.

- Participation focuses on the rights of people to be fully involved in their lives, both in decision making and doing. It is about not being excluded from everyday issues or places due to level of ability.

- Choice should be a fundamental right for everyone and not restricted by society's barriers and attitudes.

- Advocacy, empowerment, participation and choice are not infallible. Legislation, society's structures, attitudes, prejudices and ignorance can all hinder the process of people with learning disabilities being fully accepted.

- An ongoing commitment to enable people with learning disabilities is fundamental to all aspects of care and support work.

An awareness of the position of power and the need to work towards maximizing the person's own skills should be ongoing. It is important to re-examine the way we think about, talk about and treat people and to identify ways to enable all people to 'speak' for themselves.

7

Universal Human Experience in the Lives of People with Learning Disabilities

INTRODUCTION

Whilst this book predominantly explores the application of theory to practice when working with people with learning disabilities, the theories discussed are not always designed specifically for working with this client group. In this chapter we are going to consider two universal human experiences not always readily associated with people with learning disabilities: sexuality, and loss and bereavement. Each individual's sexuality is an intrinsic and defining aspect of the person. Loss and bereavement are faced by each person at some point in life. The way that sexuality and loss and bereavement are understood and approached may vary greatly from person to person. In this chapter we intend to highlight the importance of supporting and enabling people with learning disabilities to be as fully involved as possible with their own life experiences. We aim to highlight how theoretical knowledge and understanding of the universal human experiences of sexuality and loss and bereavement can be used in practice settings through the use of case studies.

SEXUALITY

INTRODUCTION

A person's sexuality needs to be recognized and accepted as an integral part of the complex characteristics of human existence. However, within the learning disabilities field this does not always appear to be the case. Literature can be found that provides information about sexuality and learning disabilities, but this often seems to focus on disability and sexuality from the perspective of it being a problem. We will endeavour to explore this perspective and also look at other implications for practice when working with people with learning disabilities.

We will start to explore the links between sexuality and gender and the influence of historic and current social pressures. We will look at the rights of people to their own sexuality, sexual relationships and sexual health. We will also examine some of the restrictions, safety structures and aspects of protection created by policies and legislation. By doing this we aim to enhance understanding of some of the complexities in working with issues of sexuality.

A BRIEF HISTORICAL PERSPECTIVE

In recent years many Government policies, initiatives and legislative changes have, to an extent, challenged the way support and care are provided for people with learning disabilities (see Chapters 1 and 10). The current community based philosophy of care has moved away from the institutionalized care synonymous with the large hospitals established around the beginning of the 1900s. We will briefly explore the impact of living in these hospitals upon the freedom, dignity and sexuality of those who were institutionalized. The Mental Deficiency Act 1913 placed a duty upon all local authorities to certify 'mental defectives' and set up certified institutions. One of the schools of thought that supported this type of care in the early decades of the 1900s was that of the Eugenic Society. Eugenic comes from the Greek *eu* meaning 'well' and *gens* meaning 'to produce'. Eugenics referred to the manipulation of breeding to 'improve' the population. By having control over people in large institutional settings, staff could make sure that the 'feebleminded' did not 'repeat their type', thus producing 'a degenerative stock' (Barker 1983). In the 1930s the Campaign for Voluntary Sterilisation began. The amount of sterilizations that were carried out is difficult to identify, whether they were voluntary or compulsory even harder to establish. In 1934 the Brock Report recommended sterilization as the best way of managing the control of birth by people who were mentally deficient. The power held by those able to make decisions about other people's lives can be clearly seen.

Many accounts can be found of the segregation that was used, including separate wards, day time separation at work and even when socializing:

You couldn't mix with the men. You could go to a dance but you'd have men on one side, women the other. You could dance with them, but they had to go back, men one side, women the other side. Even in the dance hall there were two loads of staff in the middle. (Cooper in Atkinson, Jackson and Walmsley 1997, p.25)

This level of control and segregation is still remembered by many people today. This includes care and support workers and the people with learning disabilities who were placed in the hospitals and institutional settings. Goffman looked at how the institutionalized way of life can continue when staff and patients move on from that environment (1961). The changing policies and legislation over the following decades and the introduction of Community Care have led to the closure of many of the large institutional hospitals.

The move from institutional care to community based care has not been unproblematic. The issues of segregation, control and restrictions are still apparent in some areas of care; residential units catering for men or women only are an example of this. At times it may be argued that these are in the best interest and safety of the people being supported. However, this can still restrict and impinge upon the rights of individuals. This oppression has been highlighted and challenged by the development of advocacy services (see Chapter 6). Many advocacy groups have argued against and highlighted the restrictions placed by the 'establishment' (Bateman 2000). This type of advocacy work has increased the awareness of the marginalization still faced by people with learning disabilities. It has also raised awareness of the control that can still be exerted through the medical, social and political complexities of care provision. This control continues to play a part in the issues surrounding sexuality.

WHAT IS SEXUALITY?

Sexuality can be explained in various ways, such as: 'Sexuality is not a simple or uniform phenomenon: it embraces many aspects of human existence' (Horrocks 1997, p.1). Gender, sexism and sexual discrimination can all be seen as relevant to sexuality as well as the right to have sexual feelings and sexual relationships. We will briefly explore gender, sexism and sexual discrimination and then go on to look at sexual feelings and relationships in more depth. Through this exploration we hope to provide some initial thoughts around the subject and aid consideration of some of the complex issues around sexuality.

Gender is described as 'one's sex, ...classification corresponding to sex' (Hawker and Hawkins 1996, p.130). It identifies that male and female are different with respect to gender. Gender requires further consideration when talking about people who are transsexual, also referred to as transgendered. Gender also contains 'the social and psychological characteristics attributed to men and women' (Thomas and Pierson 1996, p.157). The sex of someone is identified through a biological and medical process, whereas gender is affected by the wider social definition. Within society certain social expectations, often stereotypical, are placed on the male and female roles. This can be the cause of oppression, discrimination and conflict.

Sexism includes perspectives such as inequality, oppression and discrimination predominantly caused through male dominance. Weber (1947) talked about male 'patriarchy' and described the dominance of men within the family. This has been extended in later years to include the power of men in society as a general issue. This is drawn together in the explanation given by Bullock and Stallybrass: 'a deep-rooted, often unconscious system of beliefs, attitudes and institutions in which distinctions between people's intrinsic worth are made on the grounds of their sex and sexual roles' (Bullock and Stallybrass in Thompson 1997, p.39). Ascribed expectations may be placed upon individuals according to gender or gender stereotyping. These expectations may not be in accordance with the individual's views or wishes.

It is important to consider how we treat gender roles in our support work. For example, within day care, the majority of places on the working- or gardening-type projects may be mainly taken by men. Those taking cookery, health and beauty may predominantly be women. A person's choice must, of course, be taken into consideration; it may be an individual's decision to participate in particular sessions. However, it would be empowering to make sure that choices are available and that stereotyping does not occur.

The Sex Discrimination Act 1975 (Brayne and Martin 1997) was implemented to try to address some of the inequalities associated with gender issues: these included aspects of employment, education, housing, facilities, goods and advertising. It is questionable whether the Act has been able to achieve all of its aims and objectives in promoting equality between the sexes. It has, however, given us a framework within which to address some forms of inequality and discrimination.

It is again worthy of note that the idea of double (or multiple) discrimination may occur whilst working in the learning disabilities field. Discrimination may already be faced by people with learning disabilities and additionally through sexism, racism, ageism and disablism. The impact of multiple discrimination and oppression should not be overlooked; awareness of these factors enables challenge of them to be made.

SEXUAL FEELINGS AND SEXUAL RELATIONSHIPS

People with learning disabilities should be accepted as people who have the same capacity for loving as others in society. Loneliness and isolation may occur through the lack of opportunity to have loving relationships. There is a need to recognize the importance and complex nature of human relationships; without doing so we may ignore aspects of the whole person. People should be allowed to have their own sexual feelings and to have sexual relationships. This, of course, needs to be within the bounds of legality and between consenting adults. In no way are we supporting illegal sexual activity, such as under age or abusive sexual relationships. The issue of consent and associated factors often cause concern to the support worker. Some of the following questions may need to be considered:

- How do we know if these people are consenting?
- Do they both really want the relationship?
- Do they have enough information to be able to make an informed choice?
- Is it my role to give information?
- What if pregnancy occurs?
- What if the relationship is abusive?
- How should I support a same sex relationship?
- How will parents or carers feel?
- What will other people's perception be?
- What anxiety is there about them having a sexual relationship?
- What if it conflicts with religious or cultural beliefs?
- What are my beliefs and values and will they influence how I provide support?
- Will it be contravening agency policies or legislation?

Strategies and safeguards need to be in place to support and protect the individuals involved. Downs and Craft (1995, 1997) provide a framework of strategies and ideas of how support can be provided, in particular to people with profound and multiple impairments. Other aspects of sexuality, such as staff training and rights and responsibilities, are addressed by, for example, McCarthy and Thompson (1997, 2001).

When considering sexuality and sexual rights another aspect that requires attention is

> that under the Sexual Offences Act 1956 it is an offence for a man to have sexual intercourse with a woman knowing her to be 'of arrested or incomplete development of mind, which includes severe mental impairment of intelligence and social functioning'. Staff encouragement, or merely allowing it to happen, could be deemed 'aiding and abetting' such an offence. Thus it may be crucial to determine the degree of severity of...[a woman's] mental disability, though in practice this legislation, intended to protect from abuse or exploitation, runs counter to developments in awareness of the sexual rights of people with learning difficulties. It will still be important, however, to establish that...[a woman's] participation is voluntary and that...[she] is not being abused... (Braye and Preston-Shoot 1997, p.134)

With such legislation in mind, consent is clearly an important issue. The Human Rights Act 1998 may affect individual cases concerning sexuality and consent; time and case law will provide further insight.

None of the questions or issues raised above are particularly easy to answer. They do, however, highlight the importance of empowerment, of getting to know the person involved with well and the need to believe in the rights of people with learning disabilities. If any of the above issues raise concerns, a multi-disciplinary approach may be taken in a decision making process. Ultimately the issue of consent may have to be decided by the court. These are important aspects in the protection of vulnerable adults.

Joint working, for example, with the community nursing teams can be beneficial. Access to sex education, and sexual health and safety awareness training, through Health Action or local colleges may also prove helpful. Independent advocacy support could be used to enable the person's views to be put forward. As a support worker or carer, an awareness of legislation and agency policies is essential to ensure work remains within the legal boundaries of a role. Some agencies provide specific guidelines on how to give support in relation to issues of sexuality.

A person wanting or having a same sex relationship should, in theory, have the right to be supported. However, it is critical to be aware of and work within the legal framework that encompasses this aspect of care provision. Same sex relationships may impact upon how care and support is provided. For example, two men wishing to have a sexual relationship may be treated or supported in a different way to two women. We will explore this further, as male homosexuality may be seen as a greater threat to workers' attitudes than lesbianism. We will now look at some issues relating to male homosexuality and identify how it may impact upon practice.

Some of the legislation on male homosexuality used since the 1880s will be considered. This legislation includes the Criminal Amendment Act 1885, which criminalized all forms of sexuality between men, whether this was in public or private. More recent legislation includes the Criminal Justice and Public Order Act 1994 which specifies the age of consent between men. Lobby groups such as Stonewall continue to fight for gay and lesbian rights. At the present time partnership rights are being sought for people in same sex relationships: the right to be recognized as a couple and to have the same rights as partners in heterosexual relationships. For example, housing and pension rights or entitlement for partners of people in specific employment. Some councils have now started to recognize partnership rights. From 5 September 2001 the Greater London Authority introduced a scheme enabling any couple, same sex or otherwise, to register their partnership. This is an example of the continual striving for legislative recognition of same sex relationships.

Legislation will continue to change concerning male homosexuality and its acceptance. Thus the level of care and support that can be legally provided may also change. There are other texts that explore issues of legislation and male homosexuality in a greater depth: e.g. Brown (1998); Gooding (1992); Jeffery-Poulter (1991); Wilson (1995).

An historic resistance to accepting homosexuality is well recognized and affects many people. Heterosexuality is frequently identified as the key to sexuality: 'Heterosexism is a deeply ingrained set of ideas and practices both within and outside social work' (Thompson 1993, p.135). A person's understanding, values and religious beliefs can also affect how homosexuality is perceived. Personal beliefs can impact on responses to male homosexuality, as it may make aspects of gay male sexual activity be perceived as either morally wrong, or socially unacceptable. As explored earlier, legislation may also compound this by making certain actions criminal. This must, to an extent, inhibit or threaten the role of care and support. As a worker, the level of accountability and the risk of crossing the divide between legal and illegal support may restrict practice. All these aspects can impinge upon practice and be perceived as a threat when considering care and support concerning male homosexuality.

We are not suggesting that women wishing to have lesbian relationships are free from such restrictions of care. However, 'There has been no equivalent legislation in relation to lesbian sexual activity, as it has never been legally acknowledged in law…' (Brown Cosis 1998, p.25). This may enable care and support workers to feel less threatened by legislation when supporting women in same sex relationships. In contrast, Brown Cosis identifies other perspectives that may restrict and influence the work with, and support of, lesbians:

> …in practice, social work agencies tend to deal with lesbians in one of two ways. Either the woman's specific needs as a lesbian remain unrecognised and ignored, or her lesbianism becomes the central preoccupation, the prism through which her every word and action is interpreted. (Brown 1992, p.201)

An awareness and understanding of the different issues and perspectives affecting lesbians can help inform practice and challenge oppression and discrimination.

There are some publications that can inform this area of work in greater depth. In particular, the material concerning training packages for support staff written by McCarthy and Thompson raises many pertinent issues. These include the importance of:

- acknowledging that many people who have same sex relationships do not necessarily perceive themselves as homosexual

- the care worker being open to discussion of same sex relationships, to enable confidence, and a non-prejudiced response needs to be recognized. This is particularly important when trying to provide information to men about safer sex.

(Adapted from McCarthy and Thompson 1992)

It is important to acknowledge that general understanding, public responses and, to an extent, legislation are continually changing in relation to male homosexual and lesbian relationships.

Whether heterosexual, gay or lesbian there is a risk that a relationship may be abusive. It is critically important to make certain that any relationship is not an abusive one, that people are consenting and that care and support is provided within the legislative framework. Legislation may appear oppressive and discriminatory in some situations; however, it is also there to try to provide guidance and a legal structure that protects those at risk of abuse. The balance between supporting relationships and providing protection from abuse is often far from easy and requires careful consideration and monitoring.

Sexual relationships that are illegal or abusive must be dealt with in the appropriate manner. If at any time there is concern that there is an abusive situation it is critical that the line manager be informed immediately and appropriate action taken. Many agencies and organizations have policies that cover adult abuse and sexual abuse. Consultation of the relevant policies can provide guidance. An understanding of abuse and possible signs that abuse is taking place is a critical tool to have as a care and support worker, whether providing educational, social or medical care. Low self-esteem, depression, difficulties in developing and maintaining relationships, emotional disorders, injury or self-injury can all be an indication of abuse (Corby 1993; Finkelhor 1990; Trevithick 1993). Any concerns that abuse may have taken place, or be taking place, must be addressed immediately and the person be supported appropriately. A client centred approach involving empathy, congruence and unconditional positive regard (see Chapter 8) can often empower the person in working through issues of abuse. Time, patience and sensitivity are required in helping a person who has been abused work through the emotional issues (Copley and Forryan 1997; Corby 1993; Doyle 1997).

It is important to consider that abuse can be sexual, physical, emotional and financial and can occur at any age. Many other texts have been written that consider abuse and suggest methods of intervention. Child abuse issues can be studied through the work of, for example, Corby (1993) and Doyle (1997). Abuse against people with learning disabilities has been researched and guidance can be found in the work of, for example, Brown and Craft (1989) and C. Williams (1995). Elder abuse has been studied by, for example, Action on Elder Abuse (1995), Bennett and Kingston (1993) and Bennett, Kingston and Penhale (1997). Having an understanding and awareness of aspects of abuse can promote supportive intervention to prevent its continuance. The importance of such supportive intervention for the individuals involved should not be underestimated.

We will place some of the aspects discussed in this section into a working context through two case studies.

CASE STUDY ONE

Stefan and Barbara lived in the same supported housing for over six years. They initially formed a close friendship that deepened over time. They decided they wanted some advice concerning a sexual relationship as they were confused about some issues. Barbara was also particularly worried about getting pregnant and wished to know more about contraception.

Whilst able to give some advice and information, the residential staff asked Stefan and Barbara if they would consider a referral to the community nurse who had specialist training and knowledge. With their agreement they were also referred to their local advocacy unit for further support. Barbara's parents were not happy with the relationship; they were concerned that Barbara might be being pressurized into a sexual relationship. They discussed this with the residential staff.

Application in practice

For the staff involved one of the main issues in supporting Barbara and Stefan was that of ensuring they were both making an informed choice about their relationship. Issues were discussed with them separately on several occasions to identify their individual understanding, perspectives and wishes. Stefan was able to readily communicate his thoughts, concerns and questions, but for Barbara this was less straightforward due to her spoken communication. The staff had to establish that Barbara was consenting and that there was no abuse taking place. They took the time to establish what she wanted and discussed options of representation or an independent advocate to work with her.

The referral of the couple to the community nurse for advice enabled Stefan and Barbara to look at their relationship in more depth. They were able to think about and discuss many aspects of it. The referral to the advocacy service was another way of ensuring both Barbara and Stefan were able to individually explore their needs concerning sexuality, make informed choices and alleviate further any risk of abuse. With Barbara's permission the residential staff also worked with Barbara's parents to support them in understanding her rights to a sexual relationship. The staff were able to explain that the purpose of having an individual advocate was about ensuring informed choice for Barbara and a further safeguard for her.

A key issue to be considered is the aspect of confidentiality. Most of us are able to enjoy privacy concerning personal and sexual relationships. Barbara and Stefan not only needed to discuss theirs with residential staff but also with the community nurse and their advocates. It may be embarrassing enough to share such information with one person let alone three or more who may become involved, however positive the reasons. It is also worthy of note the power and influence that parents and carers may still have when their adult children are in residential or other forms of care. We recognize it is very important to listen carefully to parents' and carers' views and concerns. We also think it is vitally important to make sure we are listening to and advocating for the person with learning disabilities.

CASE STUDY TWO

Monique and Freda shared a supported group home with two men for several years. Initially they all got on well and went out together socially. Later, Monique and Freda formed a lesbian relationship. With their relationship strengthening and through spending more time together, the friendship with the men in the group home diminished. In the end Monique and Freda decided they wished to move into their own accommodation in the community. They spoke about this with their key worker, Alistair.

Alistair arranged for them to see a housing officer to discuss moving. They returned with forms that needed completion and sought his help. Monique and Freda wanted accessible accommodation where they could live together and were not particularly bothered about the type of accommodation. Alistair advised them to ask for two bedroom accommodation and supported them in filling out the forms accordingly.

Monique and Freda were then written to by the housing officer to say that the wait would be more than two years for two bedroom accommodation. They spoke to Alistair and said they would be happy with a one bedroom flat. Alistair advised them to wait. They were not happy with this and went to see the group home manager. They discussed what had happened with her and she supported them in talking to the housing office and in modifying their application. They were then advised of a much shorter waiting list.

Application in practice

Alistair had a problem with Monique and Freda's wishes. He was not able to acknowledge their lesbian relationship as this was in conflict with his religious and personal beliefs. His advice was based upon his personal values and not on the promotion of his clients' rights to self-determination. Alistair was disadvantaging Monique and Freda through his advice to them.

Although Alistair supported them in seeing a housing officer, they had not realized his advice had disadvantaged them. The women did not initially get the best advice due to Alistair's bias around homosexuality and lesbianism. That Monique and Freda sought help from the group home manager brought these issues to her attention. Taking into consideration Alistair's religious beliefs, the manager was then able to give Alistair appropriate supervision and look at suitable training for him on aspects of work with sexuality.

CONCLUSION

Supporting individuals within the learning disabilities field on issues of sexuality can be difficult, but should not be avoided. It is important to know where to access information to improve the support given. The perceived balance may be a fine one between supporting a happy sexual relationship and being involved in an abusive situation. Joint working and inter-agency support are crucial. Working closely with the people being supported, actively listening to what they say and acknowledging their rights and responsibilities will help the situation. As previously discussed, it is important to be aware of the policies and procedures of the organization. Above all, consideration needs to be given to the right of people with learning disabilities to have fulfilling relationships.

Key points

- Sexuality is an integral part of the complex characteristics of human existence.

- Sexuality and gender roles are both affected by historic and present day social expectations.

- People with a learning disability should be entitled to their sexuality, sexual relationships and sexual health as are other people in society.

- Legislation provides a safety structure to protect vulnerable people against abuse and inappropriate sexual activity.

- Legislation can restrict some people, in particular male homosexuals, to their right to have a same sex relationship and to receive support and guidance equal to that available to heterosexual couples.

- Informed choice is critical within all relationships.

- Any concerns of possible abusive situations must be dealt with immediately in an appropriate manner. This may be effected through the guidance of managers, policies and procedures of an agency, legislation or by police involvement.

- Joint working and inter-agency support can play a crucial role in enabling a person to achieve his or her right to sexuality and safe, respectful sexual relationships.

LOSS AND BEREAVEMENT

INTRODUCTION

It is important from the outset of this section to emphasize that by loss and bereavement we do not refer exclusively to death. We wish to address the wider context that may include the loss of personal ability, a place of work, home or friends. It is also worth noting that staff working in hospital, residential, day care or community settings often change jobs or places of work. It may have taken time to build up a working and trustful relationship with the person being supported. As the carer moves on this is often a loss to the person who is cared for. We will explore some aspects of loss and bereavement and how a person may be affected by this.

Much literature can be found that explores loss and bereavement, particularly through death (Parkes 1972; Philpot 1989; Worden 1991). However, relatively little appears to specifically relate to people with learning disabilities (Luchterhand and Murphy 1998; Oswin 1991). Hollins and Sireling (1994) provide books in a pictorial format to explore loss and bereavement. This section will explore some theoretical perspectives that were predominantly written to focus on loss through death. We aim to suggest how this knowledge can be used in supporting people with learning disabilities in various situations of loss and bereavement.

WHAT IS LOSS AND BEREAVEMENT?

Bereavement is the loss of a close and often personally significant relationship. This may be of a relative or friend and may be through death or change of circumstance. Feelings of loss usually accompany bereavement, change and separation. Grief is what we feel and mourning is the process of expressing our sorrow and adapting to our loss. A description of the function of grief is given by Buckman:

> Grief is all about letting go and saying goodbye. There are many different theories about precisely what it does, but the theme most often repeated is of the survivor letting go of her attachment to the person who dies, and, by doing that, becoming able to make attachments to other people in the future. (Buckman 1988, p.89)

Each bereavement is different, each of us will grieve in our own way. Though we experience bereavement individually there is a process which people go through when they are bereaved. This journey of grief is not an easy or straightforward process, but one with advances and regressions, each person taking their time in working towards recovery. This process is not a prescribed pathway or rigid set of stages to be strictly undertaken; rather it is a personal journey, towards readjustment and redefinition.

People with learning disabilities suffer loss and grief with the same range of emotions and reactions as the population as a whole and their needs should be fully considered. What is required by the carer, worker or supporter is an awareness of the bereavement process. There is a need to understand the time it may take and the individual's need for sensitive support to enable full participation and expression throughout his or her personal journey.

In this section we will explore this further and look at how theory can be used in practice to support people with learning disabilities through the loss and bereavement process.

LOSS AND BEREAVEMENT, THEORY AND PRACTICE

> People with learning difficulties have a right to grieve, they need opportunities to mourn, they need time to recover, and sensitive support as they go through the normal reactions of grief such as anger, weeping and depression... (Oswin in Dickenson and Johnson 1993, p.297)

This explains what may be an ideal but is not always put into practice. Initially we will explore some of the theoretical underpinnings of the process a bereaved person may undertake. There are various models and theories around the stages of bereavement and what a person may experience.

Worden (1991) suggests that four tasks of mourning have to be accomplished for equilibrium to be established:

Task I: To accept the reality of the loss.

Task II: To work through to the pain of grief.

Task III: To adjust to an environment in which the deceased is missing.

Task IV: To emotionally relocate the deceased and move on with life.

(Worden 1991, pp.10–16)

A similar process is described by Leick and Davidsen-Nielsen (1991) and Scrutton (1995). We will discuss the process as outlined by Worden and will not solely focus on death, but open the approach to other forms of loss and bereavement.

Task I: To accept the reality of the loss

Bereaved people need to accept the reality of the death or loss. Shock and disbelief are often expressed in this initial phase. Individuals may describe themselves as numb with shock or disbelief.

If the loss is through death the funeral will take place and there may be comfort in the rites of passage of religion or custom. There may also be a sense of unreality at times. Bereaved people may experience a sense of both believing and disbelieving the loss and with this mixture of emotions their behaviour may sometimes appear contradictory. Searching is part of the task of the acceptance of the reality of loss or death. Bereaved people may search in familiar or special places, in the faces of a crowd, and may also dream of the deceased. They may talk to the deceased and imagine they are present. If the fact of loss is not fully accepted and worked through then a future event may trigger feelings of the original loss. This triggering event may have no apparent significant link to the original bereavement. The original loss will need to be accepted and worked through in order to be able to move forward in life.

Task II: To work through to the pain of grief

Bereaved people need to acknowledge, feel and experience the pain of grief to accomplish this task. He or she will pass through a range of emotions, sometimes seemingly conflicting, in experiencing the pain of their grief. These emotions include sadness accompanied by crying or sobbing, feelings of anxiety, anger, guilt and remorse. Pangs or feelings of grief have been described: 'a pang of grief is an episode of severe anxiety and physiological pain' (Parkes 1996, p.43).

Task III: To adjust to an environment in which the deceased is missing

To achieve this bereaved people have to redefine their roles in life, adjust their perception of who they are and what they do, and learn new skills. The person who has died or left may have undertaken many roles in the life of the bereaved such as carer, housekeeper or budgeter. The bereaved may there-fore have to learn new skills to cope and manage in the future. At first bereaved individuals may not readily succeed in undertaking these new tasks and roles and this can lead to feelings of helplessness and failure. In gradually dealing with these events and by continuing to attempt new things comes the acquisition of knowledge and skills to enable moving forward. Some people we have worked with in the process of bereavement have discovered liberation in learning new skills that they had not previously had the opportunity to learn.

In some cases people with learning disabilities who are bereaved may have to adjust to another person taking on some roles of the deceased. Adjustment needs to take place in a variety of situations, not only following a death: when the main care provider has left home, when a long-term key worker changes job, or a residential home is shut down.

Bereaved individuals may have in some way felt themselves partly defined through the person's role or status in life and will need time to adjust to no longer being defined in such a way. 'Not only do the bereaved have to adjust to the loss of roles previously played by the deceased, but death also confronts them with the challenge of adjusting to their own sense of self' (Worden 1991, p.15).

In redefining self and through acquiring skills comes the discovery of new strengths and abilities. In time an ability to manage the roles previously fulfilled by the deceased is learnt, or a new person fulfilling that role is adjusted to.

Task IV: To emotionally relocate the deceased and move on with life

Having reached the place and time to move forward in life, bereaved individuals have spent time and energy in acceptance, mourning, adjusting, learning, acquiring skills and growing in new ways. This part of the journey is where bereaved people are able to identify a place inside themselves where memories of the deceased or person lost are held. The person who has gone is not forgotten; they remain loved or remembered, yet there is room to move on.

Exploring these tasks highlights the necessity of a flexible approach when providing support or care following a loss. There is no set time for mourning. A consensus appears to be that the process will take about two years, sometimes less, sometimes more. Each person's experience of loss is different. The period of mourning will depend upon the strength and nature of the attachment and how long it takes to work through. Recovery does not mean having to forget – it is about acceptance, adaptation and moving on.

SOME REACTIONS TO GRIEF

Sadness is experienced but is not always manifestly obvious to others. For some people there may be crying, weeping and sobbing. The pain of sadness is experienced.

Anger in realizing the reality of loss may be expressed in different ways. There may be anger directed at the deceased for abandoning the bereaved or against someone or something for allowing this to happen. Anger may be expressed against hospital staff for not saving the life of the deceased; it may also be expressed against friends or relatives for not understanding, or just because they are there.

Anxiety can occur, with the bereaved person uncertain as to whether he or she will be able to cope with the future. Anxiety may also take the form of concern about the prospect of the person's own mortality, or concern about remaining sane following the loss or death of the loved one, special person or way of life.

Guilt is frequently expressed following the loss or death of someone we love; guilt for not being there at the end, for not being able to alter the chain of events, for surviving. Given time and the ability to work through these feelings, by describing what the bereaved person actually did, may help diminish such feelings of guilt.

THEORY TO PRACTICE

When supporting people with learning disabilities through a bereavement there are various aspects to consider. Our suggestions are based on the bereavement process outlined above and on personal experience. This is, of course, not a definitive approach. Each person must be seen as individual and supported in a way that is appropriate to his or her need.

If the loss relates to death there is not a right way of providing support; this applies to most situations of loss and bereavement. The following material explores ways of working after a death; however, the principles could be transferred and used in many situations of loss.

It may be useful to have time to consider how to break the news, the words to be used and where this will take place. When breaking the news it is important to use clear and accessible language. It is best to use language that has no other meaning; words such as 'died' and 'dead'. If using sign language it is just as important to ensure there is no confusion of what is being said. In using such phrases as 'gone to sleep', 'gone on a journey' or 'passed away' mixed messages can be given. Such phrases may only serve to confuse people who have been bereaved in leading them to believe that the deceased will wake up from that sleep or return from the journey. Clear language best supports the person with a learning disability to accept the reality of the loss.

The person needs to be given time to take in what has been said. The bereaved person may wish for a time of quietness or to ask questions and may not take in the answers all at once. If the situation is of a death, the person may ask to see the body and seek support to do so. Sensitive listening plays an important role. Some people gain comfort from expression of religious beliefs and may ask about heaven or other belief. It may be useful to clarify what that means to the individual and to support him or her to explore the issue. It is important to give time and undivided attention to the bereaved person.

The importance of the genuineness of the supporter or worker – the respect demonstrated and the kindness shown – should not be under-estimated. Although support workers do not know how bereaved individuals feel, they can demonstrate empathy for their situation and feelings. This can be strengthened further by not making assumptions, by active listening and by ensuring adequate time is given to the person. In looking at the role we take, Spall and Callis say:

> Perhaps the most important thing that can be said…is that there are no right words to say. There is nothing that anyone can say that will make it right or make it better. Often just being there with the bereaved is more valuable than anything we might say. What is said is often forgotten anyway, but the sense of 'presence' may be treasured for a long time. A touch of hand or an expression of care can often be more powerful than a whole host of words. (Spall and Callis 1997, p.78)

INVOLVING THE PERSON

Some people with learning disabilities may not readily or instantly understand the concept of death or other loss. This, of course, does not stop them from feeling the bereavement. It would be wrong to assume people are not feeling a loss because they are unable to easily express it. People will absorb their loss over time in their own way and they need to be included in the mourning process to come to terms with and express their grief.

> It is critical for helpers to realize that adults with mental retardation do not have to understand the concept of death to feel loss. They are likely to experience loss and grief if people previously close are no longer in their lives. This will happen regardless of their understanding of death. (Luchterhand and Murphy 1998, p.17)

Each person is different and has different needs. As a worker or supporter, one of the fundamental points to consider is how best to enable the bereaved person to actively participate in the bereavement process. Who does it make it easier for if someone with a learning disability is excluded from part of the process of mourning? It is difficult enough to be bereaved; it is even more difficult if no one speaks of it or if a person is excluded from the process of grief and mourning.

It may be appropriate to support individuals in planning the entire funeral or it may be appropriate to consult their wishes and act on their behalf. Whatever the case, the importance of ensuring the participation of bereaved people with learning disabilities is of paramount importance: it is their loss.

EXPRESSIONS OF GRIEF

Following a loss people may suffer disruption to their usual patterns. There can be disrupted sleep with symptoms such as disturbing dreams and nightmares, and also fear of going to sleep. Eating patterns may change and loss of appetite frequently occurs. Loss of concentration, confusion and feelings of anxiety can occur. Individuals may become restless and this may take different forms; some people pace up and down whilst others may take to walking long distances. Repetition and wishing to go over an event or explanations are common behaviour in the process of working through grief.

There can be increased physical ill health with a wide variety of symptoms such as stomach upsets and asthma. Whilst symptoms are a common occurrence, they should be noted and checked. People may well need extra support in taking care of themselves and steps may need to be taken to prevent self-neglect. In recognizing these factors we can support individuals through the process and can be reassuring.

SOME DIFFICULTIES WITH THE PROCESS OF GRIEF

Denial of the reality of death or loss may occur early on in the bereavement process and is part of a self-protection strategy. Continuing denial may lead the bereaved person to become stuck and that will in turn delay the full process of mourning. There can be delayed grief where the loss is acknowledged but the emotions have yet to be worked through. Ultimately, this will delay the healing process until those emotions have been released and experienced and the pain of grief felt. If a person does not adapt to the loss then he or she may not learn how to adjust to life without the deceased or learn the skills necessary for adjustment.

Some people choose not to put themselves in the position of being hurt any further. Despite working through their feelings and emotions and adjusting to the environment without the deceased, they cannot cope with loving again as an aspect of their new life. Chronic grief occurs where people are unable to adapt to life without the deceased, lost person or way of life and see no future for themselves. Some lives may be preoccupied by memories and by missing the person with an intensity of feeling.

Usually with support the people can work through their bereavement. Sometimes individuals may become stuck in the process and it may be possible to help by suggesting tasks or by supporting visits to a particular person or place. On some occasions more specialist help such as grief counselling may be required, to enable the person to work through their thoughts and feelings.

Aspects of loss and bereavement will now be placed into a working context through the use of two case studies.

CASE STUDY ONE

Mary was in charge of an evening shift in a residential home. She received a call from a local person saying there was a man with Down's syndrome sitting in her front garden. The man would not talk to her or get up, it was very cold and she was concerned about him and asked if it was someone from the home. Mary said not but offered to come and talk to the person.

Mary introduced herself and spent time talking to the man to enable mutual trust and confidence. Mary suggested that he might like to phone somebody and he returned with her to the residential home. After some time and careful communication, Mary discovered that the man's name was Joe and that he lived in a local group home. Whilst waiting for someone to collect him, Joe kept saying 'Dad' but would not or could not elaborate further.

Application in practice

It transpired that Joe's father had died about two months previously. His family had thought it best if he did not attend the funeral as they did not want him upset and were adamant about this. Searching is a part of the early process of grief and it would seem that Joe had been literally searching for his father. He had become lost, upset and confused and ended up sitting downcast on a stranger's lawn.

Joe had been excluded not only from the funeral arrangements, but also from the funeral itself. His family had believed this to be in his best interest. Taking this course of action left Joe bereft of participating in the process of saying goodbye and in the funeral proceedings. He had not been part of the group of mourners of both family and friends and by his exclusion had become further confused.

Following this event Joe's key worker, Annie, helped alleviate the immediate situation by further talking through with Joe what happens when someone dies. She used some illustrated books borrowed from the community nurse to help explain to Joe in more detail about death and loss. She left them with him to look at and to ask any further questions when they next met.

Annie also supported Joe by encouraging his family to talk to him about his father and their happy memories as well as their sadness at his death. Joe's brother was asked to support Joe to put a memory book together, and through this they were also able to share their grief and further explore their loss. Annie also took Joe to visit his father's grave and to lay his chosen wreath upon it.

Joe had a right to grieve, to say goodbye and mourn his loss, and this was the beginning of the process of accepting the reality of the loss. It may have been a less confusing process for Joe if he had been able to fully participate in the funeral and its arrangements from the beginning of the bereavement. By discussing issues, asking questions, visiting the grave and with support from his brother, Joe was able to begin his grief work. He started to work through the process of bereavement and begin his personal journey of grief.

CASE STUDY TWO

Charmaine was 55 years of age and had always lived with her mother in the family home. Her sister Mandy had moved away to another part of the country many years before. Charmaine worked part time in a local factory that she walked to from home. She enjoyed cooking and housework and attended a local drop-in club one evening a week. Over time as her mother had become frailer, Charmaine had taken on more of the carer's role, performing domestic tasks and shopping, through to accompanying her mother on hospital appointments. They were extremely close and did not have an extensive social life outside home.

Charmaine's mother suffered a major stroke and was admitted to hospital. Following this, she did not fully recover and continued to need nursing care and was consequently admitted to a local residential home. Charmaine seemed to understand the reasons for her mother's admission and to accept the situation. She discussed the issues about her mother with the hospital social worker and was also supported by her social worker from the local community team. Charmaine seemed to cope well, and although she was sometimes weepy and quiet over the following months, showed no signs of undue distress. She seemed to adapt well to living on her own and any help she sought was on a practical level.

During a routine visit from her social worker about six months after her mother's move to residential care, Charmaine started shouting and blaming the hospital for her mother being 'taken away'. She also blamed the social worker for allowing this to happen and her sister Mandy for living away and not doing anything about it. She was angry at being left to live alone at home and angry about not being able to care for her mother.

Application in practice

An explanation for Charmaine's anger can be found within the context of bereavement theory. She was still in the process of both working through her feelings of loss and of adjusting to her loss. She missed her mother terribly and had not been able to express this fully to anyone. She had put her mother's needs first and not expressed her own needs.

Charmaine, although consulted about her mother's move to residential care, felt powerless in the situation. She also lacked her mother's constant companionship. She wanted her mother to be well cared for, but did not want someone else to care for her as well as she could.

Charmaine was able to relieve her pent-up feelings by expression of this anger, although she did not do this as a conscious measure. She was then able to express her feelings of loss of control of her situation and to explore her needs more fully. She was someone who needed kindness, understanding and support to work through her bereavement and to safely work through her feelings of anger, which she herself found quite frightening.

CONCLUSION

Loss and bereavement are complex issues requiring thoughtful support. This is highlighted by Schwartz-Borden:

> Along with the need for focus comes the need for balance. The bereaved must achieve some balance that allows them to experience their pain, sense of loss, loneliness, fear, anger, guilt, and sadness; to let in their anguish and let out their expression of such anguish; to know and feel in the very core of their souls what has happened to them; and yet to do all this in doses, so they will not be overwhelmed by such feelings. (Schwartz-Borden 1986 in Worden 1991, p. 47)

It is hoped that by having more knowledge and understanding of the under-pinning theory, the worker or care supporter will be empowered to be more supportive and empathetic. Having a realistic understanding of the process and emotions involved in the experience of loss and bereavement will enhance support and be of greater use to the person.

Key points

- Loss and bereavement are not only about death, they may also encompass loss of health or way of life, change of work or residential setting and through the loss of familiar people.

- Each bereavement is different; however, there is a process that most people will experience.

- People with a learning disability suffer loss and grief with the same range of emotions and reactions as the population as a whole and their needs should be fully considered.

- People with learning disabilities have the right to grieve, mourn, receive support and be given time to recover.

- Support should be provided in a way that is appropriate to the person's individual needs.

- There are a number of theories that can be used to help understand the process of loss and mourning.

- Respect and consideration is needed for different cultural and religious processes of mourning.

8

Values, Ethics and Contrasting Approaches: Person Centred and Behavioural

INTRODUCTION

In this chapter we will start by looking at values and ethics that inform and underpin care and support work and go on to consider two contrasting ways of working, a person centred approach and a behavioural approach. Some underpinning ideas of a person centred approach will be explored and in contrast some behavioural approaches will be looked at. In exploring behavioural approaches, consideration will be given to what is meant by behaviour, how behaviour is learnt, and some of the different ways that the approach can be used. Aspects of power difference and potential issues of control will be highlighted. Our aim is threefold: first, to highlight the importance of practising using a sound value and ethical base; second, to briefly explore aspects of person centred and behavioural approaches; and third, to reinforce the need to consider the implications of working in specific ways.

Values and ethics, person centred work and behavioural approaches will all be placed into a practice context using case studies.

VALUES AND ETHICS

INTRODUCTION

In this section, we will briefly explore values and ethics in practice. We will look at what is meant by values and ethics, and their influence in care and support work. Consideration will be given to the intricacies, conflicts and difficulties involved. Various aspects of the intrinsic nature of values and ethics within care and support work will be explored. Two case studies will be used to highlight issues discussed in this section.

VALUES

One definition of values is given as 'a belief that something is good and desirable. It defines what is important, worthwhile and worth striving for' (Thomas and Pierson 1996, p.390). This appears a sound explanation of what values should be about; however, are values really as easy and straightforward when put into practice? Banks (1995) highlights some of the difficulties that are associated with the concept of values.

> 'Values' is one of those words that tends to be used rather vaguely and has a number of different meanings. In everyday usage, 'values' is often used to refer to one or all of religious, moral, political or ideological principles, beliefs or attitudes. In the context of social work, however, it seems frequently to mean: a set of fundamental moral/ethical principles to which social workers are/should be committed. (Banks 1995, p.4)

Values are intricately involved in the role of care and support. Activities undertaken in care and support are influenced by the views of people in society and expectations of how care should be provided. The values of the society we live in influence our thinking, our actions and, to an extent, policy and legislation.

Another aspect to consider is that each of us will have our own beliefs, views and values. These beliefs, views and values will come from a variety of perspectives and be influenced by each individual's experience. Our race, cultural background, family history, perceived position and gender all play a part in how we view the world and each situation. There is a need to be aware of our personal value bases and to think how we might influence others. The influence we exert may be deliberate or inadvertent.

If we allow our personal value base to impinge upon someone we work with or support this may be both oppressive and discriminatory. Thompson's (1996) PCS Analysis considers the aspect of personal beliefs as central and the easiest to challenge. These personal beliefs are surrounded by cultural views and all are encompassed by society's views. He suggests that the place to start is by challenging our own personal views, then, when individuals have developed a sound personal value base, to move on to challenge cultural and societal views.

In principle, this appears a straightforward process, but how is a sound value base identified? In discussion of social work values, Banks outlines and explores some influential principles adapted from Biestek (1961), which are: 'Individualisation; purposeful expression of feelings; controlled emotional involvement; acceptance; non-judgmental attitude; user self determination; confidentiality' (Banks 1995, p.26). These principles can be used to inform our thinking about the meaning of values and how we encompass them in our work. Banks proposes that 'respect for the individual person as a self determining being' (1995, p.27) is a key theme running through all the above principles. If we take this key theme in relation to work with people with learning disabilities, theoretically we start with a sound basis for practice. Whatever a person's ability, each individual has the right to self-determination, and it is part of the role of the care and support worker to endeavour to find ways to best support the person in achieving this. Much care and support work is about promoting rights and choices. This may vary greatly from an individual's right to choose what to wear or what to eat, through to the promotion of independent living and the right to take risks. With such a promotion of rights comes the enabling of learning through experience for the person with a learning disability, and the ability to learn from both successful experiences and from mistakes. With the right to make choices also comes the learning about being accountable for those choices. Careful consideration needs to be given to how accountability is explained or conveyed in relation to self-determination and choice.

Banks goes on to suggest that a second key theme is '"individualisation" the recognition of each user's unique qualities based upon the right of human beings to be treated as individuals with personal differences.' (1995, p.27). Treating people as individuals with personal differences may seem an obvious statement, but this is not always evident in practice. Assumptions and generalizations about people with learning disabilities are sometimes made in ignorance or for the sake of expedience. Such assumptions or generalizations need challenging as part of the process of valuing each individual and as part of valuing difference. In this way, we reinforce values in practice and their importance to our work. We will go on to explore some of the principles outlined above in our section on person centred work.

There are various interpretations of value bases; however, for the purpose of this section we will use the value base identified by what was known as the Central Council for Education and Training in Social Work (CCETSW 1998). The value base suggested by them is still used as an intrinsic part of the training undertaken by potential social workers. The suggested values are to:

- identify and question their own values, and their implications for practice
- respect and value uniqueness and diversity, and recognize and build on strengths
- promote people's rights to choice, privacy, confidentiality and protection, while recognizing and addressing the complexities of competing rights and demands
- assist people to increase control of and improve the quality of their lives, while recognizing that control of behaviour will be required at times in order to protect children and adults from harm
- identify, analyse and take action to counter discrimination, racism, disadvantage, inequality and injustice, using strategies appropriate to role and context
- practise in a manner that does not stigmatize or disadvantage either individuals, groups or communities.

(CCETSW 1998, p.7)

Many aspects are encompassed in this value base. It recognizes difference and diversity such as ethnicity, culture, gender and sexuality and promotes the rights of individuals. It places the values in the context of the wider society in acknowledging there may be competing rights and demands. It promotes the importance of challenging discrimination whether it be against an individual, group of people, or a community. Using such a value base should promote good practice in day to day work.

In looking at our value base, we also need to consider our position within the system or organization in which we work. Our individual position and accountability as a member of that system or organization may influence us. This position is likely to affect the relationship we have with the person with whom we are working and power imbalances will almost inevitably exist. The culture of the organization may also influence our values in practice. Tensions can arise between what we wish to do, think we should do and what our role permits us to do. Our value base may influence our thinking in promoting a person's rights to a particular service, therapy or form of care but the guidelines or criteria of our organization may not allow for this. This may become a dilemma for us and the person being supported. Professional dilemmas may also arise from the conflicting needs of individuals within a family, household or other intimate setting. It may well be impossible to promote each person's rights equally in a given situation even when recognizing and addressing the complexities of competing rights and demands.

Davies (Davies, Howe and Kohli 1999, p.3) provides another aspect to think about when he suggests that social work values could be helpfully re-defined in terms of what the client values. The definition of what is of value then lies with the client and goes towards addressing the power imbalance. Perhaps in multi-disciplinary work such a definition could be more widely applied, whether in social work, educational or health settings?

Thinking about values is a complex business, which presents us with many challenges and dilemmas. We need to remain aware of our personal value base and to practise with fairness, sensitivity and consideration. In thinking about how we practise, Howe sums it up thus: '...hence the need for tolerance, and I think above all, compassion. Compassion encourages understanding, it encourages flexibility; it discourages rigidity and makes us cautious about too much moral certitude' (Davies *et al.* 1999, p.31). Having explored some aspects of values, we will now briefly look at ethics.

ETHICS

One definition of an ethical code is:

> ...a body of guiding principles for professional organisations to set the standard for good practice in relation to service delivery, client and professional relationships, and relationships between the professional and other occupational groups. (Thomas and Pierson 1996, p.140)

Ethics and values are intertwined and one informs the other. The British Association of Social Workers (BASW) has produced a code of ethics for social workers and this can provide a basis for consideration for anyone associated with the care and support of people with learning disabilities. The code suggests a framework for practice. This is a useful tool to enable us to think about our practice. The code of ethics links closely to the value base outlined earlier. The ethical guidelines suggested are:

- To value and treat each person with dignity.

- The need to encourage the self-realization of each individual person with due regard to the interests of others.

- To relieve and prevent hardship and suffering.

- The need for individual practitioners to develop and improve their skills.

- The constant evaluation of methods and policies in light of changing circumstances.

- The worker has the right and duty to bring to the attention of those in power, and of the general public, ways in which the activities of government, society or agencies create or contribute to hardship.

- These guidelines must all be balanced against the professional responsibility of the worker to the person being supported.

(Adapted from BASW 1996)

The ethical framework looks not only at the individual but also at the wider context of society and the interplay between them. The issue of an ethical base in the wider context of society, and specifically in social work, can be read in greater depth in various texts: for example, Banks (1995); Clark (2000); Gensler (1998); Hugman and Smith (1995).

The principles of ethics and values are not too hard to understand; however, placing them into practice can sometimes prove both intricate and difficult. We wish to highlight some of the possible areas of conflict and difficulty that may occur.

ETHICAL PROBLEMS AND DILEMMAS

Banks (1995) suggests that there are three fundamental issues involved in ethical problems and dilemmas:

- *Issues around an individual's rights and welfare* – a user's right to make his or her own decisions and choice; the social worker's responsibility to promote the welfare of the user.

- *Issues around public welfare* – the rights and interests of parties other than the user; the social worker's responsibility to his or her employing agency and to society; the promotion of the greatest good of the greatest number of people.

- *Issues around inequality and structural oppression* – the social worker's responsibility to challenge oppression and to work for changes in agency policy and in society. (Banks 1995, p.13)

One example of an ethical dilemma about an individual's rights and welfare may concern the person's benefits. The individual may wish to take control of his or her own benefits and decide how they are spent. The carer may deem the person with learning disability's benefits to be part of the household income and calculate it as such in the household accounting. Promoting the rights of the individual may require skilful negotiation when a family lives in relative poverty and depends upon the individual's benefits to ensure bills are paid.

There are many situations that can challenge and place values and ethics in conflict. There are the issues of accountability to the client, the organization and the public, and where our duty should lie. These issues need careful consideration before action is taken. We will use case studies to place some of these aspects into practice situations.

CASE STUDY ONE

Damon was in his forties and lived in the family home with his parents, Alice and Owen. Damon had regular respite care in a local residential hostel. Damon attended a local drop-in centre fairly regularly. Owen had dementia and Alice found it increasingly difficult to cope with supporting both her husband and Damon. The community psychiatric nurse was involved in supporting the family concerning aspects of Owen's dementia.

After some months, Alice felt unable to cope any longer and contacted social services. Initially, Alice and Owen were visited by a worker from the team for people over 65. Alice talked about feeling she was in an impossible situation. She wanted both Owen and Damon to remain at home but even with support going into the home felt overwhelmed. A worker from the learning disabilities team was also involved and visited Damon and his parents.

Damon's expressed choice was to remain in the family home with his parents. Damon's father would not even consider having respite care. Damon's mother was physically and emotionally drained and becoming ill herself. She felt something had to change; she needed to be alleviated of some of the demands of care. More regular respite care was arranged for Damon and further support put into the home, but ultimately this was not enough.

Both Damon and Owen wished to remain at home but both could not. The social workers and nurse had to support the family through this dilemma. Each person had to be listened to and his or her wishes heard. If Alice were to continue caring for either Owen or Damon then the other would have to live elsewhere. Alice felt torn. The team helped by acknowledging the difficulty of Alice's position and by supporting her to think through the options available in making this exceptionally difficult decision.

Application in practice

Alice finally decided that she must care for Owen at home and thus Damon would need to move. Her decision was made in the recognition of her own mortality and the wish to see Damon settled with appropriate care and support for the long-term future, which at that point was not an option in the family home. Damon was very upset and thought this unfair and that his wishes had not been properly considered. His social worker spent time discussing this with him and trying to help him find positive aspects of his other choices for the future.

In valuing choice, then ultimately whose choice should be respected? It was impossible to promote each person's right to choice equally within the family situation. In order to improve Alice's quality of life, Damon's quality of life had to change, not necessarily for better or worse, but change, nevertheless. However, each person was consulted, respected and treated as a unique individual.

CASE STUDY TWO

Sebena, a young Asian woman with complex needs, had lived in a private sector, purpose built house for two years. It was some distance from her family home. Sebena's family visited as often as possible but had to rely on public transport. Sebena had never felt properly settled since moving into the house and her family were not entirely satisfied with the standards of service available. They felt that despite the promises made on admission, the quality of care was barely adequate and that Sebena's cultural needs were not always considered. They were also very concerned about the high staff turnover at the home.

The family met with a worker from the local learning disabilities team to explore what choices Sebena had concerning where she was placed. The worker then visited Sebena to explore her wishes and options.

Application in practice

In reality, if Sebena wanted to stay within distance for her family to visit regularly then she had no other real choice of home that could meet her needs. If she chose to move further away then there were other possibilities; these would also depend upon the available finances to fund the change.

What the worker could do was to investigate the concerns expressed by Sebena and her family and to deal with these appropriately. She was also able to alert Sebena and her family to their right to complain and to discuss their concerns with the county's inspection and registration department.

The worker was in a position of offering support to challenge the existing provision to offer a better service. She was not able to promote a real choice of alternative accommodation to Sebena if she was to stay within visiting distance of her family.

CONCLUSION

It is important to question the values and ethics that are used to underpin day to day practice. By doing this we work towards evaluating how practice is provided and measure the standard of delivery. Whilst working within the framework of values and ethics the person being supported must remain the central focus.

Clark suggests eight rules for good practice. We would like to conclude this section with these and suggest they be used as an underpinning framework when considering values and ethics:

- be respectful

- be honest and truthful

- use a sound knowledge base and relevant theory based skills

- be careful and diligent when working

- be effective, helpful and supportive

- practise in a legitimate and authorized way

- be collaborative and accountable

- be reputable and creditable.

(Adapted from Clark 2000)

It is useful to consider each of these rules and reflect upon how they link with our own value base. This may lead to an enhanced awareness of values and ethics and their role in the development of practice.

Key points

- Values and ethics should be an intrinsic part of care and support work.

- A sound and recognized value and ethical base is critical for providing quality care.

- The CCETSW provides a value base that is still used in the training of social workers. It provides clear insight and structure.

- Our own beliefs or views could impact upon a sound value base. Recognizing and testing our individual values against a recognized framework enables validation of working practice.

- There will be a variety of external pressures that may challenge and impinge upon values. Reflection using a recognized value base and ethical framework can help in the validation of care and support work and promote anti-discriminatory and anti-oppressive practice.

A PERSON CENTRED APPROACH

INTRODUCTION

A person centred approach, particularly in the field of counselling, is often associated with Carl Rogers (1951, 1961, 1980). The approach played a part in the development of social work in the 1950s and the ideas and terminology are still influential in informing today's practice. The use of the ideas associated with a person centred approach may help us to consider different perspectives of people's actions and behaviour to better understand and support them. These ideas and their relevance will be explored throughout this section and will be illustrated in practice by two case studies.

A PERSON CENTRED APPROACH IN MORE DETAIL

As Rogers developed his style of work and person centred approach he moved away from many of the established ideas and beliefs of the time. For example, he moved away from working in a directive way, developing a non-directive approach. Rogers struggled with and debated behaviourist psychology; he believed in more than an 'unbreakable chain of cause and effect' (Rogers 1980, p.56). Rogers believed in the importance of human choice: 'I have come to realize that the basic difference between a behavioristic and a humanistic approach to human beings is a philosophical choice' (Rogers 1980, p.56).

Rogers worked in a non-directive way, promoting the counselling relationship as one that sees ideas of self as central. He demystified the therapeutic relationship and endeavoured to make it accessible to others (Thorne 1992). Mearns and Thorne, in describing the relationship between the client and counsellor, say:

> ...the client can be trusted to find his own way forward if only the counsellor can be the kind of companion who is capable of encouraging a relationship where the client can begin, however tentatively, to feel safe and to experience the first intimations of self-acceptance. (Mearns and Thorne 1998, p.6)

These ideas can be transferred and used to inform practice in a wider context than solely a counselling one. These ideas can apply to care and support work where enlightened practice can encourage the person to work towards self-acceptance and self-determination. Other people have developed a variety of interpretations of a person centred approach. England (1986) suggested that social work was a form of 'art' in its approach. Wilkes (1981) made clear links to Kantian philosophy and the rights of users to their freedom from interference and pressures of social work intervention. Howe (1987) suggested the importance of a 'client centred' approach, one that sees the person first and not as subjects to be treated or controlled. Each interpretation could be explored further; however, we will remain with our focus on the work of Rogers.

Some ideas central to Rogers' person centred approach, 'conditions of worth' and 'the locus of evaluation', will now be briefly explored. This will be followed by consideration of three of the core conditions of person centred work: congruence, unconditional positive regard and empathy. These will be considered within the ideal of respect for the person. Areas of possible conflict and difficulties in using the approach will also be explored.

Conditions of worth

son learns that to be regarded positively it may be necessary to behave certain way. If particular behaviour invokes a critical response then the rson usually learns that this behaviour needs adjusting or adapting in order to gain approval. Conditions of worth are imposed through interactions with parents or carers. If a child is told by the parent or carer that it is bad to show anger then a condition of worth has been imposed. To be loved and approved of, the child learns to live up to the conditions of worth imposed by adjusting, not showing the anger felt, or by denial of the feelings of anger.

From such interactions a self-concept and sense of worth is developed. Distress is caused by a tension between the real self and the self-concept. In extreme cases where many conditions of worth are imposed, the person may try to live up to them by denying his or her own thoughts and feelings and this can then be extremely limiting to the individual.

> A person-centred practitioner understands distress and disturbance in terms of conflict between the real self, usually referred to in person-centred theory as the organismic self, and the self-concept. The latter is the constructed, internalized, sense of self and the denials and adjustments the individual makes to gain the approval and positive regard that are essential for emotional well being. (Mabey and Sorenson 1995, p.25)

A person may decide to express his or her own thoughts or feelings and, by doing so, risk disapproval or ultimately rejection from the very person from whom approval was originally sought. In dealing with such distress and conflicts, the individual may seek the support of a counsellor to work through these feelings and conflicts. In person centred counselling it is one of the core conditions of the counselling relationship that unconditional positive regard is given to the client. The importance of unconditional positive regard is explored later in the section.

Locus of evaluation

Those who have experienced positive regard and approbation in their relationships will develop an 'internal locus of evaluation'. There is a personal strength and confidence to judge the individual's own behaviour and place it in the world. The person is able to say, 'This is what I want, this is right for me.'

On the other hand, those people who have had many conditions of worth imposed upon them will rely on others for endorsement and be less able to trust in their own judgement. They will rely upon an 'external locus of evaluation'.

> In many ways the level of dependence on an external locus of evaluation is a reliable criterion for determining the presence of psychological disturbance. Disturbed people constantly betray the lack of an internal locus and turn desperately to external authorities or find themselves trapped in a paralysis of indecision. (Thorne 1992, p.33)

The above quotation may generally hold true; however, if we place it in the context of work with people with learning disabilities it may not prove so straightforward. On occasion, some people with learning disabilities may constantly refer to external authorities or seem to be trapped in indecision. This may not necessarily be due to the imposition of conditions of self-worth. It may be due to the nature of the learning disability or it could be due to the lack of opportunity to experience decision making and the making of judgements for themselves throughout their lives. The opportunity to develop these skills and learn to fully participate and be included may be required rather than the need to work on a damaged concept of self. If all aspects are considered then a truer picture should emerge.

THE CORE CONDITIONS

When using a person centred approach there are core conditions that are considered essential in promoting change. As supporters, workers, nurses or social workers we are clearly not therapists; nevertheless, the knowledge and use of the core conditions is both relevant and recognizable and should underpin our work. The three core conditions to be addressed in this section are:

- congruence
- unconditional positive regard
- empathy.

Congruence

Congruence is also known or described as genuineness, authenticity or realness. When congruent with someone we do not hide behind a role, title, profession or position of expertise. There is no discrepancy between words, actions and emotions; responses given match what is felt inside. There is an openness and equality in the relationship and a build up of trust. The recognition that the supporter or worker is fallible enhances the congruent relationship. Congruence does not involve inappropriate self-disclosure or offloading by the worker or supporter on to the person being supported.

The worker needs to remain self-aware and be able to acknowledge negative as well as positive thoughts and feelings (Thorne 1992). In exploring congruence, Rogers said:

> Though this aspect of congruence is actually a complex one, I believe all of us recognize it in an intuitive and common sense way in individuals with whom we deal. With one individual we recognize that he not only means exactly what he says, but that his deepest feelings match what he is expressing... (Rogers 1961, p.282)

The same applies to those in the field of care work: being open about feelings can help to build up trust and mutual respect. People with learning disabilities, as is true of the majority of the population, experience congruence or authenticity and relate to this. Congruence requires skill, self-awareness and an ability to check out what belongs to the worker and what belongs to the person being supported. Congruence or genuineness is vital in our working relationships. The capacity to be intuitive about genuineness makes it all the more necessary for the worker or supporter to recognize its importance.

Unconditional positive regard

Unconditional positive regard may also be described as acceptance. The person is intrinsically valued as a human being and unconditional positive regard is given without judgement of the person. It does not mean that the worker or supporter necessarily likes or approves of the individual's behaviour, but the person is accepted. There is a paradox in that when a person feels that he or she has unconditional positive regard, and an environment of warmth and acceptance has been created, then it is possible to challenge that person in a constructive way.

Achieving unconditional positive regard is not easy and may bring us up against our own prejudices. Giving unconditional positive regard requires acceptance and may be a challenging experience.

> Defensive, aggressive, vulnerable and conflicted persons require the healing energy of unconditional positive regard if they are to discover within themselves the enormous potentialities for growth with which they lost contact perhaps in the earliest days of their existence. (Thorne 1992, p.38)

It is important to consider the meaning of unconditional positive regard to a person. By intrinsically valuing the person and distinguishing the individual from his or her behaviour there is more opportunity to develop a positive working relationship and undertake quality work.

Empathy

Empathy requires more than sympathy and having similar feelings, it involves sensing the person's world. In describing empathetic understanding Rogers said: 'To sense the client's private world as if it were your own, but without ever losing the "as if" quality – this is empathy…' (1961, p.284). The person's world is adopted and there is experience of what it is like to be that person in his or her world. However, whilst doing this the 'as if' quality is respected and an awareness of the separateness from the person is maintained. Empathy requires the use of emotional engagement in understanding the person's world; it does not mean having all the person's feelings. The person will instinctively know when there is empathy; there is an equal feeling, a common human bond.

In looking at a social work value base and the use of empathy, Thompson says:

> …this is a very skilful activity, as it involves having a degree of control over our own feelings whilst remaining open and sensitive to the other person's feelings. If we do not manage to achieve the former (a degree of control over our own feelings), then we run the risk of becoming emotionally involved at too deep a level, and also of exhausting ourselves through emotional overload. (Thompson 2000, p.114)

Empathy is an important aspect of work with people with learning disabilities. However able the person or however complex his or her needs, the use of empathy is fundamental to the working relationship and the understanding of the person.

RESPECT FOR PERSONS

Respect for persons is key to person centred work. Valuing the person and treating the individual with dignity is fundamental. Respect for persons should be an intrinsic part of everyday practice, part of empowerment, participation and choice.

Shardlow explores fundamental moral principles when looking at social work practice and how social workers act: 'Within professional social work practice, "respect for persons" is the most frequently applied principle.' Shardlow also looks at its derivation: 'As a moral principle, "respect for persons" is derived from Kant's moral principle of the *categorical imperative*'

(Shardlow in Adams, Dominelli and Payne 1998, p.28, emphasis as in original). Thompson identifies the link between respect and the basis identified in moral philosophy. Thompson acknowledges the complex nature of Kant's moral philosophy and the basis of respect for persons:

> ...the basic point is quite a simple one really, namely the importance of treating people with respect – not treating them in a way that you would object to if other people treated you like that. (Thompson 2000, p.113)

It needs to be acknowledged that within the legislative framework levels of control operate and it may be difficult to achieve Thompson's ideal. If people are at risk of harm to themselves or others, it may be necessary to place them in care. There may be limited or no choice of appropriate resources and inappropriate placements do not realistically appear to demonstrate respect for individuals. People's choices, needs and wants may be compromised by the structure that guides practice. Nevertheless, despite these difficulties and conflicts, person centred work plays a role in everyday practice. Congruence, unconditional positive regard and empathy are all of importance when working towards equality in practice.

A person centred approach can be explored further by considering its use in informing person centred planning.

PERSON CENTRED PLANNING

The person centred approach as outlined above differs from person centred planning as discussed in the White Paper *Valuing People: A New Strategy for Learning Disability for the 21st Century* (Department of Health 2001a). As mentioned earlier, the former is a non-directive humanistic approach that played a part in the development of social work in the 1950s and 1960s and was developed from a counselling perspective. The latter is a concept that places the person requiring care and support at the centre of the care planning process. The underpinning ideas suggested by Rogers (1951, 1961) are useful in informing person centred planning. Although different, both the person centred approach and person centred planning employ the idea of the person being central. With the person as central it is proposed that the support network will encompass the person to provide a 'circle of care' to meet individual need. Resources and facilities will be tailored to the individual in response to expressed needs. It is proposed that person centred planning will work alongside the care management process.

A code of practice can be found through the work of the Michigan Department of Community Health. This mental health code can be used to inform practice within the learning disabilities field:

A. Each individual has strengths, and the ability to express preferences and to make choices.

B. The individual's choices and preferences shall always be considered if not always granted.

C. Professionally trained staff will play a role in the planning and delivery of treatment and may play a role in the planning and delivery of supports. Their involvement occurs if the individual has expressed or demonstrated a need that could be met by professional intervention.

D. Treatment and supports identified through the process shall be provided in environments that promote maximum independence, community connections and quality of life.

E. A person's cultural background shall be recognized and valued in the decision making process.

(Michigan Department of Community Health 1996, p.2)

The above code reinforces the importance of the person being at the centre of the process. There are other explanations of person centred planning; each provides a similar focus of the person being central in deciding, planning and arranging the required care and support.

> Essential lifestyles planning begins with the premise that for each individual there will be a set of 'non-negotiables': key features of any service that *must* be in place for the service to work. The list of non-negotiables is developed in partnership with the individual and his or her family or supporters and is then used as a basis for specifying the service that will be needed. The process also looks for features that would be 'highly desirable' (elements of the service that ought to be in place, but which at a pinch, the person could manage without) and 'desirable' (features which the person would like, but are less critical).
> (Simons 2000, p.55)

The process of person centred planning has been described as providing a 'circle of care', with the person being supported as central and the supporters and facilitators surrounding the individual. All people involved work together in a joint, multi-agency approach to meet the needs of the person. This process draws together a diversity of service providers to ensure that the best possible care package is provided. 'Person-centred planning provides a single, multi-agency mechanism for achieving this' (Department of Health 2001a, p.5). The process should not be exclusive and should be able to be used whatever the individual's communication style. It is the importance of the participatory nature of person centred planning that draws together so many principles associated with care and support: anti-discriminatory and anti-oppressive practice, advocacy, empowerment, participation and choice.

> By definition person-centred approaches are meant to be participative; the individual with learning difficulties *has* to be at the centre of the process. Even for people without conventional ways of communicating, 'listening' to their behaviour will be a key to the process. By spending time with the person, and really getting to know them, by talking to people who know them well, by seeing people in different contexts, it is possible to build up a picture of the issues that are non-negotiable for them. (Simons 2000, p.55)

As the person centred planning process unfolds, often a personal book is completed with the person and this is the planning book that would be used throughout life. The book is owned by the individual as it is about his or her life, needs and wishes. The book provides an ongoing record and the record is envisaged as changing as the needs and wishes of the person change. Changes recorded may be about the person, life experiences, relationships or chosen activities.

> As people experience new situations and opportunities, their wishes and needs will inevitably change. Further, for people with complex needs (particularly those for whom the non-negotiables may be diffi-cult to establish), an initial person-centred planning has to be an ap-proximation. By implication, therefore, person-centred planning has to be a continuing and flexible process, with correspondingly flexible ser-vices. (Simons 2000, p.55)

All people identified as important by the individual should be able to contribute to the planning book. However, the book would only be shared with others with the consent of the individual. The book may include factors such as:

- personal details
- preferred communication methods
- people in the individual's life
- life so far

- life now
- things that are liked
- things that are disliked
- things important to the individual
- dreams
- hopes
- wishes
- support needed
- goals
- action plan.

(Adapted from personal planning material from:
South and East Belfast Health and Social Services;
Hackney Social Services; Newham Community NHS Trust)

It will be difficult to assess the success of person centred planning until the approach develops further. The process will run alongside care management and it should become clearer how the two would work together as time progresses. The principles of person centred planning are positive, making people with learning disabilities central and in control of their care. Timescales, levels of commitment, and services, resources and funding available will all affect the implementation and success of the approach. This concept may begin to bring a greater level of equality within society to a group of people who largely remain marginalized.

A person centred approach and person centred planning are an important part of the way care and support work is undertaken; however, as with many approaches, difficulties may be faced. We now intend to highlight some of the potential difficulties that may be found in practice.

DIFFICULTIES WITH A PERSON CENTRED APPROACH

It could be argued that in care and support work congruence is little more than an ideal. It may appear as something that is not achievable within the power orientated structure of care and control. The titles used such as social worker, nurse, carer and supporter all hold a level of power either perceived or real. The nature and role of care provision, delivering the services required or locating and funding the appropriate resources, may be seen as having a power imbalance. Nevertheless, congruence plays an important part. It may not be possible to eradicate fully the power of the carer or supporter; however, an awareness of the need to achieve congruence can highlight the issues of power involved. This in itself guides us towards seeing the person as central and endeavouring to achieve equality within the given framework.

The role of care and support should include unconditional positive regard as an intrinsic part of practice. The occasion may arise when work is carried out with someone who, for example, has committed a serious sexual offence or grievously injured someone. Acceptance of the person, whilst not accepting his or her behaviour, may be difficult to achieve and the worker's values challenged. The worker may achieve acceptance of the individual yet some people in the wider society may still wish to exclude the person.

Empathy is another important aspect of work with people with learning disabilities. However able the person or however complex his or her needs, the use of empathy is fundamental. The sensing of a person's private world may prove to be difficult. Trying to sense and understand how someone whose ability or methods of living or coping differ from our own may be far from easy. Aspiring to achieve empathy in practice is an important part of the working relationship and of understanding the person being supported.

The use of congruence, unconditional positive regard and empathy are all key aspects that should be an intrinsic part of everyday care and support. They are basic ideas that go towards a genuine respect for the individual.

We have highlighted some aspects of a person centred approach and have suggested some of the difficulties in practice. Concerns about the use of a humanistic approach in social care practice have been raised by others. Payne (1991) reinforces the difficulties in using humanistic approaches in the bureaucratic and control orientated framework that social care and support operates within. Banks states that humanistic views are 'underdeveloped theories for social work practice' (1995, p.61), explaining this in more depth thus:

> ...the conditions within which social work is actually practised do not lend themselves to the use of approaches and techniques based on humanistic values or assumptions about users as rational agents. Users are usually people who are in difficulty, facing crisis, in need of help and therefore less capable of rational decision-making than they or others might be in different circumstances. Social workers are often acting within the constraints of the law, agency policy, limited time and resources, and bureaucratic procedures that are more conducive to treating the user as a 'case' than as a person. (Banks 1995, p.61)

An awareness of the restrictions and obstacles that stand in the way of using a person centred approach will offer support in the challenging of such barriers. Rogers' idea of 'personal power' may help in this challenge. Rogers suggested the use of 'personal power' in community work as a way of enabling the person to challenge organizations and achieve political change. Each person holds 'personal power' and the individual can be enabled to use this to achieve change in the surrounding structures (Rogers 1977).

The development of trusting relationships is a key to success in many situations. However, consideration needs to be given to the risk of dependency within working relationships. This could be dependency on either side, dependency by those being supported or by those providing support. Working relationships should be developed in a way that enables, but minimizes a dependency risk. Joint working with others within a team, through other agencies or support networks, may be a way of achieving this. The core conditions of congruence, unconditional positive regard and empathy should be striven towards in day to day practice as a way of achieving respect for each person.

We will illustrate the use of a person centred approach in practice using two case studies.

CASE STUDY ONE

Jim lived with five other people in a voluntary sector project in the community. Each year the residents and staff went to the same holiday resort for two weeks. When the subject of booking the holiday was raised in the residents' meeting, Jim said he did not wish to go with the group. He said that he and his friend Eric had decided to go to a holiday village instead.

At the meeting questions were asked by both residents and staff about how Jim thought he would cope in a new place, particularly without staff support. Some staff were concerned about Jim's communication abilities and whether he would be able to make himself understood by strangers. Much was said about the risks involved and the fact that no one in the group had done such a thing before. Jim remained adamant; he wished to do something different without the whole group and staff. Jim said he would talk to his key worker, Dean, about this later on his own.

Application in practice

By respecting Jim and his wish to do something different away from both other residents and staff, Dean and Jim were able to look constructively at the idea of the holiday. In seeing the person and not the potential impediments, Dean was able to help Jim think about various aspects of the holiday such as travel, catering, managing money and mobility. They were then able to look at ways in which Jim could be supported.

Jim recognized there were risks involved in going on holiday without staff. Dean respected Jim's ability to make such a decision and take accountability for it. Dean had to work with several staff members who were concerned about Jim's holiday plans and about his right to try something new, providing the risks were assessed. The team were then able to look at the restrictions and barriers placed in Jim's way and at how he could be enabled to fulfil his wish.

CASE STUDY TWO

Kevin and Eddie had a fight in their group home; following this, staff had supported them to work through the situation and had reached apparent resolution. The next day, Eddie reported to Amina, a support worker, that framed photographs of his family had been smashed. He accused Kevin of doing this. Amina said to Eddie that she would talk to everyone in the house and try to find out what had happened. Amina saw each person separately to maintain confidentiality.

When Amina saw Kevin she explained the situation and they agreed to meet. Amina explained that Eddie was very upset by some smashed family photographs and asked Kevin if he knew anything about this. At first, Kevin said he did not know anything, but later said he had broken the pictures. He told Amina that he had done this as Eddie had called his sister names and he had been upset and angry.

Amina asked Kevin what he thought should be done about the situation and Kevin suggested ways he could make amends. Amina enabled Kevin and Eddie to discuss their differences, apologize for inappropriate actions and agree to discuss any future concerns to enable a resolution to be found.

Application in practice

In using unconditional positive regard in her work with Kevin and Eddie, and by respecting them as individuals, Amina enabled them to put forward their viewpoints and discuss their feelings. Amina was aware of the power accorded by her position. She did not accuse or judge, she actively listened to what both individuals said. Whilst not approving of some of the behaviour involved, Amina was able to separate this from the individuals. Through relationships built on trust and respect, both Kevin and Eddie were able to talk about what had happened and discuss their part in it. In this work, Amina was being congruent; her feelings matched her responses. She acknowledged her feelings of unhappiness at some of the behaviour and her appreciation of the individuals' wish to sort it out appropriately.

CONCLUSION

We believe that person centred work and its underpinning values are fundamental to the care and support role and are central when working with people with learning disabilities. By ensuring respect for the person and working in a non-judgemental and accepting way, we have the basis for a trusting relationship. By being congruent, giving unconditional positive regard and being empathetic, we hope to create an environment where the person feels safe and is able to develop. The use of person centred planning is a positive way of working with people with learning disabilities to identify their aspirations, wishes and goals. The process enables people to be central in making decisions about the care and support needed to achieve the identified goals. A person centred approach can be used in conjunction with many other theories; in particular, respect for persons is fundamental to anti-oppressive and anti-discriminatory practice.

Key points

- A person centred approach is often associated with counselling.

- The ideas and terminology used are relevant in the learning disabilities field.

- Respecting the person is the key to person centred work.

- The approach moves away from a directive method of working to a non-directive one.

- The person being supported is seen as central, with a focus on seeing and hearing the individual.

- The approach is underpinned by three core conditions: congruence, unconditional positive regard and empathy.

- Person centred planning is underpinned by the concepts of a person centred approach.

- A person centred approach is not infallible; issues of power, funding and legislative control may all challenge its underpinning principles.

BEHAVIOURAL APPROACHES

INTRODUCTION

Behavioural approaches provide some understanding of the various ways that behaviour can be learnt and how it can be changed, modified or adapted. Behavioural approaches provide methods of working that can be used to increase behaviours that are considered desirable and decrease or eliminate those considered undesirable. In some situations, a behavioural method of working can be useful and supportive, in others controlling and possibly manipulative. Potential aspects of oppression or discrimination through the use of behavioural approaches are highlighted in this section. The power the worker holds requires careful consideration, as does the need to work openly and in partnership with the individual concerned.

Some behavioural approaches and aspects of their use will be explored to provide an understanding of the use and power of behavioural theory. The theory will be put into practice using two case studies.

WHAT IS MEANT BY BEHAVIOUR?

One definition of behaviour is: 'Behaviour – manner of behaving or conducting oneself' (*Collins Dictionary* 1986, p.136). How people behave or conduct themselves is only one part of the larger concept of a behavioural approach; other aspects need to be considered. Behaviourism is defined as: 'A theoretical approach to explaining human development and activity, the central belief of which is that behaviour is the outcome of learning' (Thomas and Pierson 1996, p.39). Behavioural assessments may be used to gain a more comprehensive picture when an individual's behaviour is considered. A behavioural assessment requires the systematic observation of a person's behaviour and usually a detailed account of what is seen is recorded. The aim of the assessment is to analyse why a person is behaving in a certain way. If the behaviour were considered acceptable then the use of a behavioural approach would not usually be required. However, if in the opinion of the workers, support team or society, the behaviour was considered in need of change, then a method of achieving this may be sought through such means as behaviour modification. 'Behaviour modification – A method of teaching people to change their behaviour by the systematic use of reinforcements and infrequently, low-level forms of punishment. It is based in Learning Theory' (Thomas and Pierson 1996, p.39). People with learning disabilities sometimes behave in ways that conflict with society's norms and thus may not be accepted. Aspects of people's behaviour may then be worked with by using the approaches and methods discussed in this section.

BEHAVIOURAL APPROACHES IN MORE DETAIL

Behavioural approaches differ from humanistic, person centred work. Whilst person centred work focuses on the individual's thoughts and emotions, behavioural work focuses on the individual's conditioning and behaviour.

> Behaviourism…is based on a belief that feelings of distress or neurosis come about through faulty conditioning and that what needs to be changed is maladaptive behaviour. It stresses the importance of observable, testable, measurable, reproducible and objective behaviours: we are as we behave. As such, unlike psychoanalysis and humanism, behaviourism is not primarily concerned with the meaning and understanding that human beings ascribe to their thoughts and feelings. (Trevithick 2000, p.30)

Behavioural approaches have developed from a psychological underpinning. Often behavioural work is undertaken over a short term, being time limited in its application. The focus of the work is on the here and now and how to achieve change in behaviour. The change is often achieved through the worker's input and the client may have little influence on decisions about the process. On occasion, the work sometimes appears to be undertaken *on* the person rather than *with* the person. The principles behind a behavioural approach are identified by Gambrill (1995). They include acknowledgement that all behaviour is learnt and so in principle can be unlearnt. The change needs to be achieved through tried and tested methods. It should not be presumed that as a method has worked for one person that it will work for the next; each situation must be seen as individual. Gambrill suggests that the use of this approach requires warmth, empathy and a genuine understanding to enhance its chances of success. Behavioural approaches and therapies can be used in a variety of ways. Payne (1997) suggests four different approaches: 'respondent learning or classical conditioning; operant conditioning; social learning; cognitive therapy' (Payne 1997, p.116). We will now briefly explore some aspects of these approaches.

Respondent learning

Respondent learning is also sometimes referred to as 'classical' or Pavlovian conditioning (Pavlov 1927). This type of behavioural approach is predominantly used when change in a person's behaviour is required, specifically in behaviour over which a person has little conscious control, such as reflexes, anxiety and anger. Respondent learning uses a variety of methods including conditioning and counter-conditioning.

For children, the control of bed wetting can be effected through the process of respondent learning. A buzzer is connected to moisture pads in the bed and the buzzer is activated when the child urinates. The sound of the buzzer wakes the child and alerts him or her to the need to use the toilet. Gradually the child becomes conditioned so that when the bladder is felt to be full then he or she wakes up prior to the buzzer sounding. In this situation, the controlling of what a child can learn is both acceptable and helpful.

Operant conditioning

Operant conditioning is sometimes referred to as 'instrumental' or Skinnerian conditioning. Skinner (1938) is the psychologist credited with the development of theories using the approach. Unlike respondent learning that focuses on involuntary behaviour, operant conditioning is concerned with bringing about change in voluntary behaviour. This is achieved by manipulating the factors that lead up to the behaviour (called the 'antecedents') and those that follow the behaviour (the 'consequences'). This is often referred to as the 'ABC' of behaviour. The theory suggests that a person learns to do, or refrain from doing, something by experiencing the consequences of the behaviour in certain identifiable situations. An increase in the frequency of the desired behaviour can be achieved by rewarding it, referred to as reinforcing, and the behaviour can be decreased by 'punishing' or 'extinguishing' it. Different types of 'reinforcement' and 'punishment' are used in the process:

- 'Positive reinforcement' is used where desired behaviour is increased by positively rewarding it. A reward or reinforcement, such as a trip out, is offered following work towards achieving a desired outcome.

- 'Negative reinforcement' is used to reinforce desired behaviour by stopping something unpleasant happening; thus, for example, 'children may keep quiet if only to avoid the pain of being shouted at' (Coulshed and Orme 1998, p.157).

- 'Punishment' is used where undesirable behaviour is decreased by punishing it. An example of this could be a person being asked to leave a communal area when undesirable behaviour is manifest there. Undesirable behaviour may also be decreased by stopping something pleasant happening. For example, a person being asked to leave a group that he or she enjoys when the person's behaviour is considered disruptive to the group.

- 'Extinction' is used when behaviour has been positively reinforced and the reinforcements are then taken away.

Positive reinforcement of the desired behaviour is both constructive and affirming and involves some kind of pleasurable experience for the individual involved. A consequence of this approach may also be that the more time the individual spends behaving in the desired or socially valid way, then the less time will be spent behaving in undesired ways. Punishment is aimed at reducing undesirable behaviour but does not teach alternative, acceptable behaviour. In his discussion of the use of punishment in behaviour therapy, Barker asserts that 'punishment should only be used in conjunction with some positive reinforcement system or as a last resort in truly intractable cases' (Barker 1985, p.141). Thus, if punishment were to be used at all, then it would need to be used advisedly and sound reasons would be needed for its use in preference to reinforcement. In terms of valuing and respecting the individual, we believe that methods that are affirming and rewarding are preferable to methods that negatively reinforce or punish.

Operant conditioning and behaviourism have led on to applied behaviour analysis, an approach geared to individuals and involving individually tailored treatment programmes. 'Applied behaviour analysis is distinguished by its methodology for evaluating treatment effects. The focus is on intensive study of the individual subject' (Corsini and Wedding 1989, p.242).

> One of the main differences between traditional psychology and applied behavioural analysis is that most traditional psychologists analyse human behaviour by using group averages. In doing so they can lose the sensitive touch that is necessary in the analysis of individual behaviour and in the arranging of individual learning environments. In contrast, applied behavioural analysis has developed procedures specifically geared to measuring individual differences in behaviour. This has led to behaviour analysts becoming experts in tailoring individualised treatment programmes. The most important word here is 'tailored'. As with any suit of clothes, those that fit best are those that are specifically designed for the person who will wear them. (Keenan, Kerr and Dillenburger 2000, p.17)

Treatment programmes using operant conditioning such as applied behavioural analysis seek to develop socially valid and acceptable behaviours and are sometimes used to work with people with challenging behaviour.

Social learning

Social learning is used to help people modify their behaviour by modelling how to react to and learn from behaviour presented (Hudson and MacDonald 1986). For example, this approach is sometimes used when people move from institutional to community living. For a person to live within and be part of the community there are certain roles and expectations involved. To an extent, these can be learnt through a social learning process. Behaviour can be learnt by observing the behaviour of others (Bandura 1977). The tendency to learn from others is increased if:

- the person modelling the behaviour has high standing with us

- the person modelling the behaviour is moderately similar to us

- the person sees their behaviour being reinforced by others as positive

- the person has a chance to practise the behaviour soon after seeing it modelled

- positive behaviour is reinforced.

This can be achieved if the worker supporting the person:

- defines the desired behaviour clearly and ensures that attention to detail is given

- gives or arranges a demonstration

- encourages the person to copy and practise the behaviour

- gives feedback and reinforcement

- provides further support in the process if required.

(Developed from the concept of modelling:
Hudson and MacDonald 1986)

Social learning differs from other 'strict' non-cognitive therapy theories in that it assumes unobservable mental processes. Such processes include the ability to store information and to anticipate outcomes. It is a method often used in the person's environment and is used when modelling is being undertaken as part of social skills training. It is worth considering the power held by the person who is the model. The fact that the model may come from a different class or culture could influence the appropriateness of the social learning through a difference of values and beliefs.

Cognitive therapy

Cognitive therapy works on the premise that thinking, feeling and behaviour are interconnected. In this work, unhealthy emotional responses are seen as originating in the way people perceive, interpret, and are influenced by the world. The approach aims to help the person see more clearly, to interpret more accurately and to deal with issues rationally. This is achieved through exploring and changing the way a person thinks. Thus, cognitive therapies are interventions aimed at alleviating emotional distress or dysfunction due to thinking errors based on beliefs and assumptions. If the thoughts, perceptions and interpretations causing the emotional distress are dealt with, then the emotional response will cease to cause problems. The client and therapist form a collaborative relationship and between them formulate what the problem is. Unhelpful thinking is examined and questioned and a range of techniques is used to work towards the identified goals. Various texts can be found that explore this area in more depth. Material looking at conditions such as anxiety, neurosis and depression was drawn together by Ellis (1962), while the separation between mind and behaviour has been explored by Sheldon (1995). The links between emotional disorders and cognitive therapy were studied by Beck (1989).

Scott and Dryden (1996) provide a classification of four cognitive therapies that can be used: coping skills; problem solving; cognitive restructuring; and structural. Thomas and Pierson describe cognitive therapy as 'a form of therapy that aims to change the way people think about themselves and their environment' (1996, p.76). Research has shown that cognitive approaches are valid (Sheldon 1995). They can be used when dealing with emotional problems such as depression, anxiety and anger control. However, the success of cognitive approaches in the learning disabilities field is not so well documented. It could be questioned whether they are suited for use with all people with learning disabilities, as the process of thought may be impaired to an extent which could prohibit success. Expert opinion, careful planning and joint working would therefore be critical when considering the appropriateness of cognitive behavioural therapies within the learning disabilities field.

THE USE OF BEHAVIOURAL TECHNIQUES

Behavioural techniques sometimes work well in certain situations. With children, behavioural techniques may be used, for example, to work with conduct disorders, issues of toileting and phobias. With adults they may be used in anxiety problems, sexual problems or some family problems.

Additionally, the techniques may be used with adults and children with learning disabilities for skills acquisition and issues of challenging behaviour. Consistent and accurate use of the approaches is required for their success. These techniques are often used in specialist settings; these include hospital and residential units, child and adult mental health centres and establishments for children and adults with behavioural problems.

Some uses of and reservations about behavioural work have been explored above. The process is essentially about changing the behaviour of the person. The approach is used to bring about changes in the person's behaviour and we suggest it is important that these changes are wanted by the individual. Payne reinforces some concerns:

> There are also objections on ethical grounds, since the worker manipulates behaviour rather than it being under the control of the client. When using a behavioural approach the power difference could be used inappropriately in the control of an individual. This could lead to behaviourist techniques imposing workers' wishes on unwilling clients, in pursuit of social or political policies which could, at the extreme, be used for authoritarian political control. (Payne 1997, p.123)

The person should be aware when a behavioural approach is being used and should give permission for its use. Watson (1980) in Payne suggests:

> The only ethical position, which maintains clients' rights to self-determination, is to use the technique only where the client's own purpose is to free themselves from behaviour; for example, where it is compulsive, and clients cannot, but wish to, control themselves. (Payne 1997, p.123)

We acknowledge that this may not be viable in all situations. However, it cannot be ignored that power imbalances will exist between the person and the worker.

As highlighted above, there are many different approaches to behaviour therapy and ways of changing an individual's behaviour. Behavioural approaches contrast with the humanistic, person centred approach explored in the previous section, which works with emotions and feelings. However, person centred attributes such as respect, warmth and empathy should be inherent to behavioural approaches. To illustrate some of the contrasts involved we now draw some brief comparisons between one behavioural approach, cognitive therapy, and a person centred approach.

Cognitive therapy	*Person centred approach*
directive, therapy led	non-directive, client led
an agenda is set	no agenda is set
the focus is on behaviour and actions	the focus is on emotions
goals are set	no goals are set
task orientated	not task orientated
homework may be set	homework is not set
previous session is reviewed	previous session is not necessarily reviewed or even referred to
the therapist may give praise or censure while considering agreed homework	part of unconditional positive regard is that the therapist does not give praise or censure; the client feels valued for being him or herself

This brief outline of some of the contrasts between the two approaches begins to highlight some of the aspects of choice, power and control involved in them. Similar comparisons could be made with other behavioural approaches. The differences identified will need careful consideration when any work is undertaken. Working approaches can be informed and underpinned through careful use of a sound value and ethical base, as discussed at the beginning of this chapter. We will now go on to consider the use of behavioural approaches in two case studies.

CASE STUDY ONE

Maisie had lived in an institutional setting for most of her life. She had moved from a large hospital to a hostel housing 25 people. Maisie had later decided to move on to supported living in the community. Before moving to her new accommodation, Maisie lived for 12 months in a training flat where she learnt new skills and gained knowledge of local facilities. Through this experience Maisie also improved her confidence and self-esteem. During this time Maisie learned more about aspects of life such as managing money, housekeeping and accessing community facilities.

Maisie worked mainly with two support workers, Mary and Sally, who themselves also lived in the local community. She liked both women and had a good rapport with them. Maisie prioritized what she needed to learn and how to achieve this. As part of this plan, Maisie wished to access a leisure centre and was supported in doing so. On several occasions, Maisie accompanied either Mary or Sally to the centre and watched how they used the facilities, then followed their example. Through this Maisie quite quickly gained the confidence to go and use the facilities on her own.

During her time in the training flat, Maisie was also supported in making choices about her new lifestyle, including her daily occupation, where to shop, how to pay her rent and how to spend her leisure time.

Application in practice

As part of her preparation to move into supported community living, Maisie worked with Mary and Sally. There was a plan made, discussion beforehand and encouragement for Maisie to learn and participate. Part of the social learning undertaken by Maisie was through Mary and Sally's modelling of behaviour. This was reinforced by their good working relationship with Maisie and the fact that they too lived in the local community. Maisie's learning was also strengthened by being able to practise the behaviour modelled. Mary and Sally reinforced the social learning process through praise and encouragement.

CASE STUDY TWO

Samuel lived in a residential home housing six adults. The home had an adjoining respite care unit for four people. Samuel used sign language to communicate and the home was a signing environment. It had been noticed that Samuel had become agitated on several recent occasions. When staff explored whether there was a pattern to these bouts of agitation, it appeared they occurred on Wednesday evenings on a regular fortnightly basis. The staff decided to set up a systematic observation of Samuel each Wednesday for six weeks. The intention was to note any differences and particular events leading to Samuel's agitation.

Following this systematic observation, it became apparent that the evenings Samuel became agitated coincided with Vikram, a man from the respite care unit, joining Samuel's group for tea. Vikram used sign language, but during his visits the others in respite care did not sign. The visits had been set up with the residents' permission to help Vikram feel more included.

However, Vikram's presence was triggering Samuel's agitation and this had to be resolved.

Application in practice

Having communicated with Samuel and systematically observed what led up to his agitation, the situation became clearer to the staff. They noted that Wednesdays were Samuel's nights to cook, which he enjoyed. There were no problems on the Wednesdays that Vikram was absent. When Vikram came for tea, Samuel did not want him in the kitchen as he enjoyed the staff member's individual attention whilst preparing the meal. When he became agitated, he again received individual attention from the staff member. In terms of operant conditioning, the antecedent to Samuel's behaviour was the presence of Vikram. The consequence of his agitation was receiving the staff member's undivided attention.

Once this was clear, the staff were then able to work with Samuel on this issue. They recognized it was Samuel's home and reminded him he and the other residents had been asked if Vikram could come for tea. Samuel knew Vikram liked to see him and the other residents as they could sign to him. After discussion, Samuel and the staff agreed that, as usual, they would spend time individually with Samuel whilst preparing tea and Vikram could arrive later in time to eat. The staff then used the positive reinforcement of a game of cards after tea to reward Samuel if he did not become agitated by Vikram's presence. The staff explained their intentions to Vikram, saying they wished to find out what was upsetting him. They treated him with respect, warmth and genuine understanding whilst using a behavioural approach which fostered engagement and enabled rapport.

CONCLUSION

In some situations, the behavioural approach is beneficial: 'Behavioural and cognitive approaches are clearly valid and widely applicable forms of treatment whose effectiveness is supported by research' (Payne 1997, p.135). However, behavioural work uses a very structured approach and sometimes this may not sit well with the empowering and more client-led approaches often associated with social care. Whatever the intervention used, the worker holds an element of power. With behavioural approaches, the power of the worker or therapist is both visible and evident. Some nurses, social workers and care workers may struggle with the idea of the use of some behavioural techniques as they seem contrary to their value base or code of ethics. To change a person's behaviour and responses to given situations may sit less easily than exploring the feelings and emotions involved and working through them. Thus, the contrast between person centred and behavioural approaches becomes important and the power and control elements require careful thought. However, not to intervene may be a decision in itself, and this too holds power. Sheldon is potent in his assertion concerning this in relation to behavioural work:

> In which case, given that lots of things are already happening, *not* intervening is an influential decision just as much as intervening is. The decision not to intervene, or excessive procrastination about the issues raised by intervention, means that the behaviour of the individuals concerned is governed by forces which the therapist has decided *not* to try to control; not to replace with other, hopefully more benign influences; and which he has *not* taught the client how better to control himself. Sometimes it is right, or judicious, or necessary to stay out of a case, but this should be recognized as to some extent an abandonment of the client to *other* controls, and not as a simple decision not to seek control. There are no vacuums in social life and some influence or other will prevail. Therapeutic 'sins of commission' must therefore be weighed carefully against equally damning 'sins of omission'. (Sheldon 1982, p.224)

Whilst some of the dilemmas concerning power and control are not unique to behavioural work, the nature of the techniques and their effectiveness in bringing about change call for those involved to apply high ethical standards in their work.

Key points

- Behavioural approaches have been developed from psychological perspectives.

- Behaviour can be learnt and also unlearnt.

- There are various theories that help explain how the learning of behaviour is undertaken.

- There are theories that explain how behaviour can be changed by using structured theoretical approaches.

- In certain situations behavioural approaches work well.

- The person deciding to change behaviour holds much power.

- Careful consideration should be given to the reasons behaviour changes are required.

- If a person's behaviour is being changed to fit the individual into social norms, the appropriateness of the norms must first be carefully considered.

- The concern that a person's behaviour could be changed without them realizing should not be overlooked.

- Although a person centred approach appears to contrast with behavioural approaches, many aspects of behavioural work should be underpinned by the same principles of a person centred approach.

9

Practical Theories and Methods

INTRODUCTION

Whether a social worker, nurse, support worker or a person who provides care for people with learning disabilities, the support afforded is part of an ongoing process. The work may take place in a residential, day care, hospital, work or home setting. Whatever the role or setting, different methods of working are often used without consideration of the theory that underpins those methods. It would seem illogical to go about each day thinking, 'What theory shall I use now?' However, by having a working knowledge of theories and an understanding of their use in practice, support and care work can be enhanced.

There are many different theories that can be used to inform and underpin social and health care work. In this chapter we will explore four of the practical theories and methods that are often used in day to day work:

- systems theory
- task centred theory
- role theory
- crisis intervention.

Each theory/method may be used on its own or combined with others to inform practice. We will explore this further by briefly introducing the four theories/methods and then go on to present a practice based case scenario. This case scenario will set the context of how practical theories and methods can be used together to inform day to day practice. Following the case scenario each theory/method will be explored in more depth to aid understanding and provide insight into their use.

A person may have family, friends, work colleagues, attend social clubs or day services – people and places that are important to the individual. These people and places are all part of the systems that surround each of us during our lives. If an individual's systems are identified this may help to place the person in the overall context of his or her environment. This enables a more holistic view of the person whilst retaining the individual as the key focus. Later in this chapter we will consider the principles of systems theory and its application in practice.

If difficulties or problems are faced then methods of solving these problems are sought. Sometimes it appears easier to sort out the difficulties people face *for* them rather than *with* them. A task centred approach is a method of working where responsibilities are jointly negotiated and manageable tasks are taken on by the person being supported and the supporter. Through this process of shared responsibility the person is enabled to take control of the situation. This approach would not work in every case but an understanding of its principles would inform a decision for its use.

How individuals act in different situations will depend upon their role and the roles of others at that particular time. A person may behave in one way when with friends and in a very different way at work, as a family member or whilst out shopping. Other people's roles may affect how an individual acts. Role theory provides an interesting explanation of the different roles and consequent conflicts that may occur in day to day life.

It is often said that a crisis has occurred, but how is it decided that a person is in crisis? Is it really the person, or is it the staff or service that is in crisis? Insight and practical guidance can be gained by exploring the principles and use of crisis intervention theory.

The following case scenario will highlight aspects of the above four theories with the aim of drawing them together to demonstrate their practical use.

CASE SCENARIO COMBINING FOUR PRACTICAL THEORIES AND METHODS

Charlie lived in his own flat within the local community. Two mornings a week he helped out at the local coffee shop and on other days he attended the local day centre and college. Charlie could manage most things on his own but required support in some aspects of his day to day living. Charlie found washing and cooking difficult and sometimes overspent when he went shopping. Each Friday Charlie met with Chris, a community support worker, who helped him with some household tasks and shopping.

Over a period of two weeks, Chris noticed that Charlie appeared to be upset and angry. He was not interested in undertaking their normal Friday activities and would not discuss issues worrying him. On the following

Monday, Chris received a telephone call saying that Charlie had not arrived at the coffee shop and the staff were worried about him.

Chris tried to telephone Charlie but there was no response. Chris telephoned Charlie's family and other people known to Charlie including staff at the day centre, college, local shop and at the doctor's surgery. All of these were part of the 'systems' surrounding Charlie – his family, workplace, friends and those in community services. An awareness of these systems enabled Chris to network with others to try to locate Charlie.

Some time later, Chris received a call from the local resource centre saying that Charlie had just arrived there and was asking for Chris. Chris went to pick up Charlie and they started to talk through the situation. Charlie was unhappy at the coffee shop as he was only ever allowed to wash up and wanted to do other jobs. He also said he was unhappy with some of his groups at the day centre. Chris worked with Charlie to identify ways that the situation could be dealt with: talk to the coffee shop manager about doing other work, talk with the key worker at the day centre, look at other options for day care. Chris enabled Charlie to identify what was most important to him and then make a list of things to do. Charlie agreed to do some tasks and Chris others; a 'task centred approach' was being used.

Chris thought about Charlie's 'role' at the coffee shop and how Charlie saw himself. Chris also considered how Charlie might be viewed by others at the coffee shop as the 'washer up'. Charlie wanted more than this, he wanted to be thought of differently. Role theory provided a way of thinking about the role expectations of Charlie and the other staff and how these could begin to be addressed.

Chris considered Charlie's support systems, looked at his role in the coffee shop and with him jointly agreed tasks to work towards, thus averting a potential situation of crisis. On this occasion, a proactive approach avoided a crisis. If this had not been possible and Charlie had been in a crisis situation, then crisis intervention theory would have provided insight and guidance.

We will now go on to explore each of the theories/methods highlighted in the scenario in more depth in the following four sections.

SYSTEMS THEORY

INTRODUCTION

In this section we will consider the use of systems theory. This will include general and ecological systems theory – both sociologically based theories.

Systems theory is a diverse discipline; however, we will be focusing on parts relevant to social and care work. First, we will explore what is meant by a system. This will be followed by a brief exploration of where systems theory originated. We will go on to examine the way that systems theory can be used to inform practice, and examples of its use will be given in two case studies.

SYSTEMS

A system can be described as a set of objects, thoughts or feelings that are interdependent and integrated, so that together they function as a single unit. The word 'system' is frequently used in everyday life; for example, a computer system. A computer system requires a keyboard, monitor, power unit and printer to be a complete system. Each part on its own is an individual component and these components can only produce something meaningful when they work in relationship with each other. Each unit cannot function as a computer system on its own. This generalized explanation of a system can be transferred to examine further the systems that surround each of us.

In life we are all surrounded by systems that affect us in one way or another. These systems may include areas such as work, family and friends. Each one is, to an extent, related to the others; if one area (or system) changes, the other areas may be affected. The impact of changing systems can be explored. For example, the loss of a friend through bereavement may affect a person's work, social life or relationships. Systems change, however, and as the individual becomes used to the loss over time adaptation usually takes place. This will be explored further later in the chapter.

THE BACKGROUND TO SYSTEMS THEORY

There are various suggestions as to the origin of the systems approach. These are as diverse as from engineering (De Board 1997) to biological theory (von Bertalanffy 1971). Each approach has a similar core feature running through it: the idea that something is made up of many parts and each part plays a role in the overall structure. An example of this from an engineering perspective is molecules, as component parts, forming metals and these metals subsequently forming the construction of, for example, a bridge. From a biological perspective, the component cells in the organs of a body and each cell's part in the overall system of the body form a complete living person.

The systems approach that is used in social work has close links to the general systems theory (von Bertalanffy 1971). This approach considered that all organisms are part of systems, each being composed of micro-systems and sub-systems, and in turn each part belonging to a super-system. The human body can be likened to a super-system; it has need of a heart, lungs, brain, kidneys and liver as major sub-systems. It also has a circulation system comprising of fluids and cells, which form part of the micro-systems. Each part is individual but reliant on the other parts to function as a human body.

The theory of sub-systems and super-systems can be transferred and used when considering social systems. Not only do individuals have their own biological system but are also part of social systems. A person's social system may comprise friends, family, neighbours, colleagues and groups. It also comprises the other aspects of a person's place within society such as local, community, work and social settings.

In the late 19th century some social surveys were carried out. Joseph Rowntree looked at the influence of aspects of society and, in particular, the impact of poverty (Rowntree 1901). These studies started to highlight that people were affected by the systems that surrounded their day to day life and were also part of a wider systems structure. A person may be living in poverty and this may be caused by various factors such as the lack of family income or the size of the family. This may affect the person's housing situation and the health of those within the home. In turn, the health factors may affect working capabilities; the implications are immense. Change in one system can have impact on the other systems. Consideration of the systems that operate around a person enables the person to be seen as a 'whole' (Hanson 1995).Thus this does not ignore parts of a person's life that may be critical and influential. The person is considered as part of, and within, the surrounding systems.

We will now look at a different aspect of the systems approach. Consider that each system is individual; it has a boundary surrounding its physical and mental energy. This energy may be exchanged with other systems and when this happens these are called 'open systems'. If a system cannot exchange energy with others then it is a 'closed system' (Siporin 1980). This can be considered further by looking at the work of Greif and Lynch. They provide a set of concepts that offer an explanation of how systems work: 'Input, throughput, output, feedback loops, entropy' (Greif and Lynch 1983). The input is the energy being fed into a system. Whilst researching this book, the information we read was our input; this affected how we understood the theories that we have written about. The information we found was

considered and used as our throughput, as it enabled subsequent understanding of the subject to increase. The chapters written are our output – the
result of the input and throughput. As this book is read and thought about,
the issues raised and discussed, a feedback loop starts to take place. Information is taken in, thought about, shared with others and re-thought, thus
forming the loop. In contrast, entropy occurs if a system does not accept input or give output; it will eventually slow down and cease to function.

We will now look at how systems theory can be used in practice and how
it can inform day to day work with people with learning disabilities.

SYSTEMS THEORY IN PRACTICE

Systems theory was used extensively in the 1970s in social care. The aim was
to develop a single social work approach that could be applicable to all social
work settings. The idea was to look at the way people interacted and how
people depended on many different systems to meet their needs.

Each person was considered as a part of an informal system such as family, friends and neighbours. Formal systems would be those such as community groups and societal systems would be those such as schools, hospitals,
social services and the police. Whilst the systems operated in harmony, the
person retained equilibrium (Pincus and Minahan 1973). Any of these systems could break down or not provide sufficient support for the person, thus
unsettling equilibrium. In such a case, Pincus and Minahan (1973) suggested
the person's systems should be examined and the system not working effectively identified. The worker or carer could then intervene to change the in-
effective system, or support the person if change could not be made,
ultimately to restore equilibrium.

In reality, this was not always a practical way of providing support; the
approach did not progress as originally planned. However, it can still be used
to provide understanding of different situations and does highlight the importance of looking at the wider context of a person and their surrounding
systems. This enables the focus to be extended from the individual to a wider
context. It acknowledges that the situation or problem may not be solely of
the person's making and that external factors impact upon a person's life.

Germain and Gitterman (1980) suggested a 'life model' approach to social work. This played a key part in the development of ecological systems
theory. Ecological systems can provide a further perspective upon the importance and impact of social systems. This approach is described by Thomas
and Pierson as: 'A perspective in social work that emphasises the adaptive
and reciprocal relationship between people and their environment' (Thomas

and Pierson 1996, p.125). This predominantly focuses on the 'adaptive and reciprocal relationship' (Thomas and Pierson 1996) that individuals achieve in relation to their environment during their lifetime. It also considers how the person may affect the environment in which they live. The life model sees people as constantly adapting within the many aspects of their environment (Germain and Gitterman 1980). It looks at the connection between a person's problems, needs and goals and the relationship to social, economic and physical environments. Tools that can be used to help identify these relationships are ecomaps and genograms.

Ecomaps and genograms are visual methods of focusing on the network of family and support in a person's life. They provide visual diagrams of the person's systems network (Gilgun 1994). This enables a better understanding of social networks in relationship to environments. Ecomaps can be used to identify and visually describe a person's social situation. Genograms can be used to identify and visually describe a person's family tree. Genograms are particularly useful in life story work (Thomas and Pierson 1996, p.159). These visual aids are completed in partnership with the person being supported, who is the central figure. They can show those who are closest to the person and those farthest away. These methods can be used to identify and reinforce existing support networks and resources and highlight those missing.

To place this in context, let us consider someone with a learning and physical disability who wants to move from a residential unit into independent living. There are various systems that may play a part in the person's resettlement. These may include informal systems such as family, neighbours and friends. An ecological approach could also be used to identify the social systems that surround the person, such as educational facilities, and health and social support services. This approach may also highlight aspects of social exclusion, by identifying absent support structures. This would provide valuable insight when considering the appropriateness of the move, the support needs and care package that would be required. The balance between resource-led provision and needs-led support could be considered in the overall context of the person's life.

It is crucial that workers and supporters of people with learning disabilities ensure that it is the systems regarded by individuals as of importance that are fully considered. The influence of our own judgement and the perceptions of family or friends, concerning systems that are important to the individual, require careful reflection to ensure the individual's needs and wishes are properly taken into account. This may take time to achieve but avoids tokenistic working. Again, this highlights the importance of getting to know the individual and understanding his or her preferences.

The capacity of people and social systems to maintain their place in society may be influenced by various factors:

- Life transitions – developmental changes, changes in status, role or group composition.

- Environmental pressures – poverty, inequality, rigidity in the environment.

- Interpersonal processes – communication, patterns of relationship.

One of the aims of social support is to enable the person and to support the environment in changing so that compatibility can be achieved. Without identifying the systems that impose restrictions upon a person, it is difficult to effect positive change. Using the processes discussed to identify the systems that require change, a structured approach to working can be achieved.

Support work dealing with life transitions and the situations or issues that arise from them may require various methods of support, such as:

- *enabling*: strengthening the client's motivation, validating and supporting the client, helping to manage feelings

- *teaching*: helping clients learn problem-solving skills, clarifying perceptions, offering appropriate information, modelling behaviour

- *facilitating*: such as maintaining clients' freedom of action from unreasonable constraints, defining the task, mobilizing environmental supports.

(Adapted from Payne 1997, p.148)

When considering and dealing with situations or problems that arise from environmental pressures, intervention can be made through:

- *mediating*: helping the client and the system meet and deal with each other in rational and reciprocal ways

- *advocating*: pressurizing other agencies or individuals to intervene, including taking up social action

- *organizing*: such as putting the client in contact with or creating new social networks.

(Adapted from Payne 1997, p.149)

The more a support worker understands the various systems involved, the greater the information gained to inform the situation. There is a need to consider how to work, who is included or excluded, cultural expectations, experience and communication patterns.

Other theories may also inform practice when using a systems approach; for example, role theory. If a person's role is identified within a specific system, it may provide a clearer understanding of that person and his or her actions. The use of more than one theory to explore a situation can enhance understanding and the provision of care and support.

The following case studies illustrate the use of systems theory in practice.

CASE STUDY ONE

Margaret, a woman in her late thirties, had lived all her life with her father in a small country town. Margaret had a part-time job working in a cafe in a nearby town and she travelled there independently by bus. She was also a member of the local Baptist church and sang in the choir.

Over the previous six months, Margaret had begun to express a wish to move and perhaps get a flat of her own. Margaret and her father had discussed her wish for independence in some detail. Her father was concerned that Margaret might become lonely and isolated and therefore vulnerable if she lived alone. Margaret's father was also worried that she was not able to budget or pay bills. She had little experience of this, as he had always dealt with financial matters in the home. He wanted to support Margaret but was worried what independence might bring for her. They had been advised to contact social services to see what options were available, and decided to ask for a visit to discuss their next move.

Walter, a social worker on the local team for adults with learning disabilities, came to visit Margaret and her father and they discussed their hopes and fears with him. The social worker explained the need for a full assessment. This would take place over time so that the right resources and housing could be found for Margaret; this too would depend upon her skills and abilities.

In order for Walter to get an idea of Margaret's social situation, he drew up an ecomap with her. Through this work, Margaret was able to put herself figuratively in the middle of the ecomap. She then put the people and places important to her in surrounding positions, with those she felt most important to her closest and those least important farther away on the ecomap. Further discussion with Margaret and her father helped develop this theme.

Following on from Walter's initial assessment of Margaret, he then referred her to the local community support team for further assessment and support.

Application in practice

From drawing the ecomap and from their discussions, Walter was able to get a picture of the systems important to Margaret. This was used to help them consider and plan the future move. As part of her informal systems, Margaret wanted to be able to see her father with ease (and he too wanted this). She also expressed a wish to be near her close friend Shelley, whom she had known from school days and whom she met up with at least weekly. Margaret also wanted to carry on singing in the choir.

As part of her formal systems, Margaret wanted to continue her work in the cafe. Her links to societal systems were made when she and her father contacted social services for information and advice and followed this up by working with the community support team. They also linked in with the health care Margaret received from the local health trust.

The support team worked with Margaret over several months to facilitate her move and maintain contact with those she considered important to her. They enabled her to find accommodation with an appropriate level of support and encouraged this positive move. They also taught Margaret some skills that would promote her independence, such as basic budgeting. The team mediated in such ways as finding a supportive female GP with whom she could register. They organized to ensure that when she moved Margaret had familiarized herself with her new locality, that she knew the local shops and cafes, social centre and library. They advocated on Margaret's behalf with the benefits agency. Without considering the systems that surrounded Margaret, many of these important aspects could have been overlooked or ignored.

CASE STUDY TWO

Colette had lived for 15 years in a private sector hostel housing ten residents. Her friends were from the hostel and the day centre she attended; she had no family. Over time her physical condition had deteriorated, and at 52 years of age, Colette had become a wheelchair user. In the past Colette had been able to go out to the local shops alone, but since becoming a wheelchair user had been forced to rely upon others to accompany her.

Colette enjoyed her hobbies of tapestry, rug making and music. She was of a shy nature and not very assertive. Colette had two close friends within the hostel with whom she chose to spend most time. Three of the other people Colette lived with had issues of mental ill health additional to their learning disabilities. Sometimes, when their mental health deteriorated, this would have an impact upon her. These residents needed more staff attention and Colette and others therefore received less. It sometimes meant visits from outside professionals, who came into the hostel to work with individuals. Over time, Colette found herself becoming more physically vulnerable and isolated within the hostel and less able to get out.

Colette continued to attend the day centre, which she enjoyed. She was able to meet up with friends from outside the hostel and attend groups of her choosing. She also managed to get out into the community twice a week. Colette had several outbursts at the day centre followed by bouts of crying, unusual behaviour for her. Day service staff discussed this with Colette and contacted hostel staff.

With all this in mind, Colette's key worker, Narinda, discussed the issues with her and they devised a plan to maintain Colette's links to the local community. She enrolled in a tapestry night class at college that was accessible to her as a wheelchair user and she used Dial-a-Ride transport. Colette was also put in touch with, and later joined, her local PHAB (physically handicapped, able bodied) club where she could socialize, and which provided voluntary transport.

One of the things Colette most looked forward to was her summer holiday, and she saved for this from her personal allowance. Due to service policy, Colette had to fund her own holiday, including staffing costs. The impact of her deteriorating physical health and increased wheelchair use meant the rise of her holiday costs. Narinda understood Colette's wish to take a summer holiday and get away from it all. She accessed money to support the extra costs of Colette's holiday from a national charity.

Importantly, they also discussed the impact of all this upon Colette and started to explore her housing options. They looked at several, including a specially adapted group home. In the short term, Colette said she preferred to stay where she was as she was with close friends. She felt that some positive changes had been made, but decided to look at it again if circumstances changed further. She only wanted to move if she and her two close friends could be housed together.

Application in practice

For many years Colette's home system had satisfied her needs adequately. The hostel was an open system, exchanging ideas and energy with other informal systems such as the carers and families and the neighbourhood. It exchanged with societal systems such as health service workers: community psychiatric nurses, district nurses, hospital doctors and GPs. The hostel also worked with other societal systems such as social services, education and the police.

As the years went by and the residents aged, some of them had increased needs. Staffing levels were, however, not proportionately increased. Thus, whilst Colette's physical needs were met, some of her emotional and recreational needs were not. The actions of the residents with increasing mental ill health and challenging behaviour had a negative impact on Colette, making her feel vulnerable and more alone. The system had not broken down but clearly was not meeting all of her needs.

There was also the impact of the home system upon Colette's other main social system at the day centre. When day centre staff intervened, Colette had explained how she was feeling. It was apparent that her outbursts had been due to her increasing frustration and dismay with what was happening at home. From an ecological approach, the changing situation within the hostel and changing health factors had led to some social exclusion. This had been highlighted by discussion with the day centre staff. Narinda, as key worker, had recognized this and taken action to combat discrimination and disadvantage to Colette.

Concerning her holiday, the economic aspect of Colette becoming a wheelchair user disadvantaged her further. Adaptation within the system would have meant increasing her savings and having even less money to spend each week on personal items. Neither Colette nor Narinda saw this as a viable option and rather than adapt (that is, save more each week) Narinda networked and found money elsewhere to support the holiday. Narinda enabled Colette to take up this issue of holiday funding at their house meeting with the manager. She also advocated on Colette's behalf in pressurizing the management committee about the fact that those with higher needs paid more for their holidays.

CONCLUSION

We have explored systems theory by looking at general and ecological systems theory. Systems theory is a useful tool when looking at the overall situation a person is in; however, it does not tell us which system is important or needed and which is not. This can be explored further by working with the person to understand who and what is important to them. The process can be used to identify areas where support is required. The use of systems theory combined with others, such as role theory, enables a joint exploration with the person. The systems approach enables the person to remain the central focus.

Key points

- Systems theory has developed from a number of different perspectives; however, the common theme running through each is that a structure is made up of many parts and each part plays a role in the overall composition, system or arrangement.

- There are formal and informal systems, super-systems and sub-systems, and macro- and micro-systems.

- Identifying the structure of systems surrounding a person or organization can give insight into a variety of situations.

- Systems can work with each other or conflict. Being able to identify different systems can aid consideration of how the overall structure is operating.

- Systems that conflict can be challenged and change supported to enable development.

- Although systems can be identified, the theory does not tell us which systems are considered important or needed by a person. The person being cared for and supported should be consulted throughout.

- Ecomaps and genograms are good tools to show systems in a visual format and can be undertaken with the person.

- Systems theory can identify the important systems, or lack of them, surrounding a person. Other theoretical perspectives can then be used to inform ways of working to support a person or given situation.

A TASK CENTRED APPROACH

INTRODUCTION

A task centred approach can be used in many different social and care environments. It places an emphasis on the problem solving of issues that are important to the person being supported. The problems need to be identified and ways of dealing with them explored and undertaken. We will initially explore the development of task centred casework. We will go on to highlight the principles that underpin the approach, its application and limitations in practice. The use of a task centred approach will be illustrated through two case studies.

TASK CENTRED CASEWORK

In the USA during the 1960s, concerns were raised about the length of time casework took. It was suggested that social support was time consuming and ineffectual for many clients. The task centred approach was a way of changing traditional working styles. The pioneers of the task centred approach were Reid and Epstein (1972). They provided an initial explanation that described the working principles of the approach. In this section we will incorporate their ideas with the work undertaken by Doel and Marsh (1992), who provide another interpretation of task centred work.

The key features of a task centred approach can help to identify how and what the approach can be used for. The key features include:

- focusing on the here and now
- focusing on problem solving
- focusing on the outcome for the client and not for the worker
- being client centred
- being time limited
- short-term working.

When considering the key features in practice, it becomes apparent that this type of approach would only be relevant and appropriate to certain situations. Reid and Hanrahan suggested eight areas where a task centred approach could be beneficial:

1.   Interpersonal conflict.

2.   Dissatisfaction in social relations.

3. Problems with formal organizations.

4. Difficulties in role performance.

5. Problems of social transition.

6. Reactive emotional distress.

7. Inadequate resources.

8. Behavioural problems.

(Reid 1978; Reid and Hanrahan 1981 in Coulshed and Orme 1998, p.118)

These examples begin to highlight the diversity of situations in which a task centred approach could be used. An understanding of the principles that underpin the theory and explain how it works will help to identify how to use it in practice.

PRINCIPLES OF TASK CENTRED WORK

The principles of task centred work focus predominantly on the following factors:

- People are largely capable of making rational choices about what they want to do. They are the best people to make choices about themselves.

- People are more likely to achieve goals they have chosen themselves.

- Small successes build confidence and self-esteem.

- The task of the worker is to enable people to achieve their aims.

When a person has a problem or issue, then the individual concerned is often the best person to identify the nature of that problem or issue. This of course may be affected by the person's perception or understanding but, nevertheless, his or her interpretation should not be dismissed. If ability is impaired the person may still be supported in identifying the issues of concern. Task centred work relies on joint responsibility and will not work in a satisfactory way if the person concerned does not want to participate. Achieving change is more likely if the person wants to make the change and it is not something imposed by others. Involvement in identifying changes, setting targets and negotiating how work will be carried out is part of joint ownership.

When a problem appears very large or difficult to face, breaking it down into smaller, more manageable pieces or tasks is a logical way of dealing with it. Negotiation takes place to decide what tasks need to be undertaken and who is going to carry them out. Tasks can then be taken on individually whilst working towards resolution of the whole problem or issue. Achieving each task or small goal helps the person to build up self-esteem and self-confidence. If a small goal is not achieved, the failure is nowhere near as great as if the whole task were unsuccessful.

TASK CENTRED WORK IN PRACTICE

When using this approach, the initial stage is to identify the problem and establish the reason for the work (Doel and Marsh 1992). Joint working is used to explore the identified problem. Time should be spent in finding out the person's specific understanding and views. When the main problem is identified, it needs to be evaluated to see if it is resolvable. If the problem is not resolvable using a task centred approach, then other approaches may be considered to support the person to understand or accept the situation. As workers, carers or supporters, it is important that we do not impose our own agendas or those of our agencies upon the person being supported. It is also worth checking that it really is the client that wants the change, not someone from his or her family or support network.

The next step is to agree the goals and the time limits in which to achieve change. The focus of this stage is on making an agreement between the person and worker about the action to be taken (Doel and Marsh 1992). This work can then be carried out in a logical progression:

- Identify the client's problem and agree to work on this.

- If there is more than one problem then prioritize with the client.

- Be clear about the person's desired outcome.

- Set the tasks out so that they can be seen and decide which is the priority.

- Agree on the time required to carry out the tasks and set a time limit.

The planning and subsequent execution of tasks need to be undertaken and reviewed on a regular basis. Depending upon the person's ability, the tasks may involve just one thing to do or a single decision to be made. Some people may prefer to undertake a number of tasks at any given time. This highlights the importance of knowing the person concerned and having an awareness of his or her abilities. Negotiation takes place to divide tasks between client and worker. Flexibility is important in meeting individual needs.

As tasks are completed, it is critical to review progress; this allows the identification of the most successful strategies. Reviewing also gives the opportunity to analyse and then remove obstacles that may be restricting progress. Success can be reinforced with the person to promote confidence and self-esteem.

When the problem has been addressed and the desired change achieved, then an end needs to be reached. A positive approach to ending the work should include revisiting the initial problem and then evaluating the situation. This reinforces and highlights achievements and enables planning for the future. The work should then draw to an end. If, however, other problems have been identified during the work, the process may need to start again or different support sought from other agencies. Reflection upon the changes achieved is a valuable part of the task centred process.

It is useful and important to remember that a task centred approach will work best with problems that:

- the client accepts and acknowledges
- can be clearly defined
- the client wants to work on.

This theory has its limitations; the approach will not work successfully if:

- constant crises affect the client
- long-term psychological problems are the main issue affecting the client
- the client's ability to be rational is impaired
- there is a lack of motivation
- legislation or a statutory mandate is not accepted by the person
- there is a lack of openness and honesty
- an ulterior motive or hidden agenda is being used by either the person being supported or the person providing support.

A task centred approach works on strengths not weaknesses. It recognizes the ability of the person to play a major part in resolving his or her problems and it increases and strengthens the person's problem solving capacity for the future. The individual decides the change by defining the problems and goals. It is a time limited process and the person knows when the support will end. We will now explore the use of a task centred approach in the following two case studies.

CASE STUDY ONE

Leroy lived in a flat in an outlying district of town. He was settled in that area and knew people and places in the locality. He had been offered a part-time job that he really wanted on the other side of town. As this was an unfamiliar area to him, he was worried about how to get there. He was also concerned about some other issues to do with taking the job, so he contacted his local social work team for help.

Application in practice

Leroy's overall aim was to take the new job, earn more money and meet some new people. He discussed his situation with the social worker, Vanessa, and together they identified what the problems and issues were. Leroy wanted the new job but was concerned about how he would get there and the cost of travel. He also raised concerns about his benefits possibly being affected.

They discussed the possibility of different forms of transport: train, bus, taxi and bike. After some discussion, Leroy decided using his bike was not an option due to the busy town centre route he would need to take. They then set out the tasks that needed doing to find out other essential information. Leroy lacked confidence in using the phone, so they agreed the tasks as follows. Leroy would go to the bus station, get a timetable and ask about bus routes and fares. He would also go to the local taxi company and find out fare costs.

Vanessa agreed to telephone the railway station about times and fares and ask the benefits adviser how the salary offered would affect Leroy's benefits. They agreed to meet up in a couple of days to consider the options again when they knew more facts about time and costs. They could also discuss any possible effects of earnings upon Leroy's benefits. They had set a time limit to the first set of tasks.

When they met up, both had achieved their set tasks and exchanged information. Consequently, Vanessa was able to advise Leroy that his benefits would not be affected under the therapeutic earnings regulations, but could be if he earned any more money. They also discussed transport and identified the bus as being the best form of direct transport at a cost within Leroy's budget.

Leroy decided to take the job. They both agreed the next task was to enable Leroy to learn the bus route as soon as possible. The community support team agreed to undertake this with him.

CASE STUDY TWO

Alan, a man in his forties, had a joint tenancy with a friend, Deirdrie. Alan had a history of mental ill health involving anxiety and depression. Alan felt lonely and realized he was having a problem establishing friendships. Alan asked his community psychiatric nurse, Bal, for support in joining a social club as he did not know where to start.

Application in practice

During further discussion of the issue, Alan had told Bal what he wanted was a girlfriend. Bal explained to Alan that he obviously could not arrange for him to meet a girlfriend. He could, however, arrange for someone to support Alan in attending local clubs. Then Alan could see what they were like and could meet new people. They looked in the local paper and library for possible clubs of interest for Alan to attend. They identified two that were potentially suitable within town. They agreed the next step was for Alan to go and see if he enjoyed himself and, if he did, the following step would be to look at how Alan could attend independently. Bal arranged support for Alan to attend both clubs for one month and then to jointly review the situation.

When this review took place it transpired that Alan had not enjoyed attending the clubs and doing so had caused him further anxiety and depression. Bal tried to find out exactly why attending these clubs had been unsuitable for Alan. Upon further discussion, Alan told Bal that he really thought he was gay and he did not feel he fitted into the clubs he had attended.

As Alan had not been open about thinking he was gay, the focus of the task centred work had been inappropriate. This had worsened his anxiety and compounded his depression. Bal had endeavoured to support Alan with the inaccurate information he had been given. Thus, whilst the step of attending the clubs had been achieved, it was not a success. Alan's hidden agenda had prevented the success of the task centred work.

Before any further work could take place Alan needed to restore his equilibrium. He needed further advice and information and to be able to discuss gay issues. He may have needed more specialist counselling to help him resolve issues around his sexuality. Differently focused task centred work to enhance Alan's social life could only take place when these other aspects had been addressed.

CONCLUSION

The effective use of a task centred approach has been reinforced through research studies (Reid and Hanrahan 1981). The emphasis underlying this approach is on partnership with the person being supported. This partnership should underpin all aspects of task centred practice (Marsh 1990). However, it should not be forgotten that the approach provides a minimal response to the severe social problems often found in society. These may include inadequate resources, funding restrictions, poverty and social inequality. Other theories may be used to complement task centred work and enhance understanding of the presenting situation in a more holistic way.

Key points

- A task centred approach can be used in many different care and support environments.

- Work is undertaken jointly with the person rather than on or for the individual.

- The emphasis is placed on the problem solving of issues that are important to the person being supported. If the problems are large they can often be broken down into smaller, more manageable tasks.

- People are more likely to achieve goals they have set themselves.

- Throughout the work the focus remains on the person concerned, the individual is central to the process and work is undertaken to meet his or her needs.

- The task centred process needs to be structured, time focused and reviewed regularly.

- The approach works on strengths not weaknesses and this supports confidence building and personal development.

- Task centred work provides only a minimal response to severe social problems such as lack of funding, poverty and social inequality. Other theories may need to be used to underpin practice challenging such issues.

ROLE THEORY

INTRODUCTION

What is meant by role and role theory? We will have our own interpretations of what a role is and what it means. It may be seen as a part that an actor will play, a specific action, or a function that is carried out by someone. It may be the part we see ourselves fulfilling within our family, with friends, in work or in society. All of these may be accurate and, when thought about, may provide some level of explanation about how we think someone should act, how we ourselves should act and, conversely, how we should not act.

A definition taken from a social work text that provides one explanation of a role is: 'Role. Expectations and obligations to behave in a particular way, arising from a recognised social position or status' (Thomas and Pierson 1996, p.331). This places into context that expectations and obligations play a part in how a role is perceived. The point to consider is, who places these expectations and obligations and why? With this in mind we will introduce role theory.

BACKGROUND TO ROLE THEORY

Much has been written about where role theory may have originated. Some writers support its background from a sociological perspective and others from a social psychological perspective. These different perspectives are recognized by Strean (1971) and Davis (in Turner 1986) for their contribution to explaining the theory in relation to social work. We will briefly examine the sociological and social psychological perspectives to enable these ideas to be placed in the context of social work and social care.

Ralph Linton (1893–1953) in Marshal (1996) carried out studies that looked at the possible links between the relationship of personality and society. These links examined how societies function and how this impacts on the culture of society. From these studies Linton pioneered the concepts of role and status; this has provided a basis from which to explore social systems. Status gives the place in the pecking order of society and role prescribes the expected behaviours and attitudes within it. Status and role are described as any form of patterns of relationship between different things or people and are regarded as each having their individual identities.

Role theory is also related to sociology by its association with structural-functional theory. This approach considers social structure and what position a person holds within society. The position the person holds could be seen as his or her role within that society. Different expectations of how people should act and what they should or should not do are maintained; this reflects or impacts on their position within society's structure. If this approach was considered in more depth it would show that roles are always influenced in the context of their relationship with the rest of society. The role that we follow appears to create our identity in society and, along with this, the way others react to us may reinforce our own idea of our identity. An example of this is the title of Doctor. It may be a Doctor of Medicine or a Doctor of Philosophy – very different roles; however, the title of Doctor specifies a role and can convey a stereotypical identity.

In social psychology role refers to the kind of behaviour expected of a given person in a given situation (Statt 1998). The idea of social interactions is important; they occur within a context that can influence how we act. Social interactions occur at all levels: a cultural level, environmental level, through social groups, family and friends. Each can have great relevance to how we act, what we say and what we do. To explain this further, a brief understanding of scripts may help. Schank and Abelson (1977) proposed that the majority of social action in which we engage is part of planned sequences. Everything is regulated and expected; this was likened by them to the script of a play. An example of this could be taken from a visit to a hospital. The bus driver, car park attendant, receptionist, nurse, doctor, consultant, other patients and friends may all be involved. The sequence of who should do what and when is quite familiar, although these people may be strangers to us. We would know roughly what to expect at any given point – how each person should behave – and a fairly logical process will be followed. This was the underpinning of Schank and Abelson's argument that all people involved act according to the same scripts and make social interaction run fairly smoothly. The concept of role then fits in with the expected scripts that we follow. We would play our role as others would play theirs.

Roles may develop from our own or others' expectations; this is where a role is ascribed as a result of circumstances. Examples of ascribed roles are: being a woman, a man or disabled. Other roles are attained by something we have done, such as becoming a singer, politician or teacher.

Having an understanding of these different explanations of roles will support appreciation of how they can be used to inform social work practice. During an ordinary day we usually play a number of different roles. These may include long-term roles, such as being a parent, partner in a relationship or a child. Alternatively, some of our roles may be very brief, passing ones, such as going on the bus as a passenger or speaking to a stranger. On some occasions the role may be temporary but on a longer term basis; examples of this could include being a student or spending time as a patient in hospital. Each one of the roles suggested would involve specific behaviours. How a person behaved talking to a stranger may be quite different to behaviour within the family. Whilst in hospital a person would probably act differently when talking to visitors than when talking to the consultant.

Social roles are always reciprocal; in other words, the role held is always in relationship to another person. Goffman (1959) suggested that as we play roles as part of our everyday social life they gradually become internalized until they become part of the self. When we take on a new role – for example, at college – initially it all seems very unreal but after a time we fit into the role more easily. We learn our roles in life and what we expect others' roles to be; this links into social learning as described by Bandura and Walters (1973) and Bandura (1977) (see also Chapter 8 for behavioural approaches).

The principles and background of role theory have been discussed, links to everyday life shown and links with differing theories covered. Next we will consider some different aspects of the theory. Case examples will be given that place the use of role theory into the context of social work and social care within the learning disabilities field.

Some explanations of role theory show it as a type of static view of society. Of course, the reality is that society changes over time, therefore roles change. There may not be universal agreement on what a specific role entails. It does not make allowances for strong feelings that do not fit within the expectations of the framework. To inform the dilemma of change, the concept of role set was developed. As discussed above, no role exists in isolation; a role set is a collection of roles that go together in a specific social situation. Within this situation a person may take on many of the roles that it includes. For example, being a parent may be one role but the person may also be a husband, wife or partner, wage earner, son or daughter, friend, member of a club or group – the list could go on. Thus the role of being a parent may be the focal role but, in addition, the other roles relate to it as part of the role set. Each role makes a demand on the focal role; this demand is called a sent role, and may influence expectations and behaviour.

A person is usually aware of his or her role as a parent, partner, employee or friend. Others may have the same expectations of this role, and this is described as a complementary role. Different expectations, such as the amount of time that should be spent in any particular role, the level of commitment and reliability in relation to the role, may cause role conflict. Role conflict is where there is a discrepancy between these different expectations. The most common and significant cause of this is a conflict between role senders. An example of role conflict and role senders can be considered by thinking about the difficulty a person might face in trying to reconcile the balance of expectations from a child, partner or employee. Ambiguity of the role may occur when there is uncertainty about what the role entails.

Dahrendorf identified three levels of obligations associated with any given role:

- must do – functions that are essential to the role; there are definite sanctions if these functions are not performed

- should do – functions that should be performed as part of the role, but the prospect of sanctions is not as strong if these functions are not performed

- can do – these are functions that can be performed as part of the role.

(Adapted from Dahrendort 1973)

The must do, should do and can do levels can be considered in identifying the role obligations of social workers or nurses. The role obligations are guided by relevant policy, procedures, and legislative framework. Conflicts may arise between role obligations and what individual roles, scripts and beliefs are.

It is important to be aware of the role conflicts people with learning disabilities may experience through the discrepancies of expectations of others. Pressure may be exerted through these expectations; an understanding of these factors enables the focus to remain on the person being supported and gives insight into the individual's situation. Without such insight it is possible to collude with others' role expectations and, instead of supporting the individual, such collusion may lead to his or her oppression.

These ideas indicate that some behaviour can be understood as role conflict and uncertainty, and takes in a social perspective on behaviour. This gives us a useful link between behavioural problems and social environments. We should be aware that roles do not exist solely as a part of the pattern of society but also as a method of understanding individuals. Role theory does not provide methods of working to support or change role conflict, but does support its identification.

Another area of consideration should be that of negotiated roles. This incorporates the idea that social roles are not predetermined. Role players interpret and negotiate their roles together. This is often a process of gradual accommodation and change. The accommodation of roles could apply to a person receiving care and support, the carer involved and family members. An implicit part of this approach is that all successful social interaction and communication depends upon the respective participants adopting complementary roles.

This section has aimed to provide an understanding of how role theory can inform support and care work. Links to some other theoretical perspectives have been made. Two case studies will now be described; both will show how an understanding of role theory could inform practice.

CASE STUDY ONE

Jess, a 22-year-old woman with learning disabilities, had lived for three years in a supported group home housing four people. She appeared happy and settled and, over time, had formed a particularly strong friendship with Donna, one of the other women living in the house. They travelled to college together and spent most of their spare time in each other's company. Jess was generally friendly, easy-going and tended to fit in with others.

Jess had part-time work in a local shop and through this work she met Phil, who regularly came into the shop with his father. After some weeks, Jess invited Phil to a party at her local community centre; later they started going out together more seriously as partners.

After a few weeks, Donna told her key worker that she did not like Phil coming to the house so much and complained about him using their food and drinks as if he lived there. At the same time Jess's parents asked for a meeting with Jess's key worker. They were concerned that Jess was always talking about Phil and that she would no longer visit her Granny with them at weekends as she used to, something they still wanted her to do.

Application in practice

Whilst Jess was going to work, college, and spending her spare time with Donna, no role conflicts arose. Her position in her social structure was clear and known. She was a good best friend, reliable and fun; she was also a good daughter spending time with her parents and visiting her Granny at weekends. These roles were complementary, with behaviour and expectation nicely balanced.

The role conflict arose when Jess took a more independent stand and wanted to have a relationship with Phil. She was then less apt to fit in, asserted her wishes more and there was inter-role conflict between being a best friend to Donna and partner to Phil, both of whom wanted her time. Donna experienced jealousy at having to share her best friend and she needed time to adjust to this.

Jess's parents, whilst having supported her to move on and live more independently, still held a role expectation of Jess as the dutiful daughter who spent time with them as a matter of course, and this role expectation certainly did not include Jess being a sexually active woman. Jess experienced intra-role conflict through the different set of expectations held by her parents and by herself for her role as daughter.

CASE STUDY TWO

Ghita and Prem lived in a small staffed hostel housing eight people and both were in their late twenties. Both Ghita and Prem were said to have a dual diagnosis of learning disabilities and mental health issues. Ghita was additionally labelled as having challenging behaviour. They had been in a relationship for a short time.

Prem was unable to work and did not participate in any activities outside the hostel. Ghita soon ceased of attending the local drop-in centre that she had been attending somewhat erratically. They rarely spent any time with other residents, opting out of communal mealtimes, and tending to get up late and watch television most of the day. Both Prem and Ghita's key workers were concerned about them. Their perception of Ghita and Prem was of them becoming more insular due to the lack of participation in any activities; the staff worried that they were not good for each other.

One day Ghita and Prem walked in to the office and announced they were going to be married. This was discussed with their key workers, neither of whom had positive thoughts about it. Indeed the key workers went as far as trying actively to dissuade the couple from marriage, pointing out their perception of the difficulties involved. They described some of these difficulties as Prem not understanding how Ghita's mental health affected her and the difficulties both would have in managing medication.

Ghita and Prem were adamant they would marry and asked staff to help them achieve this. The local community support team were contacted and a social worker came out to see Ghita and Prem. The social worker recognized Ghita and Prem's rights to both marriage and independent living in their own style. The social worker's perspective was different from that of hostel key workers and staff. Much negotiation was undertaken by the social worker representing Ghita and Prem's interests to effect the necessary changes that would enable them to move out and marry.

Application in practice

The role expectations of the key workers then were that Ghita and Prem were in the hostel as they required a high level of support. They should behave as individual residents maintaining the status quo as it worked well enough and it did not stop them enjoying a sexual relationship. Ghita and

Prem were thus dependent upon the staff. The roles that Ghita and Prem wished to attain were those of a married couple living independently without staff telling them what to do or having to discuss each issue as it arose, however therapeutic the staff deemed this to be.

The intra-role conflict occurred between behaviour the staff expected of Ghita and Prem's position within their social structure and Ghita and Prem's ideas of their position and the possibilities for change. The hostel staff did not wish to hold Ghita and Prem back from marriage through malice, but feared their independence leading to isolation would in turn lead to deterioration of their mental health. In a sense they had accepted the labels given to Ghita and Prem. Thus, staff perpetuated their dependence without recognizing their potential for change, given the right knowledge and support, and their rights as individuals to consent to marry.

CONCLUSION

The advantage of using role theory is that its general principles can easily be understood and can therefore be applied in a wide context. Again, the importance of not seeing an individual theory as the only way of explaining a situation has been suggested. Role theory can be used to offer insight and clarity and help explain the impact and differences of roles that people may have as part of the systems surrounding them.

Key points

- Role theory is a way of understanding and gaining insight, not a method of working.

- Role theory is relatively straightforward to understand and to use.

- Role theory can be used with other theories as an additional way of helping to inform practice.

- Insight into particular behaviours may be gained through consideration of roles and role theory.

- A person's role, real or perceived, can help explain his or her position within society.

- Role theory can provide a useful and flexible approach that may offer insight into people and their situations.

CRISIS INTERVENTION

INTRODUCTION

To enable a focus on crisis intervention we will use the following definition: 'An attempt to understand the nature of episodes that people find extremely difficult or impossible to handle, and to understand how services might be organised to help people through such events' (Thomas and Pierson 1996, p.98). Who is in crisis, the person, staff, service or funders? The word 'crisis' is often used to describe a situation that is stressful or urgent. If someone is supported whilst in a stressed or urgent state the work undertaken is not necessarily crisis intervention. To claim the application of any particular theory there is a need to use the principles and techniques underpinning that theory. This provides a framework against which the actions used can be judged and measured. Therefore, understanding the principles of crisis intervention is important in order to know how the theory can be used successfully.

The theoretical principles of crisis intervention are explained in this section. We will explore the background of crisis intervention and, by doing so, aim to provide insight into the approach. Crisis intervention can be a valuable way of explaining and working with a given situation. However, on its own it does not provide a full explanation of how to support a client during a period of crisis. Other theoretical perspectives can additionally be used to inform working approaches that will enable individuals to move on from a crisis. Links to other such relevant theories and their use in crisis work will be highlighted. The case studies at the end of this section will demonstrate the use of crisis intervention in practice.

WHAT IS CRISIS INTERVENTION?

A study carried out in 1944 by Lindemann looked at the grief reactions of patients. He particularly focused on people suffering from the 'Coconut Grove fire in Boston' (Lindemann 1944). Lindemann found that the patients who handled the situation best were those who had managed and fully resolved challenges in the past.

Researching why some people dealt with severe challenges well and others not so well led a group of mental health workers to develop ideas about how people fall into crisis. Often the crisis occurred when coping or problem solving capacities became overwhelmed. Lindemann (1944) and Caplan (1965) worked towards developing ideas of how crisis can be minimized and ideally prevented and, when crisis has already occurred, how a satisfactory resolution can be achieved.

Crisis intervention additionally uses some elements of other theories in its underpinning. The principles of ego-psychology from a psychodynamic perspective can be used. This perspective focuses on people's emotional response to external events such as a crisis and their ability to deal with this rationally. Crisis intervention theory concerns itself with failures in people's capacity to effectively manage problems and challenges in life. Ideas found in systems theory such as homeostasis and equilibrium can be used in the understanding of crisis intervention.

CRISIS INTERVENTION IN CARE AND SUPPORT WORK

Crisis intervention is often used as a loose description in a variety of circumstances when care and support is required. Just because support is required it does not necessarily mean that there is a crisis. A number of important principles and techniques used in social work intervention in emergencies have been described by O'Hagen (1986, 1991, 1994).

> Crisis intervention is minimal intervention which seeks to achieve the maximum and optimum effect. Its focus of aim may be ruthlessly confined, yet its goals are nothing short of revolutionary. These are: 'to replace blind ugly passion with enlightenment and tolerance, chaos and panic with order and safety, helplessness and despair with a sense of hope'. (O'Hagen in Lishman 1994, p.155)

Golan offers a formulated approach to explain the fundamentals of crisis intervention theory. Specific key words are used by Golan in explaining each step of a crisis. These key words are placed in context as follows:

1.   A crisis begins with major problems or a series of difficulties. These are described as 'hazardous events'. These events may be 'anticipated', such as moving house. Alternatively, events may be 'unanticipated', such as sudden death, redundancy, flood or other disaster.

2.   These events pose a challenge to the ability of a person to cope competently. 'Equilibrium', the intellectual or emotional balance, is challenged.

3.   When 'equilibrium' is lost a person may enter a 'vulnerable state'.

4.   When 'equilibrium' is unbalanced, regular problem solving methods are used to deal with the problems. If these methods do not work, the person needs to find new ways of problem solving.

5.   However, if the problem solving does not work, tension and stress is suffered, increasing the state of vulnerability.

6.   If a major new challenge occurs when in a 'vulnerable state', this is known as a 'precipitating factor'. If this occurs a state of 'active crisis' may develop. This is when problem solving capabilities are overwhelmed.

(Adapted from Golan 1978)

In life, most people are in the position that a major single event or series of small events may prove too much to handle and become unmanageable. It is important to remember that it is not the event itself that is the crisis, but the inability of the person to manage the event. It is the reaction of the individual to these events that determines whether there is a crisis or not. An event that precipitates crisis for one person will not necessarily do so for another. It is the individual's perception of the event and its meaning for them that will determine whether the situation becomes a crisis or not.

Golan (1978) suggests that the more problems that have been successfully managed and dealt with in the past, the better the coping strategies available to meet new challenges. By developing these new coping strategies, the likelihood of active crisis occurring in the future diminishes. If there are unresolved problems from the past, then the person is more likely to find it difficult to cope with hazardous events and thus fall into crisis.

USING CRISIS INTERVENTION IN PRACTICE

When using crisis intervention in practice there are several aspects to consider. A crisis to one person will rarely be the same as a crisis to another. Whatever the situation, it is important to be able to promptly recognize a crisis or hazardous event and take into account its effect upon the person. To minimize the impact of the crisis and work towards resolution, support mechanisms need to be able to respond quickly and intensely.

It is also important to consider cultural issues and religious perspectives when working with someone in crisis. Different cultures may have their own particular ways of dealing with a situation: how care is provided, coping with separation or death, mourning, admitting help is needed. Sometimes what is seen in a particular situation may not provide a clear representation of what has actually happened or is happening to a person from outside. Further exploration may be required to avoid misinterpretation.

In describing aspects of Hindu death and mourning rituals, Firth says:

> For 12 days, chairs are removed from the living room and sheets spread on the floor. The bereaved relatives sit on the floor to receive the condolences of the relatives, friends and neighbours who pour into the house. Their ascetic lifestyle, sleeping on the floor, eating simple food, and having only religious music, reflects their liminal status, as they are dead to the ordinary world... (Firth 1997 in Hockey, Katz and Small 2001, p.241)

In thinking about this example it would be easy for a person outside the Hindu community, without knowledge of Hindu custom and ritual, to misunderstand or misinterpret what was happening within such a household if a visit was made during these 12 days of mourning. Careful consideration of what is happening and working closely with the person and others involved is critical.

Golan (1978) identified some key issues surrounding the support procedure during a crisis. People in crisis are often more open to being supported than those who are not in crisis. Their normal coping mechanisms have broken down and the feeling of desperation may be made easier by accepting help. Intervention in a crisis is more likely to be successful than intervention offered at other times, especially as the person wants the support. Crises often resolve themselves for better or worse in six to eight weeks; this gives a very limited amount of time to provide effective, intensive support.

It would be easy to take control of the situation and try to resolve the crisis for the person concerned. Sometimes this may be appropriate, for example, in the case of children, someone with profound disabilities or severe disruption to an individual's mental health. As always, when working in a situation that encompasses an anti-discriminatory and anti-oppressive approach, it is critical to consider methods of working. The supporter of the person in crisis needs to identify the most empowering and least restrictive way to manage the situation. Even in a crisis there is a need to work with the person throughout the situation; the more the person is actively involved, the more his or her skills can be developed for future personal management in stressful situations.

There may be barriers that restrict verbal communication – the person's understanding of the situation may prove difficult. Medication can also limit active involvement in some situations by affecting concentration or disturbing the thought process. These limiting factors need to be identified and a strategy of working developed which recognizes them.

In addition to crisis intervention, a systems theory approach can be used – working with other people that know the individual well. This may provide valuable insight into the person's life, his or her methods of communicating, and the skills and support networks involved. This information could be of benefit during the initial crisis support and in the subsequent planning of care. It is important to be open minded and to maintain the central focus of approach upon the person being supported.

There are several aspects that support successful crisis intervention. These include recognizing emotional distress, how a person responds to crisis and any changes in his or her ability to manage everyday problems. Crisis intervention uses practical tasks to help a person to readjust to the changing situation. Ultimately, this should lead to the adaptation of individual coping strategies for future use.

The main tasks in successfully finding resolution of crisis have been suggested by Golan (1978) as: 'Correct cognitive perception…, manage feelings…, developing new coping behaviours' (Golan 1978). When a person is in crisis various interpretations may be made of the situation. People in crisis need to gain a clearer and more accurate view of the events that have affected them. This will enable them to have a better understanding of what has really happened – an initial step in dealing with any crisis.

The management of feelings can be a difficult process. People who are in crisis may need to release extreme emotions and this needs to be recognized. Being empathetic and trying not to restrict such emotional release can be difficult, but is important. When someone is in the middle of an overwhelming situation, asking them not to cry or get upset may not be helpful. There is a fine balance between supporting someone to calm down in order to start to look logically at their situation, and restricting the individual from the benefit of emotional release.

Coping behaviours learnt in each situation can be used in the future. Care and support workers should enable the person to explore new ways of dealing with the crisis and of developing coping strategies. Opportunities need to be provided for the person to work through the options available to enable the way forward.

Other theories can be used in helping people move on from a crisis. Earlier, we briefly discussed the use of systems theory and the people and systems that surround the person. Systems theory can be used to form a holistic picture of the person's life and to provide additional information to enhance work with the individual. The task centred approach can also be a useful method of working when trying to progress from the crisis. The identification of specific tasks for the individual to undertake can be a positive way of managing anxiety and increasing self-esteem. The section on the task centred approach provides further insight into its use. Counselling may be beneficial to the person, depending on the nature of the crisis and the person's ability to make an informed choice to have counselling. A psychodynamic approach can, in some cases, support a person by exploring in more depth how a particular situation was arrived at. Gaining insight through a psychodynamic approach can enable a coping strategy to be developed for future use.

Crisis intervention will now be placed into a practice context with the following case studies.

CASE STUDY ONE

Christine, a woman in her late forties, had lived as a tenant in a housing association flat for five years. Christine had worked for over ten years at a local sheltered workshop and enjoyed this. She was able to cope with the pace of work and had formed a strong friendship group with the other workers there. Christine usually visited her family on Sundays and on special occasions. She was also supported by twice weekly visits from members of the local community support team. During these visits she was able to discuss issues of concern and gain support with budgeting, housekeeping and other areas as she felt necessary.

In the previous two years Christine had got into debt of over £1500. This debt was through taking out a loan on behalf of her partner, Darrell, to help him buy a car. Darrell had only made a couple of repayments to Christine when he found himself a job in another town and moved away unexpectedly, without leaving a forwarding address. Christine did not know how she would repay the loan or how to deal with the debt. She had kept these worries to herself for some time. Matters became worse as she then got into rent arrears. Christine eventually told her mother about this, who contacted the community support team.

Christine had experienced much upset and stress through the loss of her relationship with Darrell. She had also feared being put in prison due to her debt. Through this she had suffered a loss of confidence in her ability to cope living alone in the community. Having been able to discuss the situation, Christine said she felt better and, with support, was able to sort out her threatened tenancy and other financial affairs. She arranged to pay off her debt in a manageable way. Christine still felt quite lonely and continued to miss Darrell.

At this point, Christine and the other workers were informed that the sheltered workshop was to cease trading and would be closed down. They were told that all workers would be made redundant. Christine became upset and then withdrawn. She stayed at home in her flat crying most of the time and gave up visiting friends and family.

Application in practice

Before being told of her imminent redundancy, Christine had already experienced a loss of equilibrium through Darrell's leaving her and through her subsequent debt. She had entered a vulnerable state with these events. On her own she had not been able to fully solve these problems and had suffered tension and stress. After a time and with intervention, she had found encouragement and advice from her family and support workers that had enabled her to find resolutions to these problems. Christine had restored her equilibrium but remained somewhat vulnerable.

The announcement of the closure of the sheltered workshop, and that she was to be made redundant, was the major event and precipitating factor that caused an active crisis for Christine. This was about the loss of her way of life, about her role and purpose and the potential loss of support systems that surrounded her at the sheltered workshop. Christine was unable to cope with the prospect of this event. Her problem solving capabilities became overwhelmed. Christine was not managing her feelings and regular coping mechanisms were not working for her. Christine needed further support to enable her to work through the active crisis towards a satisfactory resolution.

CASE STUDY TWO

Jason, a young man with learning disabilities, had lived with his parents, two sisters and grandfather in the family home all his life. Jason generally found changes in his life quite difficult. At 19 years old, Jason had just finished the transition of moving from school to college, which had not been an easy process for him, when his grandfather unexpectedly died. He had been very close to his grandfather, who had been his main carer since childhood, and was devastated by his death.

Jason's usual easy-going behaviour altered; he had angry outbursts both at home and in public and at times became aggressive towards others. Jason kept asking where his grandfather was – his parents did their best to explain to him but seemed unable to get him to understand. This was not helped by having to cope with their own grief. A week after the bereavement, and the day before the funeral, Jason refused to leave the college classroom to return home and sat with head in hands. The staff were concerned about Jason and wished to support him in his loss, and thus contacted Jason's social worker.

Jason's social worker first listened to him and gave him time to express his grief and cry. She spent the immediate time listening to Jason and asking questions to clarify the situation, and a little later took him home. In the short term, she arranged to see him the next day and subsequently made a plan with him and his family about how to manage the next few weeks. In the longer term, she arranged a strategy in consultation with Jason for him to have specialist bereavement counselling to help him better understand and come to terms with his loss.

With the support of his family, friends, college staff and the counselling, Jason was able to work through his bereavement and in time come to terms with his grandfather's death. Two years later, Della, a friend of Jason's from childhood, became terminally ill and he was told about this. Through the experience of his grandfather's death, Jason had learnt some ways of dealing with bereavement and therefore had more personal resources to think about and deal with this subsequent event.

Application in practice

When Jason was undergoing the transition from school to college, he found this change difficult, his equilibrium was challenged and he entered a vulnerable state. Over the time of the transition, Jason found ways of adjusting to the new situation but was not yet comfortable with it. It was at this stage that his grandfather's unexpected death became the precipitating factor that pushed Jason into active crisis.

Over the days, Jason was not able to make sense of his loss and, when his grandfather did not return as he so fervently hoped he would, he became overwhelmed. In her intervention, his social worker asked Jason what had happened and then listened to his explanation. She gave him time to express his feelings and acknowledged how difficult it must be for him. She then asked him what help he would most like. Jason was able to identify being afraid of and yet wanting to attend the funeral. He also said he wanted help with certain activities that had been habitually supported by his grandfather.

Together they then drew up an initial plan with achievable tasks which enabled Jason to take back some of the control that he felt he had lost. The first task the social worker agreed to undertake was to discuss the whole situation with Jason's family, which she did when she took him home. A more detailed explanation of what would happen at the funeral was made to Jason, and one sister said she would take special care in supporting his attendance.

Jason and the social worker agreed to have weekly meetings over a six week period where tasks were identified and agreed. Through this process he was able to begin to adapt to the situation and find alternative strategies and support mechanisms to cope with life without his grandfather. In the longer term, the bereavement counselling was an additional support mechanism that enabled further growth and adaptation on Jason's part.

When the sad news of his friend's terminal illness was made known to Jason, he had some knowledge of death and some resources to draw upon. He had learned through the experience of his grandfather's death new ways of handling such a difficult situation and of adaptation over time. Jason was able to express his sadness to Della and her family and to visit her several times. Later he dealt with her death with great sadness, but without becoming overwhelmed by the event or it becoming a crisis for him.

CONCLUSION

It is critical to identify who, or what, is in crisis and how best to work with this. O'Hagen (1994) clearly identifies the risk in trying to rescue people in crisis. A structured plan is required and a methodical approach beneficial. It is important not to jump in and undertake a rescue of the person. Instead, there is a need to work with the person, supporting the individual throughout the recovery process. This can be achieved by working at the person's speed, using the individual's preferred communication methods and by using theory to inform practice. When work is undertaken with someone who is in active crisis and unable to manage, the use of crisis intervention may be beneficial. It is also important to evaluate how the person will be enabled to develop mechanisms and skills to cope.

Crisis work is demanding and the workers involved often need to commit themselves to being available during the following days to give adequate support. This can be intensive and time consuming, but if carried out effectively should achieve the best possible result for the person.

Key points

- Consideration of who is actually in crisis needs to be made, whether it is the person being supported, someone else such as the staff team or the service or organization.

- Crisis intervention can be a valuable way of explaining and working within a given situation. However, on its own it does not provide a full structure of how to support a person during a crisis.

- Other theoretical perspectives can be used to help inform ways of providing care and support for a person when they are in crisis, such as task centred work.

- Crisis intervention is not about rescuing a person but providing a structured and methodical support process.

- There are formulated approaches that can be used to help understand each step of a crisis.

- The more problems a person is able to work through and resolve during a crisis, the better the person's coping strategies will be for future situations (Golan 1978).

- Crisis intervention is provided through a quick, intensive response and only really works over a short period of time.

10

Society's Influences on Practice

INTRODUCTION

In this chapter, we will explore some of the influences that society can have on the provision of care and support – influences that can affect groups within society, including people with learning disabilities. The influences to be explored are from three specific areas: sociology, social policy and legislation.

We will start by looking at sociological development and the structure of society and go on to consider how these can influence care and support. The way that care provision has developed and how the care role is perceived will be explored in the context of today's society. In the second section, we will briefly look at social policy and political development. This will focus on the impact of Governmental power, some policies that are on the political agenda and the consequent money and resources available to meet care and support needs. The third section will focus on legislation, policy and proce-dure. These can be both supportive and controlling, either in promoting or restricting care provision. There is a legislative framework that provides guidance to care provision; however, it is not always straightforward and as-pects of this will be explored.

In looking at the influences of society, sociology lends insight into the position of people with learning disabilities within society, how this minor-ity group has been oppressed and discriminated against, and why this may occur. Through the development of social policy and legislation, ways of challenging oppression and discrimination have evolved and, in part, been implemented. Whilst such challenges go towards positive change, their aims are not always fully achieved in practice. From our brief exploration, full jus-tice to these influences cannot be accomplished. Our aim, however, is to raise awareness of the influence of society on people with learning disabilities.

This basic understanding then enables further thinking about some of the issues involved.

Issues from each section will be illustrated using two case studies.

SOCIOLOGICAL PERSPECTIVES

INTRODUCTION

Sociology is a vast and well documented discipline and in this section we intend to consider some of its aspects and their relation to practice. Initially, we will mention some of the people and perspectives that have had a major influence on the development of sociological explanations. This will be followed by some of the sociological concepts and models that can help inform or support understanding of the influence of society on the people who live within it. As mentioned in the chapter introduction, this is a theoretical perspective that can inform us about the structure and aspects of society, but does not provide a hands-on approach to practice.

We aim to consider how society's perception of an individual's place and position in the world may affect his or her life. The understanding of sociological perspectives, and how they can inform practice when working with people with learning disabilities, will be reinforced through two case studies.

SOCIOLOGY: THEORIES AND PERSPECTIVES

Sociology can be defined as 'the study of social structures and different life experiences of individuals within those social structures' (Thomas and Pierson 1996, p.359). One aspect of sociological study focuses on the different life experiences of people within social structures. Social influences that can affect social structures may include, for example, social class, gender and race. Explanations of society differ according to the perspective taken.

Haralambos and Holburn (1993) and Jones (1996), for example, provide in-depth explanations of many of the key people and sociological perspectives that have played a major part in the development and understanding of sociology as a discipline. We will mention three of the key people often quoted in sociological texts:

- Emile Durkheim (1858–1917): theory of functionalism.

- Karl Marx (1818–1913): theory of materialism/Marxism.

- Max Weber (1864–1920): theory of social action; Verstehen, theory of actors.

(Adapted from Jones 1996)

The majority of sociological theories have been developed in parallel with a changing society over a number of years. Even so, many theories can still provide insight and understanding into aspects of today's society. There are many different sociological theories and approaches, some of which are: structuralist, interpretive, structuration, postmodernism and feminism. Each theory provides its own explanation of society, structures and the people within them.

A structuralist approach is one method of understanding society. 'A "Structuralist" approach *emphasizes* the importance of social structure, and *minimizes* the importance of the actions of individuals in society' (Haralambos and Holburn 1993, p.151). Structuralism, as a general term, refers to any sociological approach which considers and regards social structure. The approach suggests that social structures influence society more than social action does. Two theoretical approaches that further explore a structuralist perspective are: functionalism (for example, Auguste Comte 1798–1857 Herbert Spencer 1820–1903) and conflict theory (for example, Karl Marx 1974).

> Functionalists stress the extent to which the different elements of the social structure fit together harmoniously. Marxists stress the lack of fit between the different parts, particularly social classes, and so emphasize the potential for social conflict. (Haralambos and Holburn 1993, p.765)

Different explanations can be found through the views of an interpretive methodology. One such explanation is:

> ...interpretive perspectives usually reject the view that society has a clear structure which directs individuals to behave in certain ways...sociologists need to understand and interpret human behaviour and discover the meanings that lie behind it. (Haralambos and Holburn 1993, p.795)

Interpretive methodologies include an interactionist approach (for example, George Herbert Mead 1863–1931 in Marshal 1996, p.318) and phenomenology, (for example, Alfred Schutz 1899–1959).

The two sociological perspectives of structuralism and interpretation, were drawn together to inform the development of structuration (Anthony Giddens 1976, 1979, 1984).

> Giddens claims that structure and action are two sides of the same coin. Neither structure nor action can exist independently; both are intimately related. Social actions create structures, and it is through social actions that structures are produced and reproduced... (Haralambos and Holburn 1993, p.815)

Thus, structuration proposes that the actions of individuals and the social structure cannot be separated.

Other explanations can be found by studying work such as post-modernism (for example, Foucault 1973) and feminism (for example, Poland 1990). There are many other combinations of ideas that contribute to the overall discipline of sociology.

The feminist perspective is useful to consider as it can help to focus on groups disempowered within society. The perspective focuses on how more power has been given to men than women in society. This power imbalance happens within many social institutions, such as the family, education, the law and the media. A feminist understanding provides insight into the many issues that can affect individuals or groups of people marginalized by society's attitudes to them. Feminist sociologists have aimed to achieve a balanced method of study and research that does not duplicate the power imbalance inherent in social structures. Feminist sociology has contributed to highlighting the multiple interpretations and interests that should be considered when trying to understand any social situation. People are often discriminated against as members of minority groups; for example, when labelled as learning disabled. Further discrimination can occur for women with learning disabilities. The feminist perspective can be useful when considering oppression and discrimination within the learning disabilities field.

The perspectives discussed are examples of different sociological theories. Consideration and use of such perspectives can highlight the relevance of sociology to care and support work. The changing political and societal structures may have an ongoing effect on the care and support of people with learning disabilities. The evaluation of people's positions in society, their views, the structures that affect them and how this may impact upon them can, in part, be informed through sociological analysis.

Sociology is a scientific discipline (Haralambos and Holburn 1993). Sociological research and studies can be carefully and fully checked and re-tested by others. This process is used to make certain that a piece of work is going to make a genuine contribution to the overall sociological knowledge base, and validates the effectiveness of sociology. Although sociology is a scientific discipline, it is also a discursive one; it examines people's understanding and experiences of the world.

In social and health care for people with learning disabilities, the support provided should encompass, or at least consider, the major aspects that affect life. Such aspects referred to could include home life, work, leisure, health and care needs. An encompassing view of care could be considered as providing care and support for the whole person. Each individual piece of care may be specific, but should be looked at within the context of the whole care. Without this overall view, one piece of work may conflict with another and do a disservice. A holistic approach supports and promotes partnership and joint working and provides the underpinning for anti-discriminatory and anti-oppressive work. Care provision is often complex and many different people play a part in it. Each care provider may impact upon and influence the person receiving care. To an extent this may also influence society's views on how people are perceived, where they are perceived to be in the hierarchy of society and how they are accepted (Haralambos and Holburn 1993).

SOCIOLOGY INFORMING PRACTICE

Sociology provides an explanation that helps to inform and illustrate the individual's place in the world: where a person is within the hierarchy of society, what a person does and how the person is viewed. Additionally, sociological studies can provide an explanation of a variety of issues:

- culture and society
- culture and behaviour
- socialization
- norms and values
- status and role
- theories of society
- views of human behaviour.

(Adapted from Haralambos and Holburn 1993)

Understanding society's influences helps to provide a different perspective from some other theories in this book. However, being aware of society's influences does not remove the moral judgements and discrimination found within society. What it can provide is a tool to identify specific influences that may affect a person's social situation – influences affecting behaviour, beliefs and attitudes on both the part of the worker and the person being cared for and supported.

In looking at the wider picture when identifying how a person manages his or her everyday life, it is possible to challenge and move on from some assumptions and expectations held within society and its structures. Detachment helps workers to stand back, reflect and evaluate the value of the care and support they contribute. Reflection and evaluation could include aspects such as culture, race, gender and ability. If a person or group of people differ from the majority, their part within society is still relevant when considering how society operates. These aspects are all part of the concept of the social phenomenon of society.

SOCIAL PHENOMENON

Human beings need to eat and sleep, need to have warmth and shelter and can make use of some, if not all, senses: sight, hearing, touch, taste and smell. People undertake tasks and do specific things for social, cultural, economic, political and psychological reasons. These are fundamental and occur throughout the world but are not always carried out in the same way. The above factors play a part in social phenomenon. Each area of social phenomenon such as culture, economics and politics can be studied.

Sociology endeavours to undertake study at a holistic level and tries to take account of the fullest possible explanation of human behaviour. Studies may inform us of many different aspects of a person within society and explain why the person may not be accepted. Although sociology helps to identify the issues, it does not in itself solve the problem being faced. However, if the problem is identified, it can be acknowledged and social and political solutions worked towards. An awareness of the impact of society on people with learning disabilities starts to provide an underpinning of how areas of oppression and discrimination can be challenged, minimized or eradicated.

To enable an understanding of social problems there is a need to carry out informed, thorough and objective analysis of the related issues. From this we begin to understand where views, attitudes, prejudices and emotions originate. It also helps to identify how people with learning disabilities have come to be in the positions that they are within society. A basic question that can be asked to help inform a situation is: 'What is happening here?' Additional questions could then be asked in order to think more widely. Such questions could include:

- What behaviour is taking place and why?
- Who or what are the influences on the situation?
- What are the gender, age, culture and race issues?
- How are people relating to each other?

By asking such questions, the effect these aspects have on the situation can be thought about. Then direct action, support or influence on a change of policy or way of working can be made. The questions and observations undertaken can be considered within the theoretical framework that informs sociologists – the framework in which observations, experience and interpretations of society are made.

EVALUATING SOCIOLOGY AND ITS USES

There are some points to consider when using sociological theory to inform practice. The diversity and abstract nature of sociology, combined with its particular terminology, can make it complex. Sociology exists to explain society, it does not provide clear and structured solutions to society's problems. The explanations can provide us with an understanding to help inform and achieve social reform and develop supportive social policies. (Social policy development can be studied in more detail in the next section of this chapter.)

From our brief exploration of some aspects of sociology we hope to have shown that, by understanding the influence of society and by looking at various interpretations, it is possible to think more widely about the position of people with learning disabilities in society and how they are perceived. Two case studies will now be used to illustrate how sociological understanding can help inform day to day practice.

CASE STUDY ONE

Serena lived in supported community living and attended her local college. As part of her college course, Serena had work experience two days per week at a local garden centre. She enjoyed this work and was able to complete most of the different tasks involved.

After a few months of her work experience, a part-time job became available at the garden centre and Serena applied for this post. She was unsuccessful in her application and was told that as she was not able to complete all the tasks necessary, she had not been appointed. The job had been given to a man.

Application in practice

From a feminist perspective looking at disempowered groups in society, Serena was affected as a woman with learning disabilities. She had proved a steady and reliable worker, but not good enough to be taken on as a paid worker. Both her learning disability and her gender proved a negative influence upon her employment. There was an expectation about the role of the garden centre worker and the need to be fit and strong. Whilst Serena fulfilled these expectations, other perceptions of her prevailed. Prior knowledge of her learning disability, and the few tasks she was unable to undertake, had also influenced the decision not to employ her.

There had not been any thought given to the structure of the organization and how it disempowered Serena as a potential paid worker. Had minimal organizational changes and small alterations to job allocation been considered, then these would have enabled Serena to realistically compete for, and satisfactorily carry out, the job.

CASE STUDY TWO

Okolie lived in supported housing and held a joint tenancy with his friend Addy. He was able to use the local shops and some nearby facilities. Okolie was unable to use public transport on his own. He therefore had to rely on others to transport and accompany him or he had to pay for taxi fares. After some months of living in supported housing, Okolie was introduced to a befriender, Alfred, who he met with once a week and who supported him in accessing leisure activities in the community.

On Friday evenings, Okolie regularly attended and enjoyed a leisure club, all of whose members had learning disabilities. He travelled there by minibus along with other group members. Okolie also enjoyed model making. Having been befriended by Alfred, Okolie was able to join a club for model makers and go there in Alfred's car.

Application in practice

Despite living in a flat in the community, there were still some barriers to Okolie's social inclusion. There was the barrier of his being unable to use public transport leading to frequent use of minibuses along with other people. This could be seen to reinforce the stereotypical image of people with learning disabilities going out and travelling in groups. It could also be seen to strengthen the perception, held by many in society, that people with learning disabilities prefer to be with others with learning disabilities.

Before being befriended by Alfred, Okolie had not known to ask about, and was unaware of, other leisure groups and clubs in his locality. The social structures he lived within were the ones he knew or had been told about. Through his friendship with Alfred, further social structures were opened up to him. Okolie was enabled to attend the club for model makers, and through this social interaction was perceived positively by group members. This in turn had a positive effect upon the perception by some members of society of the skills and abilities of people with learning disabilities. If looked at in terms of structuration both the social structure and the actions of individuals had influence on Okolie's situation.

CONCLUSION

Some of the sociological theories discussed may appear to relate to practice more readily than others. Sociological theories that deal with interpersonal relationships on a small scale may seem more pertinent to individual experiences. On the other hand, sociology that looks at the large-scale social structures may appear removed from the hands-on support for people with learning disabilities. Both small- and large-scale perspectives can help to identify differences of power, inequality and the constraints of society. Their relevance to everyday practice, and to issues such as inclusion and exclusion, may give useful insights and provide a focus for action.

Key points

- Various writers have influenced the sociological understanding of society; their ideas differ, but the majority try to provide an explanation of social structures and the people within them.

- Some sociological concepts can offer explanations and inform understanding of the impact of society upon people with learning disabilities.

- Sociological concepts can also help identify and increase understanding of an individual's place in the world.

- Social phenomena occur throughout the world but may vary due to culture, economics and political reasons.

- A feminist perspective is very useful when considering disempowered groups within society.

- Although sociology exists to explain society, it does not provide clear and structured solutions to society's problems.

- Sociology does not provide a hands-on approach to working with people with learning disabilities; however, it informs us about the structure of the society in which we live.

SOCIAL POLICY

INTRODUCTION

In this section, we will explore some of the issues surrounding social policy. Governmental policy in the area of social welfare, policy development and policy implementation may not necessarily be fully understood by support and care workers. However, the ability to analyse the impact of policy either directly or indirectly on people with learning disabilities can prove useful. Social policy affects so much: education, health, housing, benefits and social services. An understanding of the different perspectives of political parties can offer some explanations of how social policy develops. This section aims to provide a brief outline of social policy; it is not intended to explore specific polices. However, the principles of policies and how they may influence resources and support work with people with learning disabilities will be considered. Case studies highlighting the influence of social policy will be used.

BACKGROUND TO SOCIAL POLICY

In Chapter 2 a brief outline of the process of policy making was given. No further exploration will be made here into the process of policies becoming legislation. However, we will consider the social and political influences on policies that have been part of the creation of the welfare state over the past 50 years. Through this, an understanding of the development of social policy and its influence upon today's society will be provided.

Social policy is described as 'government policy in the area of welfare, and the academic study of its development, implementation and impact' (Thomas and Pierson 1996, p.350). The study of governmental policies through political science and public administration played its part in the development of social policy studies. The Government's involvement in the creation of policies, how they are implemented and their impact on individuals and society, are key to understanding social policy.

The Government played a role in pre-Second World War welfare with some involvement in pensions, state education and hospital care. However, the creation of the active welfare state is more associated with the post war period (Alcock 1996). We will initially explore some aspects of the development of the welfare state. This may appear a basic explanation of the developing social welfare system; however, it is written as a brief introduction to the concept.

A BRIEF OVERVIEW OF THE WELFARE STATE

There have been many studies about social welfare over the last one hundred years or so (for example, Midwinter 1994; Page and Silburn 1999). In this section we will briefly explore its development from the 1940s. During the Second World War there were great changes in the labour market with many men going to war and many women taking over work that was previously occupied by males. In 1942 the Beveridge Report was completed as an official report of the wartime committee for social insurance. The report, called *Social Insurance and Allied Services*, can still be seen as influencing the foundation of welfare services of today.

Beveridge identified five specific areas that needed to be tackled to provide a greater level of equality within society. The five areas identified were:

- Want.
- Disease.
- Ignorance.
- Squalor.
- Idleness.

It was proposed that the issue of want be addressed by introducing and developing a system of income maintenance – the development of a social insurance scheme that would help to support people unable to work through unemployment, sickness or through retirement. The payments would be a flat rate and financed through insurance payments, and additional support would be provided for wives and dependent children. Other proposed benefits included maternity, widows' and death grants. It was recognized that not everyone would be in a position to pay into the insurance scheme, so a means tested option would be required to provide a safety net. Beveridge made other proposals to combat the five areas he identified as problematic in society. The aims were to eliminate poverty, eliminate family poverty, promote people to work, provide comprehensive health care and avoid mass unemployment.

Many of Beveridge's proposals were implemented in the following years. The Family Allowance Act 1945, National Insurance Act 1946 and the National Assistance Act 1948 all came into force. The Government, however, rejected some of the overall proposals; for example:

- pensions being phased in over 20 years

- unemployment benefit being paid indefinitely in preference to a one year limit

- payment of benefit to people on separation from marriage.

These changes all created a greater dependency on the means tested benefit system. National Assistance was also claimed by many people to help with housing costs. People with long-term health needs and disabilities were also dependent on means tested benefits and have in reality continued to be treated as a disadvantaged group within society (Williams 1989). Beveridge's proposals reflected the majority patriarchal values of the time. As time has progressed, changing values, views and structures within society have caused Beveridge's proposals to be less satisfactory than first envisaged.

The continuing rising cost of welfare provision in the mid-1970s caused the Government to raise concerns of it being out of control. The welfare ideal of services and benefits was initially related to an expectation of full employment. Full employment would generate income through taxation and would go towards offsetting the welfare costs (Hills 1990). During the mid-1970s an oil crisis occurred, with a resulting unstable economy that made full employment very difficult to achieve. The outcome was an increase in inflation and a soaring rate of unemployment. At this time there were different political views on how welfare provision should be made. People became far less willing to fund welfare provision through taxation and used their vote to demonstrate this. The Conservative Party (New Right) introduced the idea that welfare provision could be opened up to further involve the private and voluntary sectors. If, for example, people took responsibility for their own health care and pensions through personal policies, they could purchase services to meet their needs from the independent sectors. Ideally, this would lead to less dependence upon state welfare. Additionally, the New Right argued that welfare benefits created a disincentive to work as they were too generous, causing dependency upon the state.

The National Health Service and Community Care Act 1990 was instigated during the early part of the 1990s and reinforced the need for a variety of care provision. With the opening up of the care market and subsequent changes within the statutory sector, a split occurred between the purchasers and providers of services. Statutory services such as social services would carry out assessments and then purchase care from the open market. Some schools, GP practices and hospitals became fund holders and managed themselves. Even with these schemes, the public interest in a welfare state survived. The change of government to Labour in 1997 has had its own level of impact on social welfare and its changing structure.

The idea of purchasers and providers of care still operates within the changing structure of care provision. One of the main changes the present Government has worked towards has been benefit reform. Eligibility criteria for access to local authority services and benefits changed further. More regular checks and independent assessments are carried out on claimants, fraud squads have been further developed and incentives for people to return to work introduced.

The development of social welfare and social policy is an ongoing process. The political party in power at a given time, the economy of the country, social perspectives and market forces all play a part in the process of social welfare provision. The overall costs of paying benefits and providing welfare support have continued to place a heavy burden on the government of the day. There is a focus on how the best possible services can be provided at the best possible price. The concept of 'Best Value' is one of the current initiatives in the quest for value for money and quality services where performance and provision are monitored, whether they are provided by the statutory, voluntary or private sector.

As social welfare is continually changing, it is useful to pay attention to how individual agencies are affected. Current initiatives, policy changes, resource expenditure and priorities of need may be the outcome of such changes. An understanding of social policy and its influence can help inform aspects of practice.

THE FUNDING OF TODAY'S SOCIAL WELFARE

Welfare can be described as the provision of health care, education and social services. Welfare also provides benefits including income for unemployment, sickness and old age. A large part of the provision of care and support is made without actually being directly financed. Informal care of the sick, disabled and older people is often provided by family members and relatives who receive little or no money for providing support. The formal aspect of provision is the part that needs financing; this includes payments for provision of services, benefit payments and maternity leave. Money is raised through taxation and financial balancing of the government purse. Some people elect to pay for their own care and others pay as the result of means testing. Some people receive financial support through private insurance schemes; however, many rely on the state for financing their care.

Care provision is not a limitless facility; decisions must be made about who will receive the welfare moneys available. The amount of finance available and the limitations of this play a critical part in the setting of eligibility criteria, resourcing and the outcome of provision. This raises the concern that whilst care provision remains financially led, there is a risk that individual needs will not be met. An example of how this may work in practice is that of legislation and policies instigated to ensure the needs of minority groups are met. Problems arise when the budgets allocated do not provide adequate finances to implement the services required. Thus, despite the intention to ensure culturally sensitive services, this is not necessarily achieved.

Patterns of policy and financial development for welfare provision can be found in many books looking specifically at welfare during the 20th century. We are not able to do full justice to the subject in this section and suggest additional reading could provide a more in-depth explanation of the areas highlighted. We will now briefly look at the basics of social policy in relation to disability and to people with learning disabilities.

DISABILITY AND SOCIAL POLICY

> The impact of social policy is measured against notions of quality which are culturally, structurally and bureaucratically defined. In the case of disability ideas about quality are bound up with (a) cultural values about the role of disabled people in society and (b) the social relations of welfare production in a capitalist economy. (Priestley 1999, p.11)

The impact that the medical and social models of disability have on how people are perceived within society has an influence over policy making. Disability pressure groups have been formed that have highlighted the need for social model inclusion in policy development.

The budget restrictions prevalent in services for people with learning disabilities need to be challenged if realistic, needs-led care and support are to be achieved. 'The liberation of disabled people threatens powerful professional interest groups, it brings into question the legitimacy of the welfare state and it challenges the economic imperatives of capital accumulation' (Priestley 1999, p.12). This sums up the battle facing the ongoing development of disability related social policy. A far greater insight into the complexity of disability politics and social policy development can be found in Priestley (1999) and Drake (1999).

We will highlight some of the issues relating to social policy and people with learning disabilities through the use of two case studies.

CASE STUDY ONE

Rozia lived in England with her parents until the age of 20, when she moved into a housing association flat with her own tenancy. Rozia belonged to a local advocacy group and also had access to a local independent advocacy service. Rozia attended college full time and, before the course ended, wished to think about her future options. She discussed ideas with her parents, friends, college tutors, support workers and with people in the advocacy group. Rozia was working towards attaining paid work and in the meantime wished to undertake a variety of activities, including voluntary work and training courses. Rozia had heard about direct payments and the possibility of directly purchasing care or support from agencies or individuals. She went to her local advocacy service for advice on this matter. Rozia was supported in applying for direct payments. She was told that there was a local group who had set up a support scheme for people receiving direct payments and who could help her. Rozia approached this group; they guided her through the process of finding an independent person to help set up a bank account and monitoring scheme and give support with the running of the direct payments account.

Application in practice

As part of the developing philosophy of community living, Rozia was enabled to make informed choices both about her style of living and daily activities. Due to changes in social welfare and social policy brought about by evolving social change and through pressure from disability rights activists and pressure groups, some local authorities now offer money for individuals to make direct payment for care and support. Direct payments enabled Rozia to purchase the support she had been assessed as needing from service providers of her choice, and to pay for the services herself. This gave Rozia more control over her life and more flexibility in accessing support and tailoring it to her needs. This in turn promoted Rozia's presence in society and minimized barriers to her inclusion.

CASE STUDY TWO

Rob lived at home with his parents and two brothers. Whilst he coped quite well with many aspects of his life, there were some aspects Rob needed support with, including personal care, laundry, and preparing meals. Rob's parents belonged to a carers' group and through this heard that Rob might be entitled to Disability Living Allowance (DLA). Rob and his parents completed the forms. Unfortunately, when Rob heard back from the benefits agency his application for benefit had been rejected.

Rob and his parents went to their local advocacy service for advice. Rob was then supported by an advocate in the process of appealing against the benefits agency's decision. The decision was altered and Rob was then awarded the care component of the DLA.

Application in practice

Rob applied for a social welfare benefit believing in his entitlement. In the first instance, his application was rejected. He did not feel able to self-advocate concerning his entitlement and so asked for support and advice from the advocacy service. With the support of an advocate to work through the process of appeal, Rob was ultimately able to receive the care component of the benefit.

Advocacy services are part of the developing changes in social welfare (see Chapter 6). Many people with learning disabilities have access to self-advocacy groups. Access to independent advocates is often available to support individuals with many different aspects of their lives. In England, *Valuing People: A New Strategy for Learning Disability for the 21st Century*, issued by the Department of Health (2001a), indicates the strong commitment to developing and supporting advocacy services and moneys have been allocated to achieve this in a variety of ways. The importance of social inclusion, support networks and advocacy is also reinforced in Scottish policies such as *'The Same as You?' A Review of Services for People with Learning Disabilities*

(Scottish Executive 1999). The introduction of *Valuing People* and *'The Same as You?'* are good examples of how social policy affects working issues.

CONCLUSION

In a section as short as this it is impossible to provide a complete or in-depth guide to social policy. What we have endeavoured to show is that government and social policy have a direct effect on resources available and how services are provided. The payment of benefits and the opportunity to integrate into society are influenced by social policy. We believe a strategy of including people with learning disabilities in policy development is essential.

Pressure groups and user groups supported by advocacy, empowerment and participation can play a part in the ongoing challenge of social policy. Without the acknowledgement of people's needs, social policy cannot be challenged and changed, and marginalization will continue. We believe appropriate benefits to meet needs and to enable people to live and function within society should be provided. As care and support workers, the impact of social policy on people with learning disabilities should not be underestimated, and when policies restrict people, relevant support to promote change should be considered.

Key points

- Social welfare has developed considerably over the last 60 to 70 years; welfare reform moved on following the Second World War. The Beveridge Report played a key part in the development of social welfare.

- Different perspectives may be held by political parties; these can influence social policy development.

- Welfare ideals changed during the mid-1970s; this affected how social care was provided.

- Community Care in the 1990s changed the ethos of care and brought about an increase in voluntary and private care providers.

- Social policy affects so much: education, health, housing, benefits and social services.

- The Government and social policy have a direct effect on resources and how services are provided.

- Social policy development continues to change and impact upon care and support provision.

LEGISLATION AND POLICY

INTRODUCTION

In the previous section we provided a brief summary of social policy and its impact on care provision. Governmental thinking and social policy impact upon people with learning disabilities through legislation and policies that relate to, inform and guide practice that directly affects care provision.

We will initially explore some aspects of legislation and policy. The difference between powers and duties, and how these relate to care provision, will be highlighted. This will be followed by a brief introduction to some specific pieces of legislation that may be used in practice. Legislation in England, Scotland, Wales and Northern Ireland differ in various ways, but we are not going to provide a definitive guide to each. However, what we intend to do is illustrate how legislation, wherever it has been developed, has relevance in day to day practice. The impact of policies that are used in many agencies will be considered and the conflict that may occur between care and control highlighted.

Other texts that cover legislation and policies in more depth will be referenced accordingly. Two case studies will be used placing legislation and policies into a practice setting.

THE LAW

Information about specific legislation that is used by statutory services and health, voluntary and private agencies can be presented in different formats of legal documents. Thompson (2000) provides an explanation of some of the formats:

- *Statute* This refers to actual law or Act of Parliament...a fairly detailed document, which presents the main provisions and any relevant expectations. Each Act is usually broken down into parts, sections and subsections...

- *Statutory instruments* These are minor, more specific documents that relate back to their 'parent' Act...such instruments have the status and standing of statute...

- *Statutory guidance*...documents issued by the relevant department... Such volumes of guidance offer advice on good practice in relation to specific aspects of implementation of the Act concerned... Such guidance does not have the status of statute, but there is none the less a clear expectation that the guidance will be followed...

(Thompson 2000, pp.35–36)

There are four main levels at which legislation can be interpreted: 'Statutory guidance; local policies; precedent; direct practice' (Thompson 2000, p.34). Each can influence the care that is provided for people with learning disabilities. Statutory guidance is issued by governments and directs how particular pieces of legislation are to be implemented. This informs how services are to be structured and provided. Local policies are developed by the local authorities or other agencies providing social care and support. These policies are devised by the individual agencies to provide explanations and guidance of the agency's interpretation of the law and may give procedures to follow. Precedent describes the development of law following court cases that make decisions in specific situations. This process is sometimes referred to as case law and will be explained in more depth below. In some direct practice situations, the law can provide guidelines and at times identify specific tasks to be undertaken. However, a level of individual discretion is sometimes available to workers as legislation does not provide guidance for all working situations (adapted from Thompson 2000).

Case law is where a specific piece of legislation has been challenged through the court system. The outcome of the court case can set a precedent that future court hearings would use as a basis for their decision making. This process could affect how statutory, voluntary and private agencies provide a service and may ultimately affect practice. The ongoing process of testing legislation through case law is an important part of the developing framework of legislation and its influence over practice. Case law outcomes are often published or broadcast on the television after court hearings.

Within some of the above legislative interpretations, there are aspects of direct guidance for people providing care and support; we will briefly explore this further.

WHAT HAS TO BE DONE UNDER LEGISLATION

Two main terms of guidance are found in many pieces of legislation. The first is where the legislation states that a statutory authority, such as a social services department, must/shall do something; this is referred to as a 'duty'. The second is where legislation guides what can be done, but gives the statutory authority the choice whether to undertake the task; these are referred to as 'powers'.

A duty is something that an individual or organization is obliged to undertake. An example of this can be taken from the National Health Service and Community Care Act 1990. Section 46 places a duty on every social services department to publish a community care plan for its locality and to update this at least yearly. Section 47 of the same act places a duty to assess the needs of a person in relation to community care:

> …where it appears to a local authority that any person for whom they may provide or arrange for the provision of community care services may be in need of such services…**shall** [duty] carry out an assessment of his needs for those services. (Department of Health 1989)

Duties can be found in a variety of other pieces of legislation such as the Mental Health Act 1983, Children (Scotland) Act 1995 and Children Act 1989.

In some legislation a power is granted as a way of guidance. As stated earlier, a power is different to a duty as it does not have to be carried out. It is suggested as guidance but it remains at the discretion of, for example, social services whether to undertake the outlined task or not. The National Health Service and Community Care Act 1990 gives a power in relation to services; the option is placed with the authorities about providing services:

> …where it appears to a local authority that any person for whom they may provide or arrange for the provision of community care services may be in need of such services…having regard to the results of that assessment, shall then **decide** whether his needs call for the provision by them of any services. (Department of Health 1989)

Under the Act the assessment is a duty, the provision of services a power and up to the local authority's discretion. However, it needs to be recognized that other pieces of legislation may be referenced to and used that in themselves have duties and powers. Examples of such pieces of legislation are: the National Assistance Act 1948; Chronically Sick and Disabled Persons Act 1970 (Brayne and Martin 1997).

Within some legislation there is the duty of control in a given situation. If it is assessed that a person is of risk to themselves and/or to other people, then pieces of legislation such as the Mental Health Act 1983 may be used to impose a level of controlled care. This may involve the person being admitted to hospital and detained over a period of time whilst receiving treatment. People with learning disabilities would need to fall within the categories defined by the Mental Health Act 1983 – 'mental impairment' or 'severe mental impairment' – and display 'abnormally aggressive or seriously irresponsible conduct' (The Maudsley 1999, p.6). Additionally, 'admission of a person with learning disability for treatment under the Act may also be considered if he or she also suffers from another form of mental disorder (for example mental illness)' (Department of Health and Welsh Office 1999, p.138). According to the Mental Health Act 1983 Code of Practice, 'Very few people with learning disabilities are detained under the Act' (Department of Health and Welsh Office 1999, p.138). The Mental Health Act 1983 is both subtle and complex and requires a depth of knowledge and understanding in its use and application in practice. Other features of care and control can be explored further in Brayne and Martin (1997) and Braye and Preston-Shoot (1997).

Thus it can be seen that some legislation informs the process of care and some the process of control; both might work intrinsically with the other depending upon the presenting situation.

Having briefly explored parts of the structure of legislation we will now go on to highlight some of the legislation that is used in the learning disabilities field. As mentioned in the introduction to this section, the following is not meant as a definitive guide and must be read with awareness that case law or legislative changes can occur at any point.

LEGISLATION AND PEOPLE WITH LEARNING DISABILITIES

In this short section, we are unable to cover the roles of the Scottish Executive, the National Assembly of Wales and the Northern Ireland Executive and the different legislation developed throughout the UK; thus, with careful consideration we decided to focus predominantly on English legislation as a way of showing legislative structure and its importance in informing practice.

The legislative framework that predominantly underpins the care and support role for people in England will now be briefly examined and is offered here as an example of the legislative process. Some of the legislation relates to other parts of the UK; however, if practice is undertaken predominantly in Scotland, Wales or Northern Ireland then the specific legislation relating to that area will need studying.

Today, the underpinning piece of legislation that guides working with people with learning disabilities in England is the National Health Service and Community Care Act 1990. Community Care focuses on the provision of services to people in the community, not as 'hospital inpatients'. The services should be provided to those who need them and the care co-ordinated through the care management process. Within community support settings, day centres and residential units the key tasks are primarily focused on providing support for people to enable them to live as full and independent lives as possible. Many of the care and support tasks undertaken are informed by legislation, policies or procedures, although this may not always be readily apparent. The ethos of support may differ depending on whether social or health care is the underpinning factor; whatever the factor, the process of care is similar.

The proposal for community care was not a new concept and continued to focus on how care should be provided within a flexible mixed market. What did change was the shift of emphasis from the statutory sector providing the services to managing them. It encouraged the diversity of service provision through working partnerships between social services, health services and private and voluntary sectors. Services should be responsive, flexible and cost effective in meeting individual needs and oriented towards the people using the services. Although the Act was dated 1990, it was not put into practice until 1993 in many areas (Brayne and Martin 1997).

Six objectives for the Act were identified:

1. To promote the development of domiciliary, day and respite services to enable people to live in their own homes wherever feasible and sensible;

2. To ensure that service providers make practical support for carers a high priority;

3. To make proper assessment of need and good care management the cornerstone of high quality care;

4. To promote the development of a flourishing independent sector alongside good quality public services;

5.   To clarify the responsibilities of agencies and so make it easier to hold them to account for their performance;

6.   To secure better value for taxpayers' money by introducing a new funding structure for social care.

(Department of Health 1989, p.3)

The Act proposed that there would be an accurate assessment of community care needs and individual need. With the needs assessed, careful planning for support services would then be made. The role of the care manager (sometimes referred to as social worker, commissioner or purchaser) was proposed as being:

- to identify people in need in the community

- to develop methods of referral that ensure the accessibility of services for all in the community

- to plan and secure the delivery of packages of care

- to monitor the quality of care provided

- to review service users' needs.

(Adapted from Department of Health 1989)

Services should be able to respond to individual need and be flexible in the way needs are met through service provision. There should be a choice of services available to the person receiving the support. The choice of what to access should be made with the individual and, with his or her agreement, family members, carers, and independent advocates. In principle, this sounds a positive process; in reality, the budget and resource restrictions faced by the majority of agencies may hinder the process and outcomes.

The National Health Service and Community Care Act 1990 places the duty of assessment on statutory services for people that are vulnerable and that may require support. The definition of 'vulnerable' is found in a piece of legislation that is now over 50 years old, the National Assistance Act 1948. Section 29 of the Act describes vulnerable adults as

> persons aged eighteen or over who are blind, the deaf or dumb, or who suffer from mental disorder of any description, and other persons aged eighteen or over who are substantially and permanently handicapped by illness, injury, or congenital deformity or such other disabilities as may be prescribed. (NAA 1948 in Brayne and Martin 1997, p.280)

This broad description includes people with learning disabilities. With the identification of the person's vulnerability, an assessment can be undertaken and other pieces of legislation used to inform the nature of the support required and subsequently provided.

The National Assistance Act 1948 instructs on the need to provide guidance and information about services available, sheltered employment, training facilities and residential accommodation. The Chronically Sick and Disabled Persons Act 1970 states that vulnerable adults should be supported with specific services such as practical assistance and providing or helping with adaptations or special facilities in the home. Other legislation may also be required to inform practice. Some of the Acts that may be used include:

- Carers and Disabled Children Act 2000

- Human Rights Act 1998

- Housing Act 1996

- Disability Discrimination Act 1995

- Disabled Persons (Services, Consultation and Representation) Act 1986

- Registered Homes Act 1984

- Sex Discrimination Act 1975

- Sexual Offences Act 1956

There are other pieces of legislation that may be used by or affect people with a learning disability.

Following an initial assessment, if services are required then a referral is made to the relevant team or organization. For example, the referral could involve health, housing, education and services for mental health, older age, physical disabilities or child care. Other legislation may then be used to inform practice. It is not practical to go into all of these in this section and other texts that specialize in legislation may be of interest (for example, Braye and Preston-Shoot 1997; Brayne and Martin 1997; Mandelstam 1998, 1999).

LEGISLATION AND POLICIES IN PRACTICE

Funding and the way care is commissioned may vary between geographical areas. However, there is a level of similarity in many processes. A person from a commissioning agency will assess, then purchase and fund, the support required. Whatever process of care management is being used, there is a difference between the roles of service purchasers (commissioners) and service providers. In some areas the roles and the processes of purchaser and provider are changing and a person centred approach has been introduced. This is a different way of supporting people to access their required services and in most cases will work alongside care management. A person centred approach is covered in more depth in Chapter 8.

The process of providing care that meets an individual's changing needs throughout life is one that requires careful attention, however it is accomplished. The care and resources available are often limited and funding restrictions may further affect services. Legislation and policies provide the framework for care but, alas, do not always support adequate facilities for care provision.

The legislative framework that surrounds the learning disabilities field is complex. Legislation guides and influences the provision of care. Legislation itself is influenced by social policy and society's expectations of care. Various White Papers and strategies have been published to further inform and guide practice: in England, *Valuing People: A New Strategy for Learning Disability for the 21st Century* (Department of Health 2001a); in Scotland, *'The Same as You?' A Review of Services for People with Learning Disabilities* (Scottish Executive 1999); in Wales, *Fulfilling the Promises: Proposals for a Framework for Services for People with Learning Disabilities* (Learning Disability Advisory Group 2000). Legislation is also frequently linked to the development of policies and procedures. Many statutory, voluntary and private organizations will have their own policies and procedures to be undertaken in various situations. There are many policies and procedures that are used to inform day to day practice; these include: health and safety, lifting and handling (Mandelstam 2002) and administering medication. One in particular that we will highlight as an example is risk assessment.

Risk assessments may be undertaken when assessing the chance of harm or risk occurring to a person being supported. The risk might relate to a variety of factors such as catching a bus or walking to work or concern the person's behaviour in public. The risk can be considered from two perspectives: the risk to the person when carrying out a specific task and the risk of the organization not fulfilling its duty of care. Whatever the perspective, the person undertaking the assessment holds power. There is the balance between care and control to be considered. This reinforces the importance of working in partnership with the person and, if required, in consultation with his or her family, carers or advocate. The joint approach then goes part way towards an equal balance of power. Risk assessment can be studied further through the work of, for example, Kemshall and Pritchard (1996, 1997) and Parsloe (1999).

We will now use two case studies to demonstrate the importance of legislation in practice.

CASE STUDY ONE

Connor had always lived at home with his parents, Kathy and Sean. Connor had worked for many years in a nearby local factory. He was fairly independent but required some help with personal care and some household tasks. Kathy and Sean were in their seventies and Sean was becoming quite frail through increasing ill health. Kathy and Sean became increasingly worried about their situation, their ability to cope, and how Connor would be affected in the future. They discussed this with their GP who referred them to social services.

They were visited at home by a social worker who assessed Connor's needs. Together they began to discuss Connor's preferences in thinking about the future. They also decided that Connor might benefit from certain aids and adaptations being provided in the home, and an assessment by an occupational therapist was requested. The aids and adaptations were provided a few weeks later. Kathy had been told she could be assessed in her own right as a carer. Kathy asked the social worker to undertake the carer's assessment.

Application in practice

The social worker undertook Connor's assessment of need as a duty under Section 47 of the National Health Service and Community Care Act 1990. Connor and his family were then enabled to access information about resources and services available in both the statutory and independent sectors. Later, the aids and adaptations for Connor were provided, guided by powers of the Chronically Sick and Disabled Persons Act 1970.

Kathy provided a substantial amount of care on a regular basis to Connor. Thus she was assessed as a carer in accordance with Section 1 of the Carers and Disabled Children Act 2000. This Act enables local authorities, for example, to offer carers support and provide services direct to carers. These services could include helping the carer care for the person, direct payments being made to the carer and vouchers provided for short-term breaks. These benefits might be means tested. The social worker was able to work with Kathy and Connor to identify the best way forward.

CASE STUDY TWO

Lara was a young woman with complex needs who lived at home with her mother, Anna, who was her main carer. Anna had a physical disability, which sometimes affected her mobility and her ability to meet Lara's care needs. Lara was additionally supported at home by a package of care seven days per week.

Anna was taken ill unexpectedly and required admission to hospital. In this emergency situation, Lara's needs were assessed due to the changes in her circumstances. In the short term, Lara was found accommodation in a residential home known to her from previous respite care. The social worker then worked with Lara and Anna to consider Lara's future options.

Application in practice

Following Anna's emergency admission to hospital and the change of circumstances, Lara's needs were reassessed under Section 47 of the National Health Service and Community Care Act 1990. As a person with complex needs requiring 24 hour care, Lara was assessed as meeting the criteria defining a vulnerable adult under Section 29 of the National Assistance Act 1948. In this emergency situation, a short-term place in a residential home was found under Section 21 of Part III of the National Assistance Act 1948. This allowed the social worker to arrange residential accommodation as Lara was in need of care. In the longer term, Part III accommodation was not considered the most appropriate option. In line with the aims of the National Health Service and Community Care Act 1990, Lara and Anna considered the feasibility of Lara returning home with a more intensive care package. They also looked at possible options for the future of independent supported housing offering 24 hour care.

CONCLUSION

Legislation can be interpreted at a variety of levels and either directly or indirectly informs and underpins the majority of care work. Some legislation states that there is a duty to undertake specific pieces of work and/or a power to decide if resources will be provided. Other legislation guides the development of policies and procedures that can inform and instruct specific ways of working in a variety of situations. There is also legislation that identifies the duty to control people in specific or given situations; for example, if they are a risk to themselves or others. An understanding of the diversity of how legislation can inform can help when considering its use in practice. A person can then be better informed of the legal framework and structure that underpins and guides care provision.

In the UK, legislation relating to people with learning disabilities may vary between England, Scotland, Wales and Northern Ireland. Whatever the locality, legislation is not a static subject, it will go through a process of update and change. Wherever a person works, legislation and policies will be in operation that inform and guide much of the day to day care work. Sometimes their use can be clearly seen and understood, at other times the links may seem more obscure. Nevertheless, by having an understanding of the relevance of legislation to practice, its impact upon people with learning disabilities can be better understood.

Key points

- Working within a legislative framework is a critical part of care and support within the learning disabilities field.

- Legislation and policies relate to, inform and guide practice that directly affects care provision.

- There are 'duties' which have to be undertaken and 'powers' that the provider can choose to undertake.

- Most legislation that is used today that specifically relates to people with learning disabilities dates from 1948 onwards. Some appears archaic and uses what is now considered derogatory terminology.

- Many agencies have their own specific policies about a variety of issues.

- Legislation can inform many areas including the need for an assessment, the level of care to be provided, financial support, adaptations and, in some situations, enforced control.

- Some legislation appears at face value to be supportive, but unfortunately may not stand up as well as expected.

- Legislation continues to develop and change, and is influenced by social policy.

- Legislation is developing separately in England, Scotland, Wales and Northern Ireland and may vary in some aspects.

11

The Way Forward

INTRODUCTION

As discussed in previous chapters, there are various pieces of legislation and policies relating to people with learning disabilities, including: in England, *Valuing People* (Department of Health 2001a); in Scotland, *'The Same as You?' A Review of Services for People with Learning Disabilities* (Scottish Executive 1999); in Wales, *Fulfilling the Promises: Proposals for a Framework for Services for People with Learning Disabilities* (Learning Disability Advisory Group 2000). In this chapter we will use one example of an English governmental policy to show how legislative development is playing a part in informing the way forward. For the first time in 30 years, in England, a White Paper has been produced that focuses on learning disabilities. The implications of *Valuing People: A New Strategy for Learning Disability for the 21st Century* will be looked at and its potential impact on future practice considered.

We will go on to explore research, its importance, and how it can be used effectively as a method of developing service through joint working. Links will be made with previous chapters and some of the theoretical perspectives that have been explored throughout the book. The importance and value of theory being used to inform practice will be reinforced throughout.

VALUING PEOPLE: AN ENGLISH PERSPECTIVE

Throughout the book, we have talked about the importance of seeing each person with learning disabilities as individual. A person's individuality and fundamental right to receive support to meet needs are core issues when considering valuing a person. Although care provision and acceptance of people with learning disabilities within society have moved forward considerably from the institutional care discussed in Chapters 1 and 4, there is still a long way to go.

People with learning disabilities are amongst the most vulnerable and socially excluded in our society. Very few have jobs, live in their own homes or have choice over who cares for them. This needs to change: people with learning disabilities must no longer be marginalized or excluded. (Department of Health 2001a, p.2)

The chapter on advocacy, empowerment, participation and choice (Chapter 6) explored some of the ways that advocacy can help a person become empowered within society. The need for people to be able to take control of their life choices is fundamental. The importance for people with learning disabilities to be able to achieve this has been acknowledged and the Government has stated a commitment to addressing inequalities:

Valuing People sets out how the Government will provide new opportunities for children and adults with learning disabilities and their families to live full and independent lives as part of their local communities. (Department of Health 2001a, p.2)

Valuing People identifies 11 core areas seen as major problems that need addressing to achieve inclusion within society. With an awareness of these problems, consideration can be given to the required development:

- Poorly co-ordinated services for **families with disabled children especially for those with severely disabled children**.

- **Poor planning for young disabled people at the point of transition into adulthood**.

- Insufficient support for **carers, particularly for those caring for people with complex needs**.

- People with learning disabilities often have little **choice or control** over many aspects of their lives.

- Substantial **health care** needs of people with learning disabilities are often unmet.

- **Housing choice** is limited.

- **Day services** are often not tailored to the needs and abilities of the individual.

- Limited opportunities for **employment**.

- The needs of people from **minority ethnic communities** are often overlooked.

- **Inconsistency in expenditure and service delivery.**

- Few examples of real **partnership** between health and social care or involving people with learning disabilities and carers.

(Department of Health 2001a, pp.2–3, bold as in original)

The development of facilities to meet needs is not the only issue to be considered. The whole process of care management is suggested as needing to change. The involvement of the person whose life it is should be central in identifying, considering, planning and arranging the required support. *Valuing People* identifies the key principles as 'Rights, Independence, Choice, and Inclusion'. The proposed method of achieving the key principles is through person centred casework and person centred planning, which is covered in depth in Chapter 8.

The Government has suggested that changes will be partly supported through financial investment in the development of advocacy services in the voluntary sector. The proposed investment is £1.3 million pounds a year over a three year period (Department of Health 2001a). The advocacy development could include many of the types of support groups identified in Chapter 6. Additionally, the claiming of benefits, in particular direct payments, would enable people to take more control over the purchase of care and support and how it is provided. This would move the purchasing away from the traditional care management associated with the National Health Service and Community Care Act 1990, as discussed in the sections on social policy and legislation in Chapter 10. A person centred approach is seen as an essential way of enabling people's full involvement in their own lives.

Valuing People is about valuing individuals, each unique, and each differently able. A lifelong approach is proposed that should begin by integrating services for children and their families and should go on to provide opportunities for people to develop into adult life. Improvements should be made in education, health, social services, employment, housing, support and care work for people with learning disabilities and their families and carers. Here we have used just one piece of legislation as an example of the changing structure of care. Different pieces of legislation are being used in other parts of the country and outside of the UK. Whatever legislation is being used to inform practice, it will provide guidance and a structure of how services should be changing to meet the needs of individuals.

However, the question must be raised, how is it known if these new ideas and ways of working are actually beneficial and making a difference? How are they checked and by whom? Research can be undertaken as a method of exploring new ideas and identifying the impact upon practice. Research is a powerful tool and not one that should be solely owned by the academics within society. We would now like to explore some different types of research and look at how it can be carried out as a joint process in planning and developing the way forward.

RESEARCH

Research can be used to explore a variety of issues such as the planning and development of services. Research is one way of exploring what is required and how to meet identified needs. We will initially explore research as a general process and go on to show how it can be needs led and inclusive in its approach. A fuller explanation of research can be found in specific research based texts: for example, Alston and Bowles (1998), Bell (1992), Blaxter *et al.* (1998), Everitt *et al.* (1992) and Humphries (2000). In this section, we aim to consider the differences between some research methods and suggest some approaches that can be used to undertake joint research in the learning disabilities field.

Research can be undertaken from a variety of perspectives, including social, medical or joint research, each important in its own right. There is a vast amount of medically based research undertaken that explores, for example, syndromes and their implications, why they may occur and the impact they can have on a person's development. However, we intend to look at research from a social perspective. One explanation of social research is 'the systematic observation and/or collection of information to find or impose a pattern, to make a decision or take some action' (Alston and Bowles 1998, p.6).

Research can take many different forms dependent on the beliefs, values and process/methods used by the researcher. The methods used can, of course, have some impact on the outcome of the research. Researchers may have their own agendas for carrying out a piece of work, or undertake it on behalf of others. Funding for research may be provided by organizations employing the researcher. Such aspects require careful consideration, as possible bias could affect the validity of the research and its outcomes. To enable the research process to be explored and understood further, we will briefly highlight some types of research often used in the social field; for example, quantitative, qualitative, emancipatory and feminist.

Quantitative research

Mark (1996) describes quantitative research as the oldest form of social research. It dates back to the natural science ideals held in the 18th and 19th centuries, known as 'positivism'. The idea operates on the assumption that there is an objective 'reality' that can be measured accurately within natural laws which can be 'discovered' by rigorous and objective research. Quantitative research applies a rigorous scientific approach and works to hypotheses being proved or disproved. The quantitative approach sees the researcher's influence as minimal or non-existent, with the researcher being objective and detached. Techniques that can measure quantities are predominantly used, which enables the collection and analysis of data, such as surveys and questionnaires. The approach is based upon using data in the form of numbers and undertaking work that is replicable. Quantitative research can be useful in some circumstances and can deal with large numbers. However, it does not undertake research in a way that enables a better understanding of the interpretation of the views and meanings of people. Qualitative research provides a different approach.

Qualitative research

In contrast to a quantitative approach, qualitative research does not rely on hypotheses and the development and testing of theories. Qualitative research develops from observations and experiences that are going on in the world and theories and ideas are then developed from the patterns observed: '…qualitative researchers are more interested in understanding how others experience life, in interpreting meaning and social phenomena, and in exploring new concepts and developing new theories' (Alston and Bowles 1998, p.9). Qualitative researchers acknowledge that their presence will have some impact on the research being carried out and that people's experiences and how they see life are key. Participant observation, in-depth interviews, observation and group work are some of the techniques used in qualitative research. There are many different theoretical stances that underpin qualitative research and these can be studied in more depth in many social research based books: for example, Alston and Bowles (1998) and Berg (1995).

Many people have suggested that quantitative and qualitative research can work together and are complementary to each other: for example, Babbie (1992), de Vaus (1995), Orcutt (1994) and Reid (1994), . For instance, whilst undertaking a piece of research, a researcher may wish to find out why a group of people are behaving in a specific way and the issues important to the group. A qualitative approach may be used and observations and discussions in focus groups may be undertaken. However, the researcher might also want to know the composition of males and females within the group and their ages. This is more of a quantitative approach, finding out facts and figures. It can be seen that both could prove useful and, to an extent, work hand in hand. The third form of research that we intend to explore is emancipatory research. Humphries and Truman (1994) refer to it as anti-discriminatory research.

Emancipatory research

During the 20th century, the power and use of research started to be questioned. Research may have been undertaken for the 'good' of a few but not for universal good. It had been used for political ends, the powerful researching the powerless, mainly using a top down approach. Some people being researched started to challenge the validity of the research being undertaken. Some wished to be involved and, more importantly, have a part in the decision making process about what was to be researched (Alston and Bowles 1998). As the human rights, consumer and liberation movements started to develop, some research was challenged. People from minority groups that in the past had been the 'objects' of research demanded the right of inclusion and to benefit from research undertaken. The time had come for researchers to be accountable not only to the people that funded the research projects, but also to the people that were being researched. Emancipatory research has played a part in addressing this imbalance.

Emancipatory researchers do not focus purely on studying the world, as is often associated with quantitative and qualitative research; it focuses on trying to change it (Masters 1995).

> The power of research as a tool for social change is fundamental to our understanding of the place of research... Just as the goals of social work involve not just understanding the world, but actively intervening to change things in some way, so, too, does social...research involve action, decisions and change. (Alston and Bowles 1998, p.6)

The argument that research has remained in the hands of the powerful and neglected the rights of the powerless for too long is key to the importance of the approach within many fields and, from our perspective, in the field of people with learning disabilities. Alston and Bowles sum up the role of the emancipatory researcher:

The job of the emancipatory researcher is to uncover the myths, beliefs and social constructions that contribute to the continuation of the status quo, in order to reveal how power relations are really operating to control the powerless. In the process, emancipatory researchers aim to liberate, enlighten or empower those people who are subjugated... Emancipatory researchers take for granted that research is never value free. What is important is whose side you are on. Emancipatory researchers deliberately 'take sides' with the people who are oppressed or struggling against their oppression. Thus, they are overtly political. It has been said that a mark of good research in this tradition is that it makes powerful people angry. (Alston and Bowles 1998, p.14)

The power of the approach in researching the difference between dominant and oppressed groups in society can be seen. Emancipatory research can be undertaken in a variety of ways, its main goal being that people that are oppressed or marginalized within society take a level of control over the research and benefit from it having taken place. The fourth approach to research that we will now explore is from a feminist perspective. Feminist research is an important approach within the emancipatory framework.

Feminist research

Feminist research is inclusive and participative; the researcher engages with the participants on an equal basis. It is more about the approach than the methodology and is based on egalitarian tenets. The feminist researcher will get together with participants to explore and address research questions, take data and analyse it. The researcher shares the emerging knowledge, checks it out and constantly listens to feedback. It is a shared process and credit is given to the participants. Feminist researchers uphold a code of ethics and work with informed consent as a process, not an event.

Reinharz provides ten themes of feminist research methodology:

- Feminism is a perspective, not a research method.
- Feminists use a multiplicity of research methods.
- Feminist research involves an ongoing criticism of non-feminist scholarship.
- Feminist research is guided by feminist theory.
- Feminist research may be transdisciplinary.
- Feminist research aims to create social change.
- Feminist research strives to represent human diversity.

- Feminist research frequently includes the researcher as a person.

- Feminist research frequently attempts to develop special relations with the people studied (in interactive research).

- Feminist research frequently defines a special relation with the reader.

(Reinharz 1992 in Alston and Bowles 1998, pp.15–16)

In the last two decades, feminist research has impacted upon general social research and, in particular, the role of women (Sarantakos 1993). Feminist research has exposed the male dominant sexism found within society and also within social science and research (Oakley 1985). The feminist approach has shown how traditional research methods have ignored the female viewpoint in many studies. This can be extended further to show how many viewpoints of marginalized or disadvantaged groups within society have also been ignored, silenced and controlled by those with the power to undertake the research. The feminist approach has been criticized by some who suggest that feminist research is still dominated by a middle class perspective (Gunew and Yeatman 1993). Nevertheless, the concept of groups marginalized by, and within, society being involved in and under-taking research is of great importance. We will now consider this in relation to people with learning disabilities.

RESEARCH WITH PEOPLE WITH LEARNING DISABILITIES

An emancipatory approach to research, underpinned by a feminist per-spective that highlights the difficulties and disadvantages faced by margin-alized groups within society, provides an example of how research could be approached. With a structured method of working identified, then both quantitative and qualitative methods may be used in the research process. Again, we come back to the issue that research should be undertaken *with* people with learning disabilities and not *on* them. How can this be achieved and what are the points that would need careful consideration?

Research that is being undertaken with people about their lives ideally needs to be participatory. This type of methodology promotes researching with people rather than carrying out research on them (for example, Moore, Beazley and Maelzer 1998, Oliver 1990, 1992, 1993, 1996). It acknowl-edges that the people whose lives are to be researched are the experts; they are the best people to know how they are feeling and what their views are. If the proposed research is of interest to the person or group of people, then there is a far better chance of active involvement. The starting point is the joint identification of the problem or issue to be explored or investigated. Research may be major, or focus on smaller issues of importance to participants. Some examples of research questions are:

- Is the day service providing enough activities?
- Does the residential unit have enough staff to enable people to get out?
- Do local community facilities meet the needs of people with multiple disabilities?
- Are there enough health drop-in services in the local community?
- Are local health care facilities easy to use?

The above questions were based on issues raised by people with learning disabilities. The methods subsequently used to inform and guide the research process were based on a participatory approach.

A PARTICIPATORY ACTION APPROACH TO RESEARCH

In Chapter 6, we discussed advocacy, empowerment, participation and choice. These ideas also apply when considering a participatory approach to research.

The importance of a person being able to make decisions about his or her life is a fundamental concept. Services are provided to support and enable people to achieve integration and this needs to be considered from a research perspective. At times, change and inclusion may make life more 'complicated' but this should not be a reason to deter someone from involvement. Simons (2000) argues that the more people are involved in decisions about services the better the services will become:

> Services which are geared to the wishes of those who use them are likely to be more aware of, and focused on, the reality of people's lives. They will be more responsive, flexible and efficient, providing help when people want and need it, and not when they do not. (Simons 2000, p.2)

Not only is participation important for service development, but it can also play a key part in personal development:

> By encouraging people with learning difficulties to become more con-
> fident and assertive, to take more responsibility for themselves and oth-
> ers, to make choices and to have more control over their lives, to be less
> dependent on others, and to be more informed, an effective participa-
> tion strategy has the potential to make a significant impact on the way
> people with learning difficulties see themselves. (Simons 2000, p.3)

We hope to have emphasized the importance of research and participation,
and would now like to briefly consider the drawing together of participation
and action based research. Social action and the involvement of people are
key to the approach. Action research focuses on changing or improving a
social situation and involving the people that are most affected. Two
definitions that explain participatory action research further are: 'Participatory action research is an approach to improving social practice by
changing it and learning from the consequences of change. Participatory
action research is contingent on authentic participation' (McTaggart 1989
quoted in Wadsworth 1991, p.65); and:

> Action research is defined as a process of collaborative inquiry which
> aims to enable participants in a system to develop the skills and knowl-
> edge to effect change in their own environment. (Coffey 1995, p.1)

Both explanations reinforce the importance of this collaborative and participatory approach, and this can be seen as both useful and appropriate when
applied to work with people with learning disabilities in trying to achieve
social change. Action research has often been used within a feminist research
perspective looking to achieve social change. Action research should be
viewed as an ongoing spiral process:

- initially identifying the problem or issue with those affected by it
- the issue is reflected upon, a research design is created, possibly
  using both quantitative and qualitative methods
- the research is undertaken within the field
- the findings are analysed and conclusions made
- feedback is given
- planning is carried out to implement the findings and to see how
  they have changed the initial situation
- the cycle can be repeated as many times as required. (Adapted from
  Wadsworth 1991)

All research requires time, careful planning and must be underpinned by a sound ethical framework. We will now go on to explore ethical issues in more depth.

ETHICAL ISSUES

An initial point of consideration must focus on the right of people to be able to make an informed choice about being involved in any research project. Additionally, the time required to fully involve people should be taken into consideration to avoid tokenism. Informed consent is of paramount importance; a researcher must be certain that someone who agrees to be involved in the research process is able to make an informed choice. A person's ability to be able to understand what the research project is about and how their answers would be used must be ascertained. Stalker (1998) highlighted the time implications and, at times, the need to seek and gain permission from a range of people before actually talking with people with learning disabilities. This process might include ethics committees, parents, carers and volunteer advocates. However, some aspects of talking to others could be seen as going against the process of participatory research, but necessary due to legislation.

Often an ethics committee is used as a way of judging if the correct standards and safety structure have been set up in a proposed research project. The ethical criteria would include: informed consent, confidentiality, not doing harm to anybody, doing good and positively contributing, carrying out research that is just and something that will positively contribute to knowledge in the area of study (adapted from the work of Beauchamp 1982). These points need to be considered and a strategic plan set up when considering a research project.

Making sure that people with learning disabilities have as much opportunity to make an informed choice as possible is of vital importance, and a systems theory approach (see Chapter 9) may be used to support the process. Information about the project may need to be presented in different formats: written, picture/word and widget (see Chapter 5 on communication methods). Questionnaires may need to be available in different formats, including video, to enable signing to be available. If direct interviews are taking place then a signing interpreter may be required. Many other ethical issues could be raised and discussed but the available space within this chapter restricts this. What we have tried to do is draw the reader's attention to the implications and importance of ethical issues and the way working is approached. The need for the researcher to adopt a flexible approach when enabling and supporting people with learning disabilities to participate in research studies is highlighted by Stalker (1998), Moore *et al.* (1998) and Booth (1995; Booth and Booth 1996). At times, this may mean having to include the participants in a way that may not be absolutely ideal, but does make certain that they are not completely excluded from the research study. Sometimes it may be difficult to carry out interviews that ask questions around abstract ideas. New ways of approaching the task may need to be considered so that concrete examples can be used to gain insight into people's views and understanding. Silverman (1993) reinforced the importance of being flexible and being able to change research design if information indicated this was required. This again indicates that research needs to be seen as an ongoing process and a flexible approach is the key to its success.

FINDINGS

When the research has been completed and the findings are being analysed, an inclusive approach is again important. It enables participation and inclusion during the analysis process. The findings from research can be disseminated in a variety of different formats and again we refer to Chapter 5 and communication methods. By being flexible in how the findings are produced (written word, widget, picture and word, audio tape, video tape), it tries to make certain that the research findings are open and accessible to as many people as possible. *Choosing to Change* (Lawton 2002) is a positive example of a research study being undertaken with people with differing levels of learning disabilities. It shows how issues of informed consent, ethical approval and participation were managed. Lawton presented the findings in a variety of formats to enable its accessibility. Lawton's piece of participatory action research included findings published in a full report, report summary, short report using large type and pictures, and audio/video options if required. The preparation of the findings obviously took longer than just completing a full report, but with the help and guidance of the people with learning disabilities involved in the research process, Lawton made certain that the findings were presented in ways that those involved wanted. Other studies undertaken can provide further insight into the concept of research with people with learning disabilities: for example, Moore *et al.* (1998) and Stalker (1998).

The approaches outlined above can be used in many situations. The identification of what will be studied and the research itself can be undertaken in a participatory way. This promotes empowerment and inclusion (Chapter 6) and is also person centred (Chapter 8). Many of the other theories in this book – systems theory, task centred theory, role theory – can be seen as important and informative when considering research.

The 11 core issues identified in *Valuing People* and discussed earlier in this chapter could all be explored further through participatory action research. An evidence based approach could be used to see if ideas put into practice have been successful in meeting people's needs. People's views are gained through research and the findings analysed to provide evidence of the outcomes.

An example of larger scale planned research can be seen in the proposals given by the Department of Health, who have agreed funding for a research initiative of between six and ten studies, which will cost approximately £2 million. The overall study will be called *People with Learning Disabilities: Services, Inclusion and Partnership*. It is envisaged the study will commence in 2001/02 and will be carried out over a four year period. The research will study areas such as:

- service delivery in health and social care and its effectiveness to identify elements of good practice, implementation and sustainability

- social inclusion, including access to good health care, and the factors which create disability barriers in people's lives

- organisation development to show how staff performance in learning disability services can be supported to achieve better services.

(Department of Health 2001a, p.114)

Research within the learning disabilities field will also continue through NHS research funding. At present over 130 separate research projects are being undertaken and are registered with the National Research Register (Department of Health 2001a). It is to be hoped that the research findings will provide more information and guidance on aspects such as quality of care, quality of support and joint working. The findings may then be used to provide a framework to underpin quality support and practice. Many other small-scale research projects are also being undertaken through, for example, The King's Fund, Joseph Rowntree Foundation and BILD.

Research is an ongoing process and can be used as a method for personal and practice development. Thompson suggests that 'research minded' practice provides 'a positive basis for integrating theory, research and practice, thereby contributing to an informed practice and a theory base which is not divorced from the demands of practice' (Thompson 1996, p.53). Individual workers also play a part in research development. Everitt *et al.* (1992) provide some suggestions of how individuals can be involved in an ongoing research minded approach. Two of their points, about bringing 'to the fore theories that help make sense of social need' and using theory to 'assist in decision making' and inform practice, sum up the purpose of this chapter and our complete book. The drawing together of knowledge that relates to the learning disabilities field, the understanding of how theory can inform working approaches, and the use of research in guiding and informing future development are of prime importance. This drawing together will, we hope, enable care and support workers to continue developing their working skills and move toward achieving social change.

CONCLUSION

The way forward involves change and evaluation as an ongoing process. Government proposals will continue to be made in response to consultation and by listening to what the people who use the various services and support networks want for themselves. Changing attitudes within society and public demand or pressure will also influence Government thinking.

The developmental nature of care and support work and external influences upon it provide the opportunity for services and care facilities to progress and move on. It is to be hoped that the days of institutional working are drawing to an end. An awareness of the difficulties of leaving institutional practices fully behind was identified by Goffman (1961) over 40 years ago. Some of Goffman's observations of institutional practice are still relevant today. With considered and theoretically informed practice, the remains of institutional working will be challenged and, it is hoped, eradicated during the early part of this century.

As mentioned earlier, the underpinning principles set out in legislation – for example, in England *Valuing People* (Department of Health 2001a); in Scotland *'The Same as You?' A Review of Services for People with Learning Disabilities* (Scottish Executive 1999); in Wales *Fulfilling the Promises: Proposals for a Framework for Services for People with Learning Disabilities* (Learning Disability Advisory Group 2000) – will continue to guide the way forward. The development of person centred planning, joint working, advocacy and evidence based practice provides the potential foundation for further positive changes in service structure. We would suggest that this can be supported through an awareness of individual working practice and the ability to use theoretically underpinned approaches. Drawn together, these ideas, theories and issues are key when considering the way forward.

Key points

- The structure of care is continually changing.

- Legislation and governmental guidance for working and supporting people with learning disabilities reinforces the importance of each person's uniqueness, individuality and differing abilities.

- New legislation has been introduced throughout the UK.

- In England the process of care management associated with community care is evolving and a person centred approach is being further developed.

- Research is a crucial part of service development.

- There are various approaches that researchers can use; an emancipatory approach reinforces the importance of inclusion in the research process.

- Research can be participatory and people with learning disabilities can be fully involved throughout.

- Research findings can help to shape and develop the services of tomorrow.

- There is a fundamental need to work within an anti-discriminatory and anti-oppressive framework to ensure good practice.

- Ongoing training to aid personal and professional development is always required.

- People with learning disabilities are *people* first and foremost and must be respected and treated accordingly.

Conclusion

When we first considered writing a book that would explore the links between theory and practice in the learning disabilities field, we did not fully realize what we were letting ourselves in for! On reflection, we set ourselves a difficult task in writing about the number of theories and approaches subsequently covered. Without the ongoing support of Jessica Kingsley Publishers and our 'expert readers' we may never have finished the task. However, the work carried out did reinforce to us how many differing perspectives there are, and how theories and approaches can genuinely provide insight, guidance and inform day to day practice.

We have endeavoured to explore some of the changes that have taken place within learning disabilities care and support services during the last century. New ideas have come into practice, legislative changes have taken place and public perception and understanding have altered. Different ways of working and providing care and support been used, some successful and others fashionable for a limited time. This process of progression and change has, however, provided a framework on which to further build and develop an approach, mindful of the potential dilemmas and barriers to effective practice. Care and support for people with learning disabilities should continue to move forward, striving to meet individual needs and challenging the barriers so often encountered in this field. Achieving this will not necessarily be straightforward or easy and should involve ongoing opportunities for people to make informed choices and decisions about issues affecting their lives. People with learning disabilities should also have the opportunity to be involved in the research and development of services.

People with disabilities are first and foremost individuals and should have the same opportunities to be fully involved within their local communities and society as the next person. The use of many of the theories and approaches explored in this book can help to enhance and develop working practice and enable participation and inclusion. Theory can provide a structured approach to working that promotes confidence and informs understanding for care and support work.

> Social workers [and care workers of any description], to be truly effective, need to be constantly asking why. It is in this quest for understanding about, for example, why situations arise, why people react in certain ways and why particular interventions might be utilised, that theory informs practice. (Coulshed and Orme 1998, p.9)

Thompson reinforces the need for informed practice. It is necessary to:

- do justice to the complexity of the situations social and health care workers so frequently encounter

- avoid assumptions, prejudices and stereotypes that can lead to discrimination and oppression

- lay the foundations for a *developmental* approach, one which permits and facilitates continuous personal and professional development

- ensure a high level of motivation, challenge and commitment.

(Thompson 1996, pp.1–2)

An understanding of theory does not provide a remedy or easy answers or faultless practice. However, it does help identify structured and tested ways of providing care and support for people with learning disabilities and can be used in a multitude of situations.

Thompson sums up many of our thoughts and feelings that have developed over the years working within the learning disabilities field, further reinforced during the writing of this book:

> Working in the helping professions is neither simple nor straightforward. The demands and challenges of such work are often of major proportions and can test us to the limits. Given this context, it is important that staff are as well equipped as possible to meet these challenges.
>
> Of course, no theory base can guarantee success in coping with the demands of practice. However,…a systematic and imaginative use of theory can help to prepare for the rigours of practice and help us guard against the pitfalls that stand in the way of effective and appropriate interventions. (Thompson 1996, p.125)

We sincerely hope that this book may play a part in increasing awareness and providing a range of ideas of how theory informing practice can enable empowerment, participation and inclusion to become a part of everyday life for people with learning disabilities. We believe a commitment to being open to learning and to using informed, reflective practice is a critically important part of the way forward and integral to progress.

References

Action on Elder Abuse (1995) *Everybody's Business: Taking Action on Elder Abuse*. London: Action on Elder Abuse.

Adams, R., Dominelli, L. and Payne, M. (1998) *Social Work: Themes, Issues and Critical Debates*. Basingstoke and London: Macmillan.

Ahmed, B. (1990) *Black Perspectives in Social Work*. Birmingham: Venture Press.

Ainsworth, M.D.S. (1969) 'Object Relations, Dependency and Attachment: A Theoretical Review of the Infant–Mother Relationship.' *Child Development 40*, 969–1025.

Ainsworth, M.D.S., Bell, S.M. and Dayton, D.J. (1974) 'Infant–Mother Attachment of One-Year-Olds in a Strange Situation.' In B.M. Foss (ed) *Determinants of Infant Behaviour*. London: Methuen.

Alcock, P. (1996) *Understanding Poverty* (2nd edn). London: Macmillan.

Allen, D. (1994) 'Towards Meaningful Day Activities.' In E. Emerson, P. Gill and J. Mansell (eds) *Severe Learning Disabilities and Challenging Behaviour*. London: Chapman and Hall.

Alston, M. and Bowles, W. (1998) *Research for Social Workers: An Introduction to Methods*. St Leonards, NSW: Allen and Unwin.

American Association on Mental Retardation (1992) *Mental Retardation: Definition, Classification and Systems of Support: 9th Edition*. Washington DC: American Association on Mental Retardation.

Atkinson, D., Jackson, M. and Walmsley, J. (1997) *Forgotten Lives: Exploring the History of Learning Disability*. Kidderminster: BILD Publications.

Babbie, E. (1992) *The Practice of Social Research* (6th edn). Belmont, CA: Wadsworth.

Baltes, P.B., Reece, H.W. and Lippsitt, L.P. (1980) 'Life Span Developmental Psychology.' *Annual Review of Psychology 31*, 65–110.

Bandura, A. (1977) *Social Learning Theory*. Englewood Cliffs, NJ: Prentice Hall.

Bandura, A. and Walters, R.H. (1973) *Social Learning and Personality Development*. New York: Holt, Rinehart and Winston.

Bank-Mikkelsen, N.E. (1969) 'A Metropolitan Area in Denmark: Copenhagen.' In R. Kugel and W. Wolfensberger (eds) *Changing Patterns in Residential Services for the Mentally Retarded*. Washington: President's Committee on Mental Retardation.

Bank-Mikkelsen, N. (1980) 'Denmark' in Flynn, B. and Nitsch, K.E. (eds) *Social Integration and Community Services*. Austin, TX: Pro-Ed.

Banks, S. (1995) *Ethics and Values in Social Work*. London: Macmillan.

Barber, J.G. (1986) 'The Promise and Pitfalls of Learner Helplessness Theory for Social Work Practice.' *British Journal of Social Work 16*, 5, 557–570.

Barker, D. (1983) 'How to Curb the Fertility of the Unfit: The Feeble Minded in Edwardian Britain.' *Oxford Review of Education 1983: 9*, 3 197–211.

Barker, P.J. (1985) *Behaviour Therapy Nursing.* London: Croom Helm.

Barton, L. (ed) (1996) *Disability and Society: Emerging Issues and Insights.* Harlow: Longman.

Bateman, N. (2000) *Advocacy Skills for Health and Social Care Professionals.* London: Jessica Kingsley Publishers.

Baxter, C., Poonia, K., Ward, L. and Nadirshaw, Z. (1990) *Double Discrimination: Issues and Services for People with Learning Difficulties from Black and Ethnic Minority Communities.* London: Kings Fund Centre and Commission for Racial Equality.

Beauchamp, T. (1982) *Philosophical Ethics: An Introduction to Moral Philosophy.* New York: McGraw Hill.

Beck, A.T. (1989) *Cognitive Therapy and the Emotional Disorders.* Harmondsworth: Penguin.

Becker, H.S. (1963) *Outsiders: Studies in the Sociology of Deviance.* Gencoe, IL: The Free Press.

Becker, H.S. (1964) *The Other Side: Perspectives on Deviance.* New York: The Free Press.

Bell, J. (1992) *Doing your Research Project.* Milton Keynes: Open University Press.

Bennett, G.C.J. and Kingston, P. (1993) *Elder Abuse: Concepts, Theories and Interventions.* London: Chapman and Hall

Bennet, G.C.J., Kingston, P. and Penhale, B. (1997) *The Dimensions of Elder Abuse.* London, Macmillan.

Berg, B.L. (1995) *Qualitative Research Methods for the Social Sciences.* Boston: Allyn and Bacon.

Beveridge, W.H. (1942) *Social Insurance and Allied Services.* London: HMSO.

Biestek, F. (1961) *The Case Work Relationship.* London: Allen and Unwin.

Birch, A. (1997) *Developmental Psychology from Infancy to Adulthood.* London: Macmillan.

Birdwhistell, R.L. (1973) *Kinesics and Context: Essays on Body-Motion Communications.* Harmondsworth: Penguin.

Blaxter, L., Hughes, C. and Tight, M. (1998) *How to Research.* Buckingham: Open University Press.

Blumer, H. (1969) *Symbolic Interactionalism: Perspective and Method.* Englewood Cliffs, NJ: Prentice Hall.

Booth, T. (1995) 'Sounds of Still Voices: Issues in the Use of Narrative Methods with People who have Learning Difficulties.' In L. Barton (ed) *Sociology and Disability.* London: Longmans.

Booth, T. and Booth, W. (1996) 'Sounds of Silence: Narrative Research with Inarticulate Subjects.' *Disability and Society 2*, 1, 55–69.

Bowlby, J. (1973) *Attachment and Loss, Vol. II: Separation.* London: Hogarth Press.

Bowlby, J. (1980) *Attachment and Loss, Vol. III: Loss, Sadness and Depression.* Harmondsworth: Penguin.

Braye, S. and Preston-Shoot, M. (1997) *Practising Social Work Law.* London: Macmillan.

Brayne, H. and Martin, G. (1997, 1999) *Law for Social Workers.* London: Blackstone Press.

British Association of Social Workers (BASW) (1996) *The Code of Ethics for Social Work (Revised).* Birmingham: BASW.

Brock, M. (1934) *Report of the Departmental Committee on Sterilization.* CMD 4485. London: HMSO.

Brown, H. (1996) 'Editorial.' *Tizard Learning Disability Review 1*, 2, 7–8.

Brown, H. and Craft, A. (1989) *Thinking the Unthinkable: Papers on Sexual Abuse and People with Learning Difficulties*. London: FPA Education Unit.

Brown, H.C. and Smith, H. (eds) (1998) *Normalisation: A Reader for the Nineties*. London: Routledge.

Brown, H.C. (1992) 'Lesbians, the State and Social Work Practice.' In M. Langan and L. Day (eds) *Women, Oppression and Social Work*. London: Routledge.

Brown, H.C. (1998) *Social Work and Sexuality: Working with Lesbians and Gay Men*. London: Macmillan.

Buckman, R. (1988) *I Don't Know What to Say: How to Help and Support Someone who is Dying*. London: Papermac.

Burr, V. (1998) *Gender and Social Psychology*. London: Routledge.

Bytheway, B. (1995) *Ageism*. Buckingham: Open University Press.

Caplan, G. (1965) *Principles of Preventive Psychiatry*. London: Tavistock.

CCETSW (1989) *Requirements and Regulations for the Diploma in Social Work, Paper 30*. London: CCETSW.

CCETSW (1992) *A Double Challenge: Working with People who have Both Learning Difficulties and a Mental Illness*. London: CCETSW.

CCETSW (1995) *Assuring Quality in the Diploma in Social Work – 1. Rules and Requirements for the DipSW (Revised 1995)*. London: CCETSW.

CCETSW (1996) *Assuring Quality in the Diploma in Social Work – 1. Rules and Requirements for the DipSW (Revised 1996)*. London: CCETSW.

CCETSW (1998) *Assuring Quality for Practice Teaching*. London: CCETSW.

Chappell, A. (1992) 'Towards a Sociological Critique of the Normalization Principle.' *Disability, Handicap and Society 7*, 1, 35–52.

Clark, C.L. (2000) *Social Work Ethics*. London: Macmillan.

Coffey, S. (1995) 'Action Research: The Process Phenomenon of Man.' *CQ Extension Forum 1*, April, 14 1–14.

Collins Dictionary (1986) *Collins Dictionary of The English Language*. Collins: London.

Conlan, E., Gell, C., Graley, R., Mooney, I. and Simpson, T. (1994) *Advocacy: A Code of Practice Developed by UKAN (United Kingdom Advocacy Network)*. Wetherby: Department of Health.

Copley, B. and Forryan, B. (1997) *Therapeutic Work with Children and Young People*. London: Cassell.

Corby, B. (1993) *Child Abuse: Towards a Knowledge Base*. Buckingham: Open University Press.

Corsini, R.J. and Wedding, D. (eds) (1989) *Case Studies in Psychotherapy*. Itasca, IL: FE Peacock Publishers.

Coulshed, V. and Orme, J. (1998) *Social Work Practice: An Introduction*. London: Macmillan.

Croft, S. and Beresford, P. (1990) *From Paternalism to Participation: Involving People in Social Services*. London: Joseph Rowntree Foundation.

Croft, S. and Beresford, P. (1994) 'A Participatory Approach to Social Work.' In C. Hanvey and T. Philpot (eds) *Practising Social Work*. London: Routledge.

Dahrendorf, R. (1973) *Homo Sociologies*. London: Routledge.

Dalrymple, J. and Burke, B. (1995) *Anti-Oppressive Practice: Social Care and the Law*. Buckingham: Open University Press.

Daniel, B., Wassell, S. and Gilligan, R. (1999) *Child Development for Child Care and Protection Workers*. London: Jessica Kingsley Publishers.

Davenport, G.C. (1996) *An Introduction to Child Development*. London: Collins Educational.

Davies, M., Howe, D. and Kohli, R. (1999) *Assessing Competence and Values in Social Work Practice*. Norwich: UEA Social Work Monographs.

Daw, R. (2000) *The Impact of the Human Rights Act on Disabled People*. London: Disability Rights Commission.

De Board, R. (1997) *The Psychoanalysis of Organizations: A Psychoanalytic Approach to Behaviour in Groups and Organizations*. London: Routledge.

de Vaus, D.A. (1995) *Surveys in Social Research*. Sydney: Allen and Unwin.

Department of Health and Social Security (1969) *Report of the Committee of Enquiry into Allegations of Ill-treatment of Patients and Other Irregularities at the Ely Hospital, Cardiff*. CMND 3795. London: HMSO.

Department of Health (1989) *Caring for People: Community Care in the Next Decade and Beyond*. London: HMSO.

Department of Health (1992) *Social Care for Adults with Learning Disabilities (Mental Handicap) LAC (92) 15*. London: HMSO.

Department of Health (1993) *DoH Circular (93) 10*. London: HMSO.

Department of Health (2001a) *Valuing People: A New Strategy for Learning Disability for the 21st Century. Cm5086*. London: HMSO.

Department of Health (2001b) *Nothing About Us Without Us: The Report from the Service Users Advisory Group*. London: HMSO.

Department of Health (2001c) *Family Matters, Counting Families In*. London: HMSO.

Department of Health (2001d) *Learning Difficulties and Ethnicity*. London: HMSO.

Department of Health and Welsh Office (1999) *Code of Practice, Mental Health Act 1983*. London: HMSO.

DHSS and Welsh Office (1971) *Better Services for the Mentally Handicapped*. London: HMSO.

Doel, M. and Marsh, P. (1992) *Task Centred Work*. Aldershot: Arena.

Dollard, J., Doob, L.W., Miller, N.E., Mowrer, O.H. and Sears, R.R. (1939) *Social Representations*. Cambridge: Cambridge University Press.

Dominelli, L. (1997a) *Anti-Racist Social Work. London: Macmillan.*

Dominelli, L. (1997b) *Sociology for Social Work* London: Macmillan.

Downs, C. and Craft, A. (1995) *Sex in Context. Part 1: Strategies and Safeguards Relating to the Sexuality of Children and Adults with Profound and Multiple Impairments*. Brighton: Pavilion Publishing.

Downs, C. and Craft, A. (1997) *Sex in Context. Part 2: Staff Development and Working Effectively with Parents and Carers*. Brighton: Pavilion Publishing.

Doyle, C. (1997) *Working with Abused Children*. Basingstoke: Macmillan/BASW.

Drake, R.F. (1999) *Understanding Disability Policies*. London: Macmillan.

Dybwad, G. (1969) 'Action Implications, USA Today.' In R. Kugel and W. Wolfensberger (eds) *Changing Patterns in Residential Services for the Mentally Retarded*. Washington: President's Committee on Mental Retardation.

Ellis, A. (1962) *Reason and Emotion in Psychotherapy*. Seacus, NJ: Lyle Stuart.

England, H. (1986) *Social Work as Art: Making Sense for Good Practice*. London: Allen and Unwin.

Evans, P. (1975) *Motivation*. London: Methuen.

Everitt, A., Hardiker, P., Littlewood, J. and Mullender, A. (1992) *Applied Research for Better Practice*. London: Macmillan.

Faculty of Health and Community Care (2002) at http://www.hce.uce.ac.uk/cpsu/packs/LD/learning.htm

Finkelhor, D. (1990) 'Early and Long-Term Effects of Child Sexual Abuse.' *Professional Psychology: Research and Practice 21*, 325–330.

Foucault, M. (1973) *The Birth of the Clinic: An Archaeology of Medical Perception*. London: Tavistock.

Foundation for People with Learning Disabilities (2001) *Learning Disabilities: The Fundamental Facts*. London: The Mental Health Foundation.

Freed, A.O. (1988) 'Interviewing through an Interpreter.' *Social Work 33*, 4, 315–319.

Gaag, A.U. and Dormandy, K. (1993) *Communication and Adults with Learning Disabilities*. London: Wurr Publishers.

Gambrill, E. (1995) 'Behavioural Social Work: Past, Present and Future.' *Research on Social Work Practice 5*, 4, 460–484.

Gensler, H.J. (1998) *Ethics: A Contemporary Introduction*. London: Routledge.

Germain, C.B. and Gitterman, A. (1980) *The Life Model of Social Work Practice*. New York: Columbia University Press.

Giddens, A. (1976) *New Rules of Sociological Method*. London: Hutchinson.

Giddens, A. (1979) *Central Problems in Social Theory*. London: Macmillan.

Giddens, A. (1984) *The Constitution of Society*. Cambridge: Polity Press.

Gilgun, J.F. (1994) 'An Ecosystemic Approach to Assessment.' In R. Compton and B. Galaway (eds) *Social Work Processes* (5th edn). Pacific Grove, CA: Brookes Cole.

Glaser, B. and Strauss, A. (1967) *The Discovery of Grounded Theory*. Chicago: Aldine Publishing Company.

Goffman, E. (1959) *The Presentation of Self in Everyday Life*. Harmondsworth: Penguin.

Goffman, E. (1961) *Asylums*. New York: Anchor.

Golan, N. (1978) *Treatment in Crisis Situations*. New York: Free Press.

Gooding, C. (1992) *Trouble with the Law: A Legal Handbook for Lesbians and Gay Men*. London: GMP.

Gooding, C. (1995) *Blackstone's Guide to the Disability Discrimination Act 1995*. London: Blackstone.

Gray, B. and Jackson, R. (2001) *Advocacy and Learning Disability*. London: Jessica Kingsley Publishers.

Greif, G.L. and Lynch, A.A. (1983) 'The Eco-System Perspective.' In C.H. Meyer (ed) *Clinical Social Work in the Eco-Systems Perspective*. New York: Columbia University Press.

Grossman, H.J. (ed) (1983) *Classification in Mental Retardation*. Washington, DC: American Association on Mental Deficiency.

Gunew, S. and Yeatman, A. (1993) *Feminism and the Politics of Difference*. St Leonards: Allen and Unwin.

Hanson, B.G. (1995) *General Systems Theory: Beginning with Wholes*. Washington: Taylor and Francis.

Haralambos, M. and Holburn, M. (1991) *Sociology: Themes and Perspectives*. London: Collins Educational.

Haralambos, M. and Holburn, M. (1993) *Sociology: Themes and Perspectives* (3rd ed). London: Collins Educational.

Hawker, S. and Hawkins, J.M. (1996) *The Oxford Popular Dictionary*. Oxford: Parragon.

Hawkins-Shepard, C. (1994) *Mental Retardation*. Reston, VA: Educational Resources Information Center.

Hayes, N. (1996a) *Principles of Social Psychology*. Hove: Psychology Press.

Hayes, N. (1996b) *Foundations of Psychology: An Introductory Text*. Walton-on- Thames: Thomas Nelson & Sons.

Herbert, M. (1981) *Psychology for Social Workers*. Basingstoke: Macmillan and British Psychological Society.

Hills, J. (ed) (1990) *The State of Welfare: The Welfare State in Britain since 1974*. Oxford: Oxford University Press.

HMSO (1957) *Royal Commission on the Law Relating to Mental Illness and Mental Deficiency: Report and Minutes of Evidence. Cmnd 169*. London: HMSO.

Hockey, J., Katz, J. and Small, N. (2001) *Facing Death: Grief, Mourning and Death Ritual*. Buckingham: Open University Press.

Hollins, S. and Sireling, L. (1994) *When Dad Died/When Mum Died*. London: St George's Mental Health Library.

Holt, G., Kon, Y. and Bouras, N. (1995) *Mental Health in Learning Disabilities*. Brighton: Pavilion Publishing.

Horrocks, R. (1997) *An Introduction to the Study of Sexuality*. London: Macmillan.

Howe, D. (1987) *A Introduction to Social Work Theory*. Aldershot: Wildwood House.

Howe, D. (1994) 'Modernity, Post Modernity and Social Work.' *British Journal of Social Work 24*, 5, 513–532.

Hudson, B. and MacDonald, G. (1986) *Behavioural Social Work: An Introduction*. London: Macmillan.

Hugman, R. and Smith, D. (1995) *Ethical Issues in Social Work*. London: Routledge.

Hume, I. and Pryce, W.T.R. (eds) (1986) *The Welsh and their Country*. Dyfed: Gomer.

Humphries, B. (ed) (2000) *Research in Social Care and Social Welfare*. London: Jessica Kingsley Publishers.

Humphries, B. and Truman, C. (1994) *Re-Thinking Social Research*. Aldershot: Avebury.

Hutt, C. and Bhavnani, R. (1972) 'Predictions from Play.' *Nature 237*, 171–172.

Iphofen, R. and Poland, F. (1998) *Sociology in Practice for Health Care Professionals*. London: Macmillan.

Jeffery-Poulter, S. (1991) *Peers, Queers and Commons: The Struggle for Gay Law Reform from 1950 to the Present*. London: Routledge.

Jones, P. (1996) *Studying Society: Sociological Theories and Research Practices*. London: Collins Educational.

Keenan, M., Kerr, K.P. and Dillenburger, K. (eds) (2000) *Parents' Education as Autism Therapists: Applied Behaviour Analysis in Context*. London: Jessica Kingsley Publishers.

Kemshall, H. and Littlechild, R. (2000) *User Involvement and Participation in Social Care*. London: Jessica Kingsley Publishers.

Kemshall, H. and Pritchard, J. (1996) *Good Practice in Risk Assessment and Risk Management*. London: Jessica Kingsley Publishers.

Kemshall, H. and Pritchard, J. (1997) *Good Practice in Risk Assessment and Risk Management 2*. London: Jessica Kingsley Publishers.

Kings Fund Centre (1980) *An Ordinary Life: Comprehensive Locally Based Residential Services for Mentally Handicapped People.* London: Kings Fund Centre.

Kings Fund Centre (1984) *An Ordinary Working Life: Vocational Services for People with Mental Handicap.* London: Kings Fund Centre.

Kings Fund Centre (1988) *Ties and Connections: An Ordinary Community Life for People with Learning Difficulties.* London: Kings Fund Centre.

Kugel, R. and Wolfensberger, W. (1969) *Changing Patterns in Residential Services for the Mentally Retarded.* Washington: President's Committee on Mental Retardation.

Langan, M. and Lee, P. (eds) (1989) *Radical Social Work Today.* London: Unwin Hyman.

Law, J. and Parkinson, A. (eds) (1999) *Communication Difficulties in Childhood: A Practical Guide.* London: Radcliffe Medical Press.

Lawton, A. (2002) *Choosing to Change.* Luton: Health Action Zone.

Learning Disability Advisory Group (2000) *Fulfilling the Promises: Proposals for a Framework for Services for People with Learning Disabilities.* Learning Disability Advisory Group: www.wales.gov.uk

Leick, N. and Davidsen-Neilsen, M. (1991) *Healing Pain: Attachment, Loss and Grief Therapy.* London: Routledge.

Lemert, E. (1967, 1972) *Human Deviance, Social Problems and Social Control.* Englewood Cliffs, NJ: Prentice Hall.

Lindemann, E. (1944) 'Symptomatology and Management of Acute Grief.' In H.J. Parad (ed) (1965) *Crisis Interventions: Selected Readings.* New York: Family Service Association of America.

Lishman, J. (ed) (1994) *Handbook of Theory for Practice Teachers in Social Work.* London: Jessica Kingsley Publishers.

Louis, M.R. (1980) 'Organizations as Culture-Bearing Milieux.' In L.R. Pondy, P.J. Frost, G. Morgan and T.C. Dandridge (eds) *Organisational Symbolism.* Grenwich, CT: JAI Press.

Luchterhand, C. and Murphy, N. (1998) *Helping Adults with Mental Retardation Grieve a Death Loss.* New York: Taylor & Francis.

Mabey, J. and Sorenson, B. (1995) *Counselling for Young People.* Buckingham: Open University Press.

Macmillan, B. (1937) *Law and Other Things.* Cambridge: Cambridge University Press.

Malin, N. (ed) (1987) *Reassessing Community Care.* London: Croom Helm.

Mandelstam, M. (1998) *An A–Z of Community Care Law.* London: Jessica Kingsley Publishers.

Mandelstam, M. (1999) *Community Care Practice and the Law.* London: Jessica Kingsley Publishers.

Mandelstam, M. (2002) *Manual Handling in Health and Social Care: An A–Z of Law and Practice.* London: Jessica Kingsley Publishers.

Mark, R. (1996) *Research Made Simple: A Handbook for Social Workers.* Thousand Oaks, CA: Sage Publications.

Marsh, P. (1990) *Outline of Social Work in Partnership Research.* Sheffield: Social Work in Partnership Programme.

Marshal, G. (1996) *Concise Dictionary of Sociology.* Oxford: Oxford University Press.

Marx, K. (1974) *Capitol, Vol. III.* London: Lawrence and Wishart.

Masters, J. (1995) 'The History of Action Research.' *Action Research Electronic Reader.* http://www.cchs.su.edu.au/AROW/masters.htm

McCarthy, M. and Thompson, D. (1992) *Sex and the 3R's. Rights, Responsibilities and Risks: A Sex Education Package for Working with People with Learning Difficulties.* Hove: Pavilion Publishing.

McCarthy, M. and Thompson, D. (1997) *Sex and Staff Training.* Brighton: Pavilion Publishing.

McCarthy, M. and Thompson, D. (2001) *Sex and the 3R's. Rights, Responsibilities, Risks.* Brighton: Pavilion Publishing.

McKuisick, V.A. (1988) *Mendelian Inheritance in Man.* Baltimore: Johns Hopkins University Press.

McLeod, J. (1993) *Introduction to Counselling.* Buckingham: Open University Press.

Mead, G.H. (1934) *Mind, Self and Society.* Chicago: University of Chicago Press.

Mearns, D. and Thorne, B. (1998) *Person-Centred Counselling in Action.* London: Sage.

Mencap (2002) *Accessibility Services* at: http://www.mencap.org.uk/html/services/accessibility.services.htm.

Messer, D. and Jones, F. (eds) (1999) *Psychology for Social Care.* London: Macmillan.

Michigan Department of Community Health (MDCH) (1996) *Person-Centered Planning: Practice Guidelines.* Lansing, MI: Michigan Department of Mental Health.

Midwinter, E. (1994) *The Development of Social Welfare in Britain.* Buckingham: Open University Press.

Moore, M., Beazley, S. and Maelzer, J. (1998) *Researching Disability Issues.* Buckingham: Open University Press.

National Development Group (1977) *Day Services for Mentally Handicapped People, Pamphlet No. 5.* London: HMSO.

Nelsen, J.C. (1980) *Communication Theory and Social Work Practice.* Chicago: University of Chicago Press.

Nelsen, J.C. (1986) 'Communication Theory and Social Work Treatment.' In F.J. Turner (ed) *Social Work Treatment: Interlocking Theoretical Approaches.* New York: Free Press.

Nirje, B. (1969) 'The Normalization Principle and its Human Management Implications.' In R. Kugel and W. Wolfensberger (eds) *Changing Patterns in Residential Services for the Mentally Retarded.* Washington: President's Committee on Mental Retardation.

Northern Ireland Executive (2001) *Improving Civil Rights for Disabled People – Northern Ireland Executive Response to the Disability Rights Task Force.* Northern Ireland Executive: http://www.ofmdfmni.gov.uk/equality/drtf_response/index.htm

Norton, D.G. (1978) *The Dual Perspective: Inclusion of Ethnic Minority Context in the Social Work Curriculum.* Washington DC: Council on Social Work Education.

Ntebe, A. (1994) 'Effective Intervention Roles of South African Social Workers in an Appropriate, Relevant and Progressive Social Welfare Model.' *Journal of Social Development in Africa 9,* 1, 41–50.

Oakley, A. (1985) *The Sociology of Housework.* London: Basil Blackwell.

O'Brien, J. (1981) *The Principle of Normalisation. A Foundation for Effective Services.* Atlanta, GA: Georgia Advocacy Office.

O'Brien, J. (1987a) 'A Guide to Life Style Planning: Using the Activities Catalogue to Integrate Services and Natural Support Systems.' In B.W. Wilcox and G.T. Bellamy (eds) *The Activities Catalogue: An Alternative Curriculum for Youth and Adult with Severe Disabilities*. Baltimore: Brookes Publishing.

O'Brien, J. (1987b) *Learning from Citizen Advocacy Programs*. Atlanta: Georgia Advocacy Office.

O'Hagen, K. (1986) *Crisis Intervention in Social Services*. London: Macmillan.

O'Hagen, K. (1991) 'Crisis Intervention in Social Work.' In J. Lishman (ed) *Handbook of Theory for Practice Teachers in Social Work*. London: Jessica Kingsley Publishers.

O'Hagen, K. (1994) 'Crisis Intervention: Changing Perspectives.' In C. Harvey and T. Philpot (eds) *Practising Social Work*. London: Routledge.

Oliver, M. (1990) *The Politics of Disablement*. London: Macmillan.

Oliver, M. (1992) 'Changing the Social Relations of Research Production?' *Disability, Handicap and Society 7*, 2, 101–114.

Oliver, M. (1993) 'Re-Defining Disability: A Challenge to Research.' In J. Swain, V. Finkelstein, S. French and M. Oliver (eds) *Disabling Barriers: Enabling Environments*. London: Sage.

Oliver, M. (1996) *Understanding Disability: From Theory to Practice*. London: Macmillan.

Orcutt, B.A. (1994) 'Commentry on Reid's "Reframing the Epistemological Debate".' In E. Sharman and W.J. Reid (eds) *Qualitative Research in Social Work*. New York: Columbia University Press.

Oswin, M. (1991) *Am I Allowed to Cry? A Study of Bereavement amongst People who have Learning Difficulties*. London: Macmillan.

Page, M. and Silburn, R. (1999) *British Social Welfare in the Twentieth Century*. London: Macmillan.

Parkes, C.M. (1996) *Bereavement: Studies of Grief in Adult Life*. London: Penguin.

Parsloe, P. (ed) (1999) *Risk Assessment in Social Care and Social Work*. London: Jessica Kingsley Publishers.

Pavlov, I. (1927) *Conditioned Reflexes*. New York: Oxford University Press.

Payne, M. (1991, 1997) *Modern Social Work Theory*. London: Macmillan.

Philpot, T. (1989) *Last Things: Social Work with the Dying and Bereaved*. Oxford: Reed Business Publishers.

Pincus, A. and Minahan, A. (1973) *Social Work Practice: Model and Method*. Itasca: Peacock.

Poland, F. (1990) 'Breaking the Rules: Assessing the Assessment of a Girls' Project.' In E. Stanley (ed) *Feminist Praxis*. London: Routledge.

Priestley, M. (1999) *Disability Politics and Community Care*. London: Jessica Kingsley Publishers.

Quality Assurance Agency for Higher Education (2000) *Social Policy and Administration and Social Work*. Gloucester: Quality Assurance Agency for Higher Education.

Reid, W.J. (1994) 'Reframing the Epistemological Debate.' In E. Sharman and W.J. Reid (eds) *Qualitative Research in Social Work*. New York: Columbia University Press.

Reid, W.J. and Epstein, L. (1972) *Task Centred Casework*. New York: Columbia University Press.

Reid, W.J. and Hanrahan, P. (1981) 'The Effectiveness of Social Work: Recent Evidence.' In E.M. Goldberg and N. Connelly (eds) *Evaluation Research in Social Care*. London: Policy Studies Institute.

Robinson, L. (1995) *Psychology for Social Workers*. London: Routledge.

Rogers, C.R. (1951) *Client-Centred Therapy: Its Current Practice, Implications and Theory.* London: Constable.

Rogers, C.R. (1961) *On Becoming a Person: A Therapist's View of Psychotherapy.* New York: Houghton Mifflin Company.

Rogers, C.R. (1977) *Carl Rogers on Personal Power.* London: Constable.

Rogers, C.R. (1980) *A Way of Being.* Boston, MA: Houghton Mifflin Company.

Rosengreen, K.E. (2000) *Communication: An Introduction.* London: Sage.

Rosenham, D.L. (1973) 'On Being Sane in Insane Places.' *Science 179,* 250–258.

Rowitz, L. (1974) 'A Sociological Perspective on Labelling.' *American Journal of Mental Deficiency 79,* 265–267.

Rowntree, J. (1901) *Poverty: A Study of Town Life.* York: Joseph Rowntree Trust.

Royal Commission (1908) *Care and control of the feebleminded.* London: HMSO.

Russell, O. (1985) *Mental Handicap.* Edinburgh: Churchill Livingstone.

Sarantakos, S. (1993) *Social Research.* Melbourne: Macmillan.

Satir, V. (1972) *Peoplemaking.* Palo Alto, CA: Science and Behavior.

Schaffer, H.R. (1977) *Mothering.* London: Fontana/Open Books.

Schank, R. and Abelson, R. (1977) *Scripts, Plans, Goals and Understanding: An Enquiry into Human Knowledge.* Hillsdale, NJ: Lawrence Erlbaum.

Schank, R.L., Stark, J.A., Snell, M.E., Coulter, D.L., Polloway, E.A., Luckasson, R., Reiss, S. and Spitalnik, D.M. (1994) 'The Changing Conception of Mental Retardation: Implications for the Field.' *Mental Retardation 32,* 181–193.

Scheflen, A.E. (1972) *Body Language and Social Order.* Englewood Cliffs, NJ: Prentice Hall.

Scott, M.J. and Dryden, W. (1996) 'The Cognitive-Behavioural Paradigm.' In R. Woolfe and W. Dryden (eds) *Handbook of Counselling Psychology.* London: Sage.

Scottish Executive (1999) *'The Same as You?' A Review of Services for People with Learning Disabilities.* Edinburgh: Scottish Executive.

Scottish Home and Health Department (1972) *Services for the Mentally Handicapped (The Blue Book).* Edinburgh: The Scottish Office.

Scrutton, S. (1995) *Bereavement and Grief: Supporting Older People through Loss.* London: Edward Arnold/Age Concern.

Seligman, M.E.P. (1975) *Helplessness: On Depression, Development and Death.* San Francisco: Freeman.

Sheldon, B. (1982) *Behaviour Modification: Theory, Practice, and Philosophy.* London: Tavistock.

Sheldon, B. (1995) *Cognitive-Behavioural Therapy: Research, Practice and Philosophy.* London: Routledge.

Silverman, D. (1993) *Interpreting Qualitative Data.* London: Sage.

Simons, K. (1993) *Sticking Up for Yourself.* York: Joseph Rowntree Foundation.

Simons, K. (2000) *A Place at the Table.* Kidderminster: British Institute of Learning Disabilities.

Siporin, M. (1980) 'Ecological Systems Theory in Social Work.' *Journal of Sociology and Social Welfare 7,* 4, 507–532.

Skinner, B.F. (1938) *The Behaviour of Organisms.* New York: Appleton-Century-Crofts.

Smith, C.K. (1990) 'Legal Review: Informed Consent – A Shift from Paternalism to Self Determination.' *Topics in Health Record Management 9,* 71–75.

Spall, B. and Callis, S. (1997) *Loss, Bereavement and Grief: A Guide to Effective Caring.* Cheltenham: Stanley Thornes.

Stalker, K. (1998) 'Some Ethical and Methodological Issues in Research with People with Learning Difficulties.' *Disability and Society 1*, 5–19.

Statt, D.A. (1998) *The Concise Dictionary of Psychology.* London: Routledge.

Stern, D. (1977) *The First Relationship: Infant and Mother.* London: Fontana.

Strauss, A. (1990) *Qualitative Analysis for Social Scientists.* Melbourne: Cambridge University Press.

Strean, H.S. (1971) *Social Casework: Theories in Action.* Metuchen, NJ: Scarecrow Press.

Taylor, P. and Daly, C. (eds) (1995) *Gender Dilemmas in Social Work: Issues Affecting Women in the Profession.* Toronto: Canadian Scholars Press.

The Arc (1982) *The Prevalence of Mental Retardation.* Silver Spring, MD: The Arc.

The Arc (2001) at http://www.thearc.org/faqs/mrga.html

The Maudsley (1999) *The Maze: Mental Health Act 1983 Guidelines (Revised 1999).* London: The Bethlem and Maudsley NHS Trust.

The New Penguin English Dictionary (2001) Edited by R. Allen. London: Penguin Group.

The World Health Report (2001) at http://www.who.int/whr/2001/main/en/chapter2/002eb.htm

Thomas, M. and Pierson, J. (1996) *Dictionary of Social Work.* London: Collins Educational.

Thompson, N (1993) *Anti-Discrimination Practice.* London: MacMillan.

Thompson, N. (1996) *Theory and Practice in Health and Social Welfare.* Buckingham: Open University Press.

Thompson, N. (1997) *Anti-Discriminatory Practice.* London: Macmillan.

Thompson, N. (2000) *Understanding Social Work.* London: Macmillan.

Thorndike, E.L. (1913) *Educational Psychology.* New York: Columbia University Press.

Thorne, B. (1991) *Person-Centred Counselling: Therapeutic and Spiritual Dimensions.* London: Whurr.

Thorne, B. (1992) *Carl Rogers.* London: Sage.

Todd, M. and Gilbert, T. (eds) (1995) *Learning Disabilities: Practice Issues in Health Settings.* London: Routledge.

Trevithick, P. (1993) 'Surviving Childhood Sexual and Physical Abuse.' In H. Ferguson, R. Gilligan, and R. Torode (eds) *Surviving Childhood Adversity: Issues for Policy and Practice.* Dublin: Social Studies Press.

Trevithick, P. (2000) *Social Work Skills: A Practice Handbook.* Buckingham: Open University Press.

Turner, F.J. (ed) (1986) *Social Work Treatment: Interlocking Theoretical Approaches.* New York: Free Press.

Tyne, A. and O'Brien, J. (1981) *The Principles of Normalization: Campaign for Mental Handicap/Campaign for Mental Handicap Education and Research Association.* London: CMH/ERA.

UKCC (1992) *Code of Professional Conduct.* London: UKCC.

Union of Physically Impaired Against Segregation (UPIAS) (1976) *Fundamental Principles of Disability.* London: UPIAS and the Disability Alliance.

von Bertalanffy, L. (1971) *General System Theory: Foundations, Development, Application.* London: Allen Lane.

Wadsworth, Y. (1991) *Everyday Evaluation on the Run*. Melbourne: Action Research Issues Association.

Weber, M. (1947) *The Theory of Social and Economic Organisations*. New York: Free Press.

Wilkes, R. (1981) *Social Work with Undervalued Groups*. London: Tavistock.

Williams, C. (1995) *Invisible Victims: Crime and Abuse against People with Learning Disabilities*. London: Jessica Kingsley Publishers.

Williams, F. (1989) *Social Policy: A Critical Introduction*. Cambridge: Polity Press.

Williams, P. (1995) 'Residential and Day Services.' In N. Malin (ed) *Services for People with Learning Disabilities*. London: Routledge.

Wilson, A.R. (ed) (1995) *A Simple Matter of Justice?* London: Cassell.

Wolfensberger, W. (1972) *The Principles of Normalisation in Human Services*. Toronto: National Institute on Mental Retardation.

Wolfensberger, W. (1977) *A Multicomponent Advocacy and Protection Scheme*. Toronto: Canadian Association for the Mentally Retarded.

Wolfensberger, W. (1983) 'Social Role Valorization: A Proposed New Term for the Principle of Normalization.' *Mental Retardation 21*, 6, 234–239.

Wolfensberger, W. and Thomas, S. (1983) *Passing Program Analysis of Services Systems' Implementation of Normalization Goals*. Toronto: Canadian National Institute of Mental Retardation.

Worden, W.J. (1991) *Grief Counselling and Grief Therapy: A Handbook for the Mental Health Practitioner*. London: Tavistock/Routledge.

World Health Organisation (1991) *Internal Classification of Disease and Related Health Problems (ICD)/Diagnostic Criteria for Research (DCR), 10th edition*. Geneva: World Health Organisation.

World Health Organisation (2000) *International Classification of Functioning and Disability*. Geneva: World Health Organisation.

Wright-Mills, C. (1959) *The Sociological Imagination*. New York: OUP.

Subject Index

Author Index